Before Military Intervention

Timothy Clack · Robert Johnson
Editors

Before Military Intervention

Upstream Stabilisation in Theory and Practice

palgrave
macmillan

Editors
Timothy Clack
St Peter's College
University of Oxford
Oxford, UK

Robert Johnson
Pembroke College
University of Oxford
Oxford, UK

ISBN 978-3-030-07494-4 ISBN 978-3-319-98437-7 (eBook)
https://doi.org/10.1007/978-3-319-98437-7

Softcover re-print of the Hardcover 1st edition 2019

Cover image: A soldier from 4th Battalion The Rifles (4 RIFLES) rushes through a stream during a training exercise at the British Army Training Unit Kenya (BATUK). © Crown Copyright
Cover design: Akihiro Nakayama

This Palgrave Macmillan imprint is published by the registered company Springer Nature Switzerland AG
The registered company address is: Gewerbestrasse 11, 6330 Cham, Switzerland

Foreword

Almost two decades into the twenty-first century, the only certainty is that the strategic outlook will continue to be extremely uncertain. The pace of political, technological and demographic change continues to accelerate, and their compound effects frustrate forecasters. There is no shortage of threats with which we need to contend, whether resurgent or emergent state actors, or the multiplicity of rapidly mutating substate groups. Coupled with environmental change and population flows, these threats and hazards combine as potent cocktails of human suffering. Even when adequate governance is in place, the consequences are very rarely contained by local or regional boundaries. And if local governance is inadequate these crises rapidly escalate, usually presenting trans-regional (and occasionally global) challenges, particularly once amplified by penetrating, persistent and increasingly politicised media coverage.

With this in mind, this book explores recent stabilisation efforts, with a view to identifying what has worked in the past and what might work in the future. As prevention is always cheaper than the crisis of state collapse or civil war, upstream stabilisation operations retain enduring appeal. However, the unpredictability and variability of state instability require governments and militaries to adopt a diversity of diagnosis, conceptualisation and approach. Offering perspectives from both theorists and practitioners, the chapters in this collection provide important insights into military roles and capabilities; opportunities, risks and limitations; doctrine, strategy and tactics; and critically, measures of effect relevant to operations in upstream environments. This book will appeal to both researchers and operators hoping to understand past conflicts with a view to preventing future ones.

Crucially, this book is in part a product of the British Army's continuing efforts to understand the causes of, and possible antidotes to, instability. Academic engagement such as this is one way to access the widest variety of perspectives on past and future challenges, minimising the likelihood of convergent thinking and its attendant dangers.

Upavon, UK

Major-General Tom Copinger-Symes
CBE, GOC Force Troops Command

Preface

This volume explores the nature of recent efforts to stabilise states and threats to those practices which appear to be on the future horizon, a prospect often labelled as 'upstream'. As prevention is always cheaper than the costs of state collapse or civil war, it seems likely that states will invariably favour upstream stabilisation operations. Nevertheless, the future character of conflict makes the execution of this policy look very uncertain indeed. The unpredictability and variability of state instability require governments and militaries to adopt diverse approaches. This makes conceptualization problematic, and even the epistemology of stabilisation appears to be complex and contested. Offering perspectives from theory and practice, the chapters in this collection provide crucial insight into policy options, military roles and capabilities, and the opportunities, risks, and limitations of practice. It illustrates points that will influence policy, doctrine, strategy, and even tactical issues of 'ground truth'. It points to measures of effect relevant to operations in upstream environments for both civil and military practitioners. This volume will appeal to both researchers and professional military personnel seeking to understand, with the benefit of recent and historical cases, how to navigate their way through current and future conflict scenarios.

This book would not exist without the support of Sarah Roughley at Palgrave. Her championing of the project has been crucial and we are incredibly grateful for her vision and assistance. Mary Fata at Palgrave was extremely helpful and efficient during the book's production for which many thanks are due.

This book emerged from the Upstream Effects: Capacity Building, Stabilisation and Counter-Terrorism Workshop, 8–9 December 2015 at Merton College, Oxford University. Organised by the editors, the workshop explored conflict and stabilisation drivers in a number of theatres in light of current and historical military interventions. The workshop also attempted to draw out tactical and operational lessons from case study interventions. Using the dialogue of theory and practice, participants at the event included academics from the UK, Canada, Norway, and the USA and serving military personnel from UK, Denmark, Germany, and the USA. Even though not all of their respective contributions appear in the chapters that follow, the enthusiasm and intellectual inputs of the participants shaped this volume significantly. We have not been able to do justice to the determination to see improvement in intervention and conflict prevention that was evident at that conference, but we have at least established a record of some of the ideas, which, we hope, other scholars will be able to take up and develop. It is not possible to name all of those who participated, but particular thanks are owed to: Prof. David Anderson; Sir Rodric Braithwaite; Edward Canfor-Dumas; Prof. Dawn Chatty; Prof. Toby Dodge; Col (Ret'd) Graham Fairclough; Prof. David Galbreath; Dr. Elisabeth Kendall; Dr. Oliver Lewis; Prof. Roger Mac Ginty; Tom Rodwell; and Maj-Gen (Ret'd) Andrew Sharpe.

We are indebted to the British Army's 1st Intelligence, Surveillance and Reconnaissance Brigade (1ISR Bde) for funding the initial event, and to David Lacey, Ruth Murray, Liz Robson and Geoff Wood for their respective administrative contributions. Institutionally, the British Army, Cabinet Office, Defence Academy, Foreign and Commonwealth Office (FCO), Royal Military Academy Sandhurst (RMAS), and Stabilisation Unit (SU) provided assistance of one form or another, both at the event and in its aftermath, and deserve recognition.

Most importantly, we are appreciative of the contributors to this volume who have been loyal, patient, and steadfast in their commitment to the book's production. At 1ISR Bde, Lt Col Al Bowman and Lt Col Anna Janes were strong advocates of academic input into military understanding. Their encouragement went a long way in facilitating the depth of analyses presented in this work.

During the volume's production, a number of individuals assisted with an assortment of activities from the reading of drafts to chasing up references to finalising permissions. Of these, Allan Hall deserves special thanks for his help in each of these areas and expert navigation of institutional bureaucracies. Shane Wilkinson, at Army Media and Comms, and Capt Charles Ashington-Pickett helped source the images. However, any errors are the responsibility of the editors.

As editors, we are grateful to Oxford University's Changing Character of War Centre (CCW) and the Land Intelligence Fusion Centre (LIFC) for hosting elements of this research but also, more importantly, for the intellectual communities and camaraderie both institutions have provided over the past decade. The fusion of ideas, backgrounds, thinking and common purpose lies at the heart of what we do.

This book is dedicated to those individuals, both military and civilian, who hazard their lives to make the world more secure, peaceful and just.

Oxford, UK

Timothy Clack
Robert Johnson

Contents

Notes on Contributors

Dr. Timothy Clack is Fellow and Lecturer of St Peter's College and Senior Research Fellow of the Changing Character of War Centre, University of Oxford. He is a specialist in cultural identity, media and conflict, primarily related to areas of sub-Saharan Africa and Central Asia. He is co-editor, with Dr. Robert Johnson, of *At the End of Military Intervention: Historical, Theoretical and Applied Approaches to Transition, Handover and Withdrawal* (2014).

Dr. Aaron Edwards is Senior Lecturer in Defence and International Affairs at the Royal Military Academy Sandhurst. He is the author of *Mad Mitch's Tribal Law: Aden and the End of Empire* (2014) and *Defending the Realm? The Politics of Britain's Small Wars Since 1945* (2012).

Dr. Annette Idler is the Director of Studies at the Changing Character of War Centre and Senior Research Fellow of Pembroke College, University of Oxford. She is a specialist in conflict, security, transnational organised crime and peacebuilding, with a specific interest in violent non-state actors. She is the author of *Borderlands: Violent Non-state Groups and Insecurity on the Edges of Colombia* (2018).

Dr. Robert Johnson is Director of the Changing Character of War Centre and Senior Research Fellow of Pembroke College, University of Oxford. A former army officer, he specialises in historical and current conflicts in Asia and the Middle East. He is the author of works on strategy and war in history, including *The Great War and the Middle East* (2016), and partnering local forces, in *True to Their Salt* (2017).

Dr. Simon Mabon is Lecturer in International Relations at the University of Lancaster, the Director of the Richardson Institute and a Research Associate at the Foreign Policy Centre. He is the author of *Saudi Arabia and Iran: Soft Power Rivalry in the Middle East* (2013), and co-author of *Hezbollah: From Islamic Resistance to Government* (2016), and *The Origins of ISIS* (2017).

Prof. William Reno is Professor at Northwestern University. He specialises in the politics of conflict, the behaviour and organisation of non-state armed groups, and the politics of international intervention. He has extensive fieldwork experience in Africa, with expertise in warlordism. He is the author of *Warfare in Independent Africa* (2011) and *Warlord Politics and African States* (1998).

Prof. Paul Schulte is Honorary Professor at the Institute for Conflict, Cooperation and Security, University of Birmingham, UK. A specialist on disarmament, just war theory, drone warfare, and deterrence, he was the founding Head of the UK's interdepartmental Post Conflict Reconstruction Unit (now the Stabilisation Unit), which deployed to Afghanistan. He has published extensively, including 'Motives and Methods of Future Political Violence: Landscapes of the Early 21st Century' in Brad Roberts (ed.) *Hype or Reality? The "New Terrorism" and Mass Casualty Attacks* (2000).

Prof. Gareth Stansfield is Professor of Middle East Politics and the Al-Qasimi Chair of Arab Gulf Studies at the University of Exeter. He is the Director of Middle East Studies and Senior Associate Fellow of the Royal United Services Institution. He has extensive field experience of Iraq, especially as a special advisor on the Kurds, and he is the author of works on Iraq and the Kurds, including the co-edited, with N. Caspersen. *Unrecognized States in the International System* (2010).

Dr. Susanna D. Wing is Associate Professor of Political Science at Haverford College. She holds a Ph.D. in Political Science and an M.A. in African Area Studies from the University of California, Los Angeles. She is the author of the award-winning monograph *Constructing Democracy in Africa*. Her work has appeared in leading journals including *Journal of Modern African Studies*; *African Affairs*; *Polity* and *Foreign Affairs*.

List of Figures

List of Tables

CHAPTER 1

Introduction: Anticipating Future Stabilisation

Robert Johnson and Timothy Clack

In 2015, the British Chief of Defence Staff, General Sir Nicholas Houghton, asserted that: 'Armed forces should be much more about avoiding, preventing and deterring war; maintaining the stability of the world order so as to permit the exploitation of opportunity in pursuit of prosperity; whilst mitigating those recurring threats and security related crises'. Prevention is better than cure. The acceptance of this and similar logic has resulted in the recognition, principally among Western governments, that it is better to invest lesser amounts of resources early to deliver conflict prevention than vast amounts later in fighting a greater threat. Stabilisation efforts must thus recognise the diffuse nature of upstream threats, difficulties in measuring success and effects, the potential for situational mismanagement, and, in the event of perceived deficiencies, the loss of domestic support for action. Consequently, in this introductory chapter, we examine the problems in the definition of

R. Johnson (✉) · T. Clack
University of Oxford, Oxford, UK
e-mail: robert.johnson@history.ox.ac.uk

T. Clack
e-mail: timothy.clack@arch.ox.ac.uk

T. Clack and R. Johnson (eds.), *Before Military Intervention*,
https://doi.org/10.1007/978-3-319-98437-7_1

stabilisation, theories of stabilisation in different disciplines, the challenges and criticisms of the practice, especially in upstream contexts, and the various approaches to stabilisation, specifically the military role. The introduction offers an outline of a voluminous literature on the subject, showing the context and value of the case studies and chapters that follow.

The interventions of 2001–2014 in Afghanistan and Iraq demonstrated limits to Anglo-American military capabilities in stabilisation. Yet planning for preventative operations has a tendency to grossly overestimate the capacity of what can be achieved with the resources available in peacetime (Dodge 2012). Part of the problem is that assumptions in government are based on what can be achieved with the available assets, and the potential to roll in more resources as and when required. It does not make financial sense to hold ready large reserves of personnel and material for low-priority missions, and ruthless decisions have to be made about more pressing requirements and the need to create a balanced force. The result is that armed forces and defence capabilities are rarely, if ever, adequate before or at the start of a stabilisation mission of any magnitude (Johnson and Clack, 2015). There are usually too few personnel with the necessary in-country knowledge to engage key leaders, especially those remote from the local government's apparatus. Non-Governmental Organisations (NGOs) and the commercial sector will often have a better picture of the initial conflict, although here too there are limits. There is often friction with host-nation governments or local leaders. There can be expectations and anxieties to manage among the local population. There can be clandestine spoiling tactics at all levels, while criminal or terrorist networks use connections on an informal and covert basis and deliberately seek to hide their operations from any supervision. Alternative networks need to be understood for any effective action to be taken, and here local government and civil society agencies are invaluable. Nevertheless, there can be high levels of collusion between the state and non-state actors, corruption, or state abuse of the population to contend with.

In defence, it is widely acknowledged that stabilising states is a complex, long-term and multi-agency activity (Ritchie, 2011). The doctrine of Understand to Prevent: The Military Contribution to the Prevention of Violent Conflict asserts: 'To determine the appropriate approach to upstream engagement, we must not only understand the nature of the conflict, but also who acts and what actions are best taken at each level' (Multinational Capability Development Campaign 2014: 30). Many armed services personnel regard stabilisation with some trepidation, seeing it as a low-priority compared with warfighting and associated with the problematic outcomes of operations in Iraq and Afghanistan. For civilian organisations, there are significant differences in how one even defines stabilisation. Most scholars, particularly economists, regard stabilisation as a form of structural economic readjustment, and not necessarily related to conflict (Franicevic and Kraft 1997; Gomulka 1994). Aid agencies and NGOs define stabilisation as recovery from an immediate humanitarian crisis, and do not regard a state's role as particularly important. By contrast, government departments would see the state's role as the essential one, and the ability of national, regional and local government to deliver services would be their definition of a stabilised polity.

To make definitions even more problematic, there have been significant changes over the last few decades which have altered what is meant and intended, in theory and practice, by the term stabilisation. In the immediate aftermath of the Second World War, a particular model of state reconstruction tended to set the agenda of subsequent planning assumptions (Rynold 2011; Chandra 1996). In light of European decolonisation and a greater awareness of developing world humanitarian crises, and as the UN and other organisations struggled to deliver the appropriate level of support without creating a neocolonial dependence, definitions were altered significantly. Stabilisation and state-building became interchangeable again after the end of the Cold War, although certain regions were thought to be in particular need throughout the twentieth century (Paris and Sisk 2009). In the late 1990s, the popularity of humanitarian intervention reached its peak with UN endorsement of the 'responsibility to protect' (R2P), an issue the British Prime Minister Tony Blair championed in a speech at Chicago in 2000. More recently, in light of the armed interventions by Western Coalitions into Iraq and Afghanistan, and the debilitating experience of countering local insurgencies, it seems less likely that the West would be willing to intervene. Indeed, the phrase in widespread use after 2014 was 'upstream prevention', reflecting a hope that stabilisation could be achieved before a large-scale military intervention became necessary. This policy shift was more apparent than real, as prevention was a long-standing policy aspiration in US and UK governments. The UN had set the agenda for decades, but the UN Secretary General, Boutros-Ghali, articulated the Agenda for Peace in 1992, and this was reinforced by the Brahimi Report (2000), after the UN Special Envoy Lakhdar Brahimi, the

Millennium Report, and then by Ban Ki-Moon's reports which constituted 'R2P Pillar II'. The UN Security Council had consistently called for prevention, peacebuilding and stabilisation, and both the United States and the United Kingdom have been champions of these efforts. American and British armed forces have also examined measures to implement conflict prevention in peacekeeping, peace support, and stabilisation (Doctrine Publications 2014–2017).

The context of Western powers' willingness to intervene is that international institutions or other non-Western nations may be obligated to take action, which has geostrategic consequences. China already plays a more significant role in peacekeeping, for example, but may come to be seen as a regional 'policeman' for East Asia. Yet, China, like the West, is inherently cautious and is aware of the risks in trying to stabilise states where order is collapsing. Above all, the UN and all its member states are conscious of the question of Westphalian sovereignty, which limits intervention. This issue is not new and has been a source of discussion for many decades (Rath 1964; Pugh et al. 2008). What also concerns most states, NGOs and scholars is the degree of effectiveness of interventions to stabilise. Any attempt to engage can, potentially, destabilise, creating turbulence that can cause the very conflict it sought to avert. There is little sign in Yemen, for example, that years of Western preventative engagement could halt the unrest that developed after 2011 or the intervention of regional actors.

Since at least the 1970s, the character of conflict has shifted 'inwards' from interstate to civil wars. This period has been mirrored by 'outward' trends in global governance and conflict management, i.e. from the nation state to coalitions and international fora (Pogodda et al. 2015). At the multinational level, Western concepts and approaches have been afforded primacy and shaped the agenda, albeit not without contest (Hurrell 2016). Relatedly, the uncritical application of Western concepts and approaches to conflict prevention in non-Western theatres is problematic. There are a number of reasons why this is the case. From the outset, the complex and dynamic global security landscape indicates the impracticality of a 'universal' or 'uniform' approach. The unpredictability and variability of forms of instability require diverse approaches. It requires a versatility in conceptualisation but precision over the episteme of 'stabilisation'. Thus, in practice, cultural, temporal, spatial and perceptual dissonance undermines the possibility of a strategic or operational calculus, effective in all situations. Solutions must be based on

Fig. 1.1 A Chinook from the Joint Helicopter Support Unit (JHSU), manned by members of 27 Squadron, preparing to deliver humanitarian aid in the highlands of Pakistan in 2005 (*Credit* Crown Copyright)

Fig. 1.2 A soldier from D Company, 5 RIFLES operating in dense forest whilst taking part in a multinational exercise in Estonia as part of NATO's eFP (enhanced Forward Presence) (*Credit* Crown Copyright)

contextualisation. Furthermore, culture and identity are also often paramount drivers in conflict (Eagleton 2008; Eller 1999; Mach 1993). This is, of course, also evident in the destruction of cultural property during conflict (Sørensen and Vienjo-Rose 2015; Turku 2017; Welasek 2018). Considering this multi-scaler cultural variability alone, 'one size fits all' approaches to conflict prevention are to be eschewed. Indeed, the catalytic role of cultural identities in conflicts, often tied to historic grievances and traumas, has resulted in conflict prevention discourses linked to social constructivism (Checkel 1998; Conteh-Morgan 2005) and participatory methods and local agency (MacGinty 2017; MacGinty and Firchow 2016).

Despite on face value growing global interdependence offering the possibility of a unified approach to preventative interventions, in reality these processes exacerbate problems. As argued by Robert Keohane (2002), transnational relationships often have the ability to exert effects over great distances. Indeed, the state's exclusivity on security has been, in many contexts, undermined by an array of inter and subnational

Fig. 1.3 British soldiers from the Liaison Support Team providing medical training to Nigerian soldiers in Maiduguri, NE Nigeria (*Credit* Major Tom Clack and Crown Copyright)

actors, including multinational corporations, NGOs and political organisations. Similarly, the implications of amplified economic integration (see Friedman 2005; Held and Koenig-Archibugi 2003; see also Jomo and Baudot 2007) and interdependence of nations states (Keohane 1984, 2002) have both improved and denuded ontological and physical security. International organisations, such as the UN, have sought to encourage cooperation around complementary interests with what Anne Marie Slaughter (2000: 203) has described as, 'disaggregated sovereignty'. However, even as a collective, state actors cannot maintain monopolies on interaction or communication. Moreover, contemporary forms of interdependence precipitate the conditions whereby actors can pursue strategies of cost externalisation. Naturally, those bearing these externalities, state or non-state, may retaliate and conflicts result. Again,

Fig. 1.4 A British soldier from 1 SCOTS mentors Somali National Army soldiers in the use of combat torniques Baidoa, Somalia in 2018 (*Credit* Crown Copyright)

the fluidity and nuance of these conditions in different localities makes the bulk translation and export of Western concepts to other arenas unsuitable.

Given this multiplicity of interpretations and dilemmas, this volume offers some examples of stabilisation, including both theoretical literature and practical advice on the subject, and highlights the key emerging issues. For the sake of clarity, we include in our definition early intervention (in the widest sense of the term, over both short- and long term) with activities relating to: state stabilisation; deterrence; humanitarian assistance (Fig. 1.1); counterterrorism; arms limitation; countering organised crime; security sector reform; the deployment of loan service personnel; joint exercises (Fig. 1.2); defence industry cooperation; and capacity building (Figs. 1.3, 1.4 and 1.5). Despite this generalisation, we take the view that, in order to be effective, each intervention will be necessarily tailored to its context, and dependent on the environment, level of threat, and resources. The differences require considerable flexibility in planning and approach.

Fig. 1.5 British soldier from 1 SCOTS teaching weapons handling drills to soldiers from the Somali National Army in Baidoa, Somalia in 2018 (*Credit* Crown Copyright)

Theories of Stabilisation

The literature on stabilisation is extensive but divided between a number of themes and approaches. Economists tend to limit their interpretation to the restructuring of economies and their effects, whereas international relations scholars are more concerned with state organisation and the relationship with international institutions. Peace studies and development studies are again distinctive, being focused on the resolution of conflict and the impact on civilians, often at a micro level. A useful starting point in the latter field is Thomas G. Weiss, 'Researching Humanitarian Intervention: Some Lessons' and Yuri Barsegov and Rustem Khairov's 'A Study of the Problems of Peace' (Weiss 2001; Barsegov and Khairov 1973).

There are some studies that attempt to cross the disciplinary boundaries and examine how state decomposition, or our interpretations of it, affect approaches (Miller 2009; Albert et al. 2008; Varden

2011). Among the more recent works, the debate on what constituted a 'failed, failing or fragile' state elicited some interesting studies, merging economic failures, illicit financing, and government abuses of power. Of note are Pierre Englebert and Denis M. Tull's article of 2008, 'Postconflict Reconstruction in Africa: Flawed Ideas About Failed States', and Richard Snyder and Ravi Bhavnani's (2005) publication 'Diamonds, Blood, and Taxes: A Revenue-Centered Framework for Explaining Political Order' (Engelbert and Tull 2008; Snyder and Bhavnani 2005).

Typifying the local, micro-level stabilisation are works such as Yossef Ben-Meir, 'National Sovereignty Through Decentralization: A Community-Level Approach' and Jeff Haynes, Trevor W. Parfitt and Stephen Riley, 'Debt in Sub-Saharan Africa: The Local Politics of Stabilisation' (Ben-Meir 2008; Haynes et al. 1987). At the other end of the spectrum, showing how regional and international stabilisation can be achieved through diplomacy, and therefore the sovereignty of a nation, are works such as Aida Abzhaparova, 'Denuclearisation practices of Kazakhstan: performing sovereign identity, preserving national security' (Abzhaparova 2011).

The majority of scholarly works on stabilisation deal with its economic aspects. Paul Collier's work on the drivers of civil war includes detailed examples of the immediate post-conflict stabilisation problems from an economic point of view (Collier and Duponchel 2013). Tilman Brück, Wim Naudé and Philip Verwimp, examine the private sector's role in 'Business under Fire: Entrepreneurship and Violent Conflict in Developing Countries' while Tor Benjaminsen has examined the legacy of scarcity in holding back stabilisation in the case of Mali (Brück et al. 2013; Benjaminsen 2008). Under-development as a more general challenge for stabilisation was the subject of Jeffrey Herbst's 'War and the State in Africa' and Richard Sandbrook's 'Hobbled Leviathans: Constraints on State Formation in Africa' (Herbst 1990; Sandbrook 1986).

Unsurprisingly, there is a considerable volume of research on the efforts of the UN in stabilisation. The objectives of the UN are the feature of articles by Laura J. Shepherd, "'To Save Succeeding Generations from the Scourge of War': The US, UN and the Violence of Security", (Shepherd 2008) and Alex J. Bellamy and Paul D. Williams, 'Who's Keeping the Peace?: Regionalization and Contemporary Peace Operations' (Bellamy and Williams 2005). Yet the role of institutions has been challenged by those who seek to examine the effects of UN operations. The local reactions to peacekeeping are the subject of studies by Andrea Ruggeri, Theodora-Ismene Gizelis and Han Dorussen (Ruggeri et al. 2013) and Declan Power (Power 2013) and especially Han Dorussen and Theodora-Ismene Gizelis, 'Into the Lion's Den: Local responses to UN peacekeeping' (Dorussen and Gizelis 2013).

In government departments and the armed services, there are different concerns from the scholars, and their perspectives are on issues of time, space and scale. To governments, a preventative approach can mean 'early' in relation to the conflict curve, but it can also relate to geography with conflict-prone or 'at risk' nations located in particular regions. Upstream and downstream have also become shorthand descriptors among some Western practitioners to denote proximity and direction of travel of threats to the home nation. Furthermore, small overseas engagements are considered more 'upstream' than larger interventions. The term 'defence engagement', which is in common use, does not entirely cover the definition since this can be applied to states with no threat of instability, being considered 'defence diplomacy', that is, keeping alive alliance partnerships, rehearsing operational tasks and providing mutual reassurance of support. In sum, we have very different civil and military interpretations, and academic perspectives, of what we mean by stabilisation and preventative intervention.

Critiques of Western Policies of Intervention

Intervention to conduct stabilisation has attracted a number of critical studies. Some of these are related to the expeditionary campaigns in Afghanistan and Iraq, but the majority consider structural economic inequalities or the geostrategic balance of power. The most noteworthy are Roland Paris, 'Saving liberal peacebuilding' (Paris 2010) and Joseph A. Camilleri, 'Globalization of Insecurity: The Democratic Imperative' (Camilleri 2001) while critics of Western policies related to the 'war on terror' include Paul Rogers, "The 'War on Terror' and International Security" (Rogers 2011), Dennis Florig (2010) and Christopher Layne (Layne 2009).

Nevertheless, there are critics of intervention who also challenge the neo-liberal assumptions of Western stabilisation, or, given the enthusiasm to install democracy as part of stabilisation practice, the notion of a democratic peace (Chandler 2006; Richter 2005; Paris 2002). Despite the cacophony of criticism, there still seems to be some faith in the idea of neutral international institutions being able to intervene, even though their track record in stabilisation has been notoriously poor (Hasenclever and Weiffen 2006).

The challenges of stabilisation are considerable, and, as a result of hard-won experience, it is possible to identify some of the more significant themes, such as: elections, water, energy, militancy, economic injustice or maldistribution, security sector reform, cooperation and coordination between government and non-government organisations, local armed groups and sustaining peace. Let us briefly examine each of these in turn.

It has always been felt that, in intervening to conduct stabilisation, power should be returned as quickly as possible to the local population through elections, but in the midst of a civil war or insurgency, this is far harder to achieve in practice, as Cyril K. Daddieh noted in his 2001 study of Côte d'Ivoire (Daddieh 2001). Climatic challenges and conflict impose particular pressure on essential resources, including water, as aid agencies know well (Palanisami et al. 2010). Other forms of economic injustice and maldistribution, sometimes the result of long-term infrastructural problems or short-term crises, can sustain conflicts and hamper stabilisation efforts (Dunning 2005; Custers 2006) which, in the case of deliberate social inequalities and acute environmental stress, some critics believe can amount to a genocide (Chossudovsky 1996).

A conflict of priorities can obstruct the delivery of stabilisation, and while some of these may be the result of local authorities' malign or incompetent leadership, simple bureaucratic problems can delay or duplicate unnecessarily even the most vital service provision. Daniel Ehrenfeld, Shira Yael Kogut and Hilary Hove are more typical in their concern that some governments wish to make aid conditional on some other benefit to their national interests (Ehrenfeld et al. 2003). Aid agencies are not above rivalries and coordination problems, and can antagonise governments seeking to defeat insurgents by insisting on offering unconditional aid to rebel groups, or the civilians in their areas of control. NGOs could pay more attention to the driving forces of unrest in this regard (Shapiro and Fair 2009).

In the scholarly literature and in professional journals, a considerable volume of work is dedicated to Security Sector Reform (SSR) and two edited works, both containing a number of case examples, are worthy of further examination in this regard, namely Security Sector

Reconstruction and Reform in Peace Support Operations edited by Michael Brzoska and David Law (Brzoska and Law 2007) and Security Sector Reform and Post-Conflict Peacebulding edited by Albrecht Schnabel and Hans-Georg Erhart (Schnabel and Erhart 2005). One of the chief problems of SSR is the existence of militias and armed groups which challenge the government's monopoly of violence. But not all local armed groups oppose the government. Sabine C. Carey, Neil J. Mitchell and Will Lowe identify 332 pro-government militias (PGMs) in their work and show how they are linked to a governing political party, individual leaders, or the military. Their conclusion is that such groups increase the risk of civil war, but historical examples indicate that local armed groups could often provide a short-term security solution and successful post-conflict reform is achievable (Carey et al. 2013). Sustaining peace, even where a conflict has been brought to an end, in order to ensure the continued stabilisation of a state, is also the subject of much of the scholarly literature. Of the work, three studies merit further consideration: Jenny Pearce, 'From Civil War to 'Civil Society': Has the End of the Cold War Brought Peace to Central America?' (Pearce 1998); Beyond Settlement: Making Peace Last After Civil Conflict by Vanessa E. Shields, Nicholas D. J. Baldwin (Shields and Baldwin 2008) and Securing the Peace: The Durable Settlement of Civil Wars by Monica Duffy Toft (Toft 2009).

Routes to Success in Stabilisation

The Comprehensive Approach, as it was known to British government personnel, is dependent on a close coordination of effort. This requires an open dialogue between the armed forces, government departments and their political leaders, with international and local NGOs, and with the host-nation authorities. Early interventions, ahead of a crisis, offer better prospects for change and reform which has the consent of the local government and population. On the other hand, a lack of deep understanding of a region, which often characterises early interventions, can lead to errors of policy and misunderstanding. Moreover, any attempt to offer limited support risks the gradual increase of demands without proper planning, a form of 'mission creep'. The result is often ineffectiveness in the initial projects stemming from unrealisable objectives and under-resourcing. Continuous modulated engagement, underpinned by long-term relationships, ensures more enduring progress, better situational awareness and mutual understanding. Good relations and knowledge are likely to improve influence both from the stabilising authorities and the local agencies on the ground.

Formal coordination should take place between diplomatic, economic, military, NGO and civil society elements in a series of regular meetings, aligned to a comprehensive and constantly updated plan. This means 'reaching out' consciously to a range of actors and stakeholders. For this, qualified diplomatic and liaison staff are required. Wherever possible, different lines of activity should be mutually supporting. Recent interventions have demonstrated that, for reasons of legitimacy, host-nation invitation and military support to a civilian lead are crucial (Rundell 2015). There must be alignment between military missions and a clear set of political objectives, emphasising outcomes rather than outputs. In the UK, for example, military activities should also be linked formally to the FCO's country plans for respective areas.

Getting the policy and doctrine right is essential, and, as noted earlier, much will depend on the context for the appropriate level, scale and depth of stabilisation. Being aware of the structural obstacles to development and stabilisation can assist in avoiding the usual planning problems or their consequences (Barry et al. 2010). Suitably trained staff are also vital (Mann and Derleth 2011) especially if one is to avoid the sort of controversies that surrounded the employment of civilian anthropologists and government engagement with NGOs which characterised the early operations in Iraq between 2004 and 2008 (Gusterson 2007; Robbin 2010). Equally, government personnel needs to be aware that experienced civilians in NGOs and aid agencies have their own agendas, which do not necessarily accord with the stabilisation plans laid out, and they may still insist on protection when things go wrong (Ward 2007).

In the short term, the primary role of the military may be to provide some level of security, but longer-term demands might include 'advise and assist' training missions or the implementation of peace agreements. Such tasks require a significant level of preparation and understanding (DeRouen et al. 2010). The military task may also include the enforcement of arms control, and J. 'Bayo Adekanye's review article, covering Somalia by Clement Adibe; Rhodesia/Zimbabwe by Jeremy Ginifer; Croatia and Bosnia-Herzegovina by Barbara Ekwall-Uebelhart and Andrei Raevsky; Cambodia by Jianwei Wang; and Mozambique by Eric Berman, provides a useful starting point in this extensive subject (Adekanye 1997).

Another key military task in stabilisation is ex-combatants' reintegration. Again, this task is far from straightforward when all sides regard a peace initiative as temporary or unproven. Suspicion will characterise relationships, and there is often ample opportunity for spoilers and opportunists to disrupt stabilisation efforts to seize short-term advantages. These problems and their resolution feature in works by Katherine Glassmyer and Nicholas Sambanis; Mark Knight and Alpaslan Özerdem; and Walt Kilroy (Glassmyer and Sambanis 2008; Knight and Özerdem 2004; Kilroy 2011). A related field is in the education and training of young people formerly involved in or affected by conflict, or subject to long-term segregation (Olaifa 2012; Torsti 2009).

Justice is often a subject that is raised by local populations and which is regarded as a vital prerequisite for government. The ability to stabilise a state will often depend on the quality and access of the public to the justice system, although overcoming prejudices against an existing or imposed justice structure brings its own challenges (Binningsbø et al. 2012). The international court can be a useful mechanism to salve legacies of injustice (Mernik 2005).

In parts of the developing world, access to resources and energy can be significant drivers of conflict, and resolving disputes become important to stabilisation activities. Land reform is an example of a task that must be in local government hands, but proved the key to stabilising or destabilising a state (Albertus and Kaplan 2013; Unruh 2001; Prosterman et al. 1981).

There is little doubt that understanding and knowledge is vital to success in stabilisation operations. For practitioners, in-country knowledge can determine success or failure. For scholars, case studies are an equally important tool in comparative study and in the testing of theory. To that end, this edited collection contains several case examples. Readers wishing to extend their understanding of stabilisation might also consider three works on Iraq: Benjamin Sovacool and Saul Halfon, 'Reconstructing Iraq: Merging Discourses of Security and Development' (Sovacool and Halfon 2007); Robert E. Looney, 'The Iraqi Impasse: Sustaining Economic Reconstruction During War-Time' (Looney 2006); and for the cautionary tale of the political consequences of stabilisation and intervention, Caroline Kennedy-Pipe and Rhiannon Vickers, "'Blowback' for Britain? Blair, Bush, and the War in Iraq" (Kennedy-Pipe and Vickers 2007).

Operations in Afghanistan provide a rich seam of work on stabilisation, and they illustrate the importance of a clear strategy (Indurthy

2011), the elusive nature of peace settlements in civil wars (Beautement 2015; Nathan and Toft 2011); the foundation of counter-insurgency on stabilisation and political settlements (Griffin 2011; Chaudhuri and Farrell 2011; King 2010; and Egnell 2011). Caroline Leprince has written, from a Canadian perspective, on the concept of Provincial Reconstruction Team, an important aspect of stabilisation efforts in Afghanistan (Leprince 2013). Seth Jones reminded us of the importance of the insurgents in denying or disrupting efforts at stabilisation throughout the conflict there (Jones 2008).

There are considerable variations with these studies of Iraq and Afghanistan to be found in other parts of the world, underscoring the variety of stabilisation approaches. There are articles which deal with attempts to end the conflict in Colombia (Camacho and Rodriguez 2013), the efforts of the European Union as an international institution to stabilise Kosovo (Shepherd 2009), the economic stabilisation of Sri Lanka during its protracted civil war (Dunham and Kelegama 1998) and both macro-scale and micro-scale studies of stabilisation in South Africa (Beall et al. 2005; Tropp 2003). An edited volume of particular value when analysing the endeavour to restore local security in Sierra Leone is Paul Jackson and Peter Albrecht Reconstructing Security after Conflict (Jackson and Albrecht 2011). Taken together, these studies offer a useful data set for understanding the challenges and possible routes to stabilisation.

The Military Role in Stabilisation

There are several aspects of stabilisation which appear to be specific to military forces, or to law enforcement agencies and private security contractors. The most obvious of these is providing physical security but this aspect is well-established and need not be covered in more detail here. The additional operations of training and mentoring, stand-off interventions with air power, building capacity and operational investment are less well understood and are given some further explanation.

Training and Mentoring: Advise and Assist

Mentoring and training of local security forces or law enforcement agencies, are important elements of capacity building. Mentoring is often considered a second-tier activity compared with warfighting operations, but while the pressures are certainly less, the complexity of the mentoring tasks requires specific skills and dedication. There are different demands for training, mentoring and advising. Much effort is required to build working relationships, to generate output of the appropriate standard, to gauge the right approach, and to plan the duration and progression of the mentored organisations (Phillips and Phillips 2016). The British mentoring mission in Afghanistan, which included the Afghan National Army Officers' Academy, required both security and diplomatic skills, and the ability to negotiate state-to-state and military-to-military. Since the aptitude for mentoring and language training are not always found in the same people, it is clear that the right mix and the most appropriate numbers to be deployed are important. History shows that preparation for these roles has to be comprehensive, not least in language and cultural training. Career tracks for the personnel involved have to be recognised as a specific distinction, and not regarded as a departure from any fast-track promotion route.

Military personnel also have to understand the political and diplomatic limitations that might be placed on their mission. In Iraq in the period 2016–2017, when this collection was in production, British trainers were prevented from going forward with the local forces they had schooled, and the only solutions were realistic training packages and efforts to stay in touch, were through remote communications, with those on the front line. The constraints evidently frustrated some officers, but political leaders had to manage the disquiet, if not outright public opposition, that would accompany any proactive frontline operation.

The development of a central training hub in the UK, for example, to teach mentoring, including languages and institutional development, to military units also seems paramount, if history is any guide. In training soldiers 'how' to mentor, the different talents of the 'warfighter' and 'mentor' can be optimised in advance of each deployment. Furthermore, a reduced dependency on translators enhances relationships and helps reduce the 'insider threat', where frustrated local forces turn their anger on their trainers.

Stand-Off Interventions

For reasons of cost and technological asymmetry, remote capabilities are likely to figure substantially in future stabilisation operations. Air missions, influence operations, cyber and electronic activities, and psychological operations are widely anticipated. The reconnaissance, surveillance and even strike roles of Remotely-Piloted Air Systems (RPAS)/Unmanned Aerial Vehicles (UAVs) are also thought to be of increasing importance in the next two decades (United Nations 2014). RPAS provide a number of military options, some of which could support other stabilisation activities, such as the delivery of air strikes to protect local forces, and surveillance assistance to partner governments to control illicit economic activity. RPAS are cheaper to deploy in comparison with piloted aircraft. Their commercial availability would reduce the appeal of offers from developed countries. On the other hand, even 'tokens of assistance' promote intelligence sharing and cooperation, but the capabilities can be withdrawn efficiently when the stabilisation requirement is completed.

Unsurprisingly, there are problems. First, the use coercive air power can make it genuinely hard to distinguish between preventative and more committed operations. Establishing a limit might seem sound in theory but in practice is impossible to define. By far the most effective role of air power and RPAS is in constant surveillance monitoring and intelligence collection, but there remains the tension between what one can do technologically and what one would prefer to do militarily, and constraints are to be expected. Second, while it is the 'responsibility to protect' which can often act as the primary driver for intervention, and where air power can deliver humanitarian aid, it cannot on its own ensure stabilisation. Third, the internal drivers of conflict are usually beyond the capacity of technological resources available against them. Consequently, when a civil disorder has broken out and threatens to engulf a country in a more serious conflict, 'air policing' is highly unlikely to prevent it (Boon and Lovelace 2014).

Building Capacity and Operational Investment

Occasionally, a relatively small intervention at a precise juncture in time and under certain conditions can create a disproportionate and beneficial strategic effect. Local government, commercial enterprises and NGO actors, for example, often have long-term reach into local communities and their knowledge can be vital in identifying where the strategic leverage points might be. While sharing information might compromise the humanitarian principle of neutrality, and therefore preclude some aid organisations, simple coordination can avoid conflicts. In one case in East Africa, the mere presence of a regular military force deterred predatory militias and enabled one NGO to assist civilians in need as a result. They did not 'cooperate' but there was mutual benefit nonetheless.

Working through local partners is frequently problematic, especially when there are inevitably a variety of competing agendas at work. If a number of external actors attempt to deliver support in the same fragile context, the effect can actually be detrimental and counterproductive. Mitigation strategies should be considered in case of disruption to a host state's capacity. As always, close cooperation is crucial.

The challenges of future stabilisation environments, especially when constrained by limited resources, will necessitate some bold innovations and improvisation. Nevertheless, there is great merit in adequate preparation and planning. Career specialists, with the relevant training and experience, are invaluable. Recruitment will involve the identification of suitable individuals, their education, promotion, and engagement on familiarisation tours to the private sector, and international or national attachments. At the very least, a cadre of civilian and military specialists should be developed to engage with area experts when particular crises intensify, or, better still, ahead of them. To consolidate regional specialism, suitable military candidates should undergo selection and be sent on secondments to academic, NGO and industrial institutions (DfID 2014). Specialisms might include: institution-building, counter-corruption, logistics, procurement, law, pay and conditions expertise, peacebuilding and reconciliation, construction, emergency relief, mass evacuation and decontamination.

Contrary to many expectations, preventative interventions and stabilisation are not low-cost options. Nevertheless, the right 'investment' and acknowledgement that a long-term engagement demonstrates a commitment to host communities, can offset the 'cost' of obligation. Above all, prevention is always cheaper than the crisis of state collapse or civil war.

The contributors to this volume offer a variety of themes to amplify the general context outlined in the introduction. Paul Schulte questions the 'Discreet Indispensability of Unpiloted Assistance' in his examination of remote aerial capabilities in upstream preventative stabilisation. Will Reno takes one area, the Horn of Africa, to assess the 'Politics of Security Assistance', while Aaron Edwards surveys the limitations on the use of force in neighbouring Yemen. Susannah Wing looks at intervention during counterterrorism crises in the Sahel. Annette Idler takes us into another region, Colombia and its 'illicitly governed' borderlands, to assess 'Upstream Engagement' there. Robert Johnson moves the debate into the challenges and problems of future stabilisation strategy based on likely scenarios in Syria and the Middle East. Simon Mabon suggests current challenges to state stability, as demonstrated by Daesh, reflect an apocalyptic and sectarian alternative, based on their own interpretations of identity, an intolerable social situation and a philosophical alternative. Finally, Gareth Stansfield focuses on the unintended consequences of Western upstreaming in Iraq since 2014. As editors, we have enjoyed the thought-provoking perspectives offered by such diverse chapters, and, as readers, we hope you derive similar satisfaction from thinking through the challenges to the Anglo-American orthodoxies of defence thinking presented here.

References

Abzhaparova, A. 2011. Denuclearisation Practices of Kazakhstan: Performing Sovereign Identity, Preserving National Security. *Review of International Studies*, 37 (4), 1537–1553.

Adekanye, J. B. 1997. Review Article 'Arms and Reconstruction in Post-Conflict Societies'. *Journal of Peace Research*, 34 (3), 359–366.

Albert, M., Kessler, O., and Stetter, S. 2008. On Order and Conflict: International Relations and the 'Communicative Turn'. *Review of International Studies*, 34, 43–67.

Albertus, M., and Kaplan, O. 2013. Land Reform as a Counterinsurgency Policy: Evidence from Colombia. *The Journal of Conflict Resolution*, 57 (2), 198–231.

Barry, F., King, M., and Matthews, A. 2010. Policy Coherence for Development: Five Challenges. *Irish Studies in International Affairs*, 21, 207–223.

Barsegov, Y., and Khairov, R. 1973. A Study of the Problems of Peace. *Journal of Peace Research*, 10 (1), 71–80.

Beall, J., Gelb, S., and Hassim, S. 2005. Fragile Stability: State and Society in Democratic South Africa. *Journal of Southern African Studies*, 31 (4), 681–700.

Beautement, M. 2015. Negotiated Agreements in Tactical Transitions: The Sangin Accord, 2011. In Johnson, R. and T. Clack, eds. *At the End of Military Intervention*. Oxford: Oxford University Press, pp. 323–359.

Bellamy A. J., and Williams, P. 2005. Who's Keeping the Peace? Regionalization and Contemporary Peace Operations. *International Security*, 29 (4), 157–195.

Benjaminsen, T. A. 2008. Does Supply-Induced Scarcity Drive Violent Conflicts in the African Sahel? The Case of the Tuareg Rebellion in Northern Mali. *Journal of Peace Research*, 45 (6), 819–836.

Ben-Meir, Y. 2008. National Sovereignty Through Decentralization: A Community-Level Approach. *International Journal on World Peace*, 25 (1), 59–71.

Binningsbø, H., Malmin, L., Cyanne E., Gates, S., and Elster, J. 2012. Armed Conflict and Post-Conflict Justice, 1946–2006: A Dataset. *Journal of Peace Research*, 49 (5), 731–740.

Boon, K., and Lovelace, D. 2014. *The Drone Wars of the Twenty-First Century*. Oxford: Oxford University Press.

Brück, T., Naudé, W., and Verwimp, P. 2013. Business Under Fire: Entrepreneurship and Violent Conflict in Developing Countries. *The Journal of Conflict Resolution*, 57 (1), 3–19.

Brzoska, M., and Law, D. 2007. *Security Sector Reconstruction and Reform in Peace Support Operations*. London: Routledge.

Camacho, A., and Rodriguez, C. 2013. Firm Exit and Armed Conflict in Colombia. *The Journal of Conflict Resolution*, 57 (1), 89–116.

Camilleri, J. A. 2001. Globalization of Insecurity: The Democratic Imperative. *International Journal on World Peace*, 18 (4), 3–36.

Carey, C., Mitchell, N., and Lowe, W. 2013. States, the Security Sector, and the Monopoly of Violence: A New Database on Pro-Government Militias. *Journal of Peace Research*, 50 (2), 249–258.

Chandler, D. 2006. Back to the Future? The Limits of Neo-Wilsonian Ideals of Exporting Democracy. *Review of International Studies*, 32 (3), 475–494.

Chandra, N. 1996. Marshall Plan, German Unification and Economics of Transition. *Economic and Political Weekly*, 31 (22), 1307–1310.

Chaudhuri, R., and Farrell, T. 2011. Campaign Disconnect: Operational Progress and Strategic Obstacles in Afghanistan, 2009–2011. *International Affairs*, 87 (2), 271–296.

Chekel, J. T. 1998. The Constructivist Turn in International Relations Theory. *World Politics*, 50, 324–348.

Chossudovsky, M. 1996. Economic Genocide in Rwanda. *Economic and Political Weekly*, 31 (15), 938–941.

Collier, P., and Duponchel, M. 2013. The Economic Legacy of Civil War: Firm-Level Evidence from Sierra Leone. *The Journal of Conflict Resolution*, 57 (1), 65–88.

Conteh-Morgan, E. 2005. Peacebuilding and Human Security: A Constructivist Perspective. *International Journal of Peace Studies*, 10 (1), 16–29.

Custers, P. 2006. Globalisation and War in Ivory Coast. *Economic and Political Weekly*, 41 (19), 1844–1846.

Daddieh, C. K. 2001. Elections and Ethnic Violence in Côte d'Ivoire: The Unfinished Business of Succession and Democratic Transition. *African Issues*, 29 (1/2), 14–19.

DeRouen Jr., K., Ferguson, M. J., Norton, S., Park, Y., Lea, J., and Streat-Bartlett, A. 2010. Civil War Peace Agreement Implementation and State Capacity. *Journal of Peace Research*, 47 (3), 333–346.
DfID Engagement with Private Sector and NGOs, at Emily Darko, ODI. 2014. http://r4d.dfid.gov.uk/pdf/outputs/EPS/Private_Sector_and_NGO_Engagement.pdf. Accessed 22 August 2017.
Doctrine Publications. 2014–2017. Joint Warfare Publication 3-50. The Military Contribution to Peace Support Operations. 2004. The British Army Field Manual AFM-10 Countering Insurgency. 2009. Joint Doctrine Note 5/11 Peacekeeping: An Evolving Role for Military Forces. 2011. Army Doctrine Publication ADP-3 'Operations'. 2010. Army Doctrine Publication AC71940 'Land Operations'. 2017. Joint Doctrine Publication 'Maritime Power'. 2017.
Dodge, T. 2012. Iraq. In R. Caplan, ed. *Exit Strategies and State Building*. Oxford: Oxford University Press.
Dorussen, H., and Gizelis, T. 2013. 'Into the Lion's Den: Local Responses to UN Peacekeeping. *Journal of Peace Research*, 50 (6), 691–706.
Dunham, D., and Kelegama, S. 1998. Stabilisation and Adjustment: Sri Lankan Experience, 1977–1993. *Economic and Political Weekly*, 33 (24), 1475–1482.
Dunning, T. 2005. Resource Dependence, Economic Performance, and Political Stability. *Conflict Resolution*, 49 (4), 451–482.
Eagleton, T. 2008. Culture Conundrum. *The Guardian*, 21 May. https://www.theguardian.com/commentisfree/2008/may/21/1. Accessed 4 April 2018.
Egnell, R. 2011. Lessons from Helmand, Afghanistan: What Now for British Counterinsurgency? *International Affairs*, 87 (2), 297–315.
Ehrenfeld, D., Kogut, S., and Hove, H. 2003. Aid Conditionality and the Peace Process: An Analysis of Its Implementation. *International Journal on World Peace*, 20 (4), 59–96.
Eller, J. D. 1999. *From Culture to Ethnicity to Conflict*. Ann Arbor: Michigan University Press.
Englebert, P., and Tull, D. 2008. Postconflict Reconstruction in Africa: Flawed Ideas About Failed States. *International Security*, 32 (4), 106–139.
Florig, D. 2010. Hegemonic Overreach vs. Imperial Overstretch. *Review of International Studies*, 36 (4), 1103–1119.
Franicevic, V., and Kraft, E. 1997. Croatia's Economy After Stabilisation. *Europe-Asia Studies*, 49 (4), 669–691.
Friedman, T. 2005. *The World Is Flat: A Brief History of the Twenty-First Century*. London: Farrar Straus Giroux.
Glassmyer, K., and Sambanis, N. 2008. Rebel: Military Integration and Civil War Termination. *Journal of Peace Research*, 45 (3), 365–384.
Griffin, S. 2011. Iraq, Afghanistan and the Future of British Military Doctrine: From Counterinsurgency to Stabilization. *International Affairs*, 87 (2), 317–333.

Gomulka, S. 1994. A Gap in Transition Models? A Reply. *Europe-Asia Studies*, 46 (5), 871–873.
Gusterson, H. 2007. Anthropology and Militarism. *Annual Review of Anthropology*, 36, 155–175.
Hasenclever, A., and Weiffen, B. 2006. International Institutions Are the Key: A New Perspective on the Democratic Peace. *Review of International Studies*, 32 (4), 563–585.
Haynes, J., Parfitt, T. W., and Riley, S. 1987. Debt in Sub-Saharan Africa: The Local Politics of Stabilisation. *African Affairs*, 86 (344), 343–366.
Held, D., and Koenig-Archibugi, M. 2003. *Taming Globalisation: Frontiers of Governance*. London: Polity.
Herbst, J. 1990. War and the State in Africa. *International Security*, 14 (4), 117–139.
Houghton, N. 2015. *Interesting Times*. General Sir Nick Houghton, Chief of the Defence Staff, RUSI Christmas Speech, 16 December 2015. https://www.gov.uk/government/speeches/interesting-times. Accessed 4 April 2018.
Hurrell, A. 2016. Towards the Global Study of International Relations. *Revista Brasileira de política internacional*, 59 (2), http://www.scielo.br/pdf/rbpi/v59n2/1983-3121-rbpi-59-02-e008.pdf. Accessed 3 April 2018.
Indurthy, R. 2011. The Obama Administration's Strategy in Afghanistan. *International Journal on World Peace*, 28 (3), 7–52.
Jackson, P., and Albrecht, P. 2011. *Reconstructing Security After Conflict: Security Sector Reform in Sierra Leone*. New York and Basingstoke: Palgrave.
JDP-3-40 Security and Stabilisation: The Military Component.
Johnson, R., and Clack, T. 2015. Introduction. In R. Johnson and T. Clack, eds. *At the End of Military Intervention*. Oxford: Oxford University Press, 1–50.
Jomo, K. S., and Baudot, J. 2007. *Flat World, Big Gaps: Economic Liberalization, Globalization, Poverty and Inequality*. London: Zed Books.
Jones, S. G. 2008. The Rise of Afghanistan's Insurgency: State Failure and Jihad. *International Security*, 32 (4), 7–40.
Kennedy-Pipe, C., and Vickers, R. 2007. Blowback for Britain? Blair, Bush, and the war in Iraq. *Review of International Studies*, 33 (2), 205–221.
Keohane, R. O. 1984. *After Hegemony: Cooperation and Discord in the World Political Economy*. Princeton, NJ: Princeton University Press.
Keohane, R. O. 2002. *Power and Governance in a Partially Globalised World*. London: Routledge.
Kilroy, W. 2011. From Conflict to Ownership: Participatory Approaches to the Re-Integration of Ex-Combatants in Sierra Leone. *Irish Studies in International Affairs*, 22, 127–144.
King, A. 2010. Understanding the Helmand Campaign: British Military Operations in Afghanistan. *International Affairs*, 86 (2), 311–332.

Knight, M., and Özerdem, A. 2004. Guns, Camps and Cash: Disarmament, Demobilization and Reinsertion of Former Combatants in Transitions from War to Peace. *Journal of Peace Research*, 41 (4), 499–516.

Layne, C. 2009. America's Middle East Grand Strategy After Iraq: The Moment for Offshore Balancing Has Arrived. *Review of International Studies*, 35 (1), 5–25.

Leprince, C. 2013. The Canadian-Led Kandahar Provincial Reconstruction Team: A Success Story? *International Journal*, 68 (2), 359–377.

Looney, R. E. 2006. The Iraqi Impasse: Sustaining Economic Reconstruction During War-Time. *International Journal on World Peace*, 23 (4), 3–31.

Mac Ginty, R. 2017. Everyday Social Practices and Boundary-Making in Deeply Divided Societies. *Civil Wars*, 19 (1), 4–25.

Mac Ginty, R., and Firchow, P. 2016. Top-Down and Bottom-Up Narratives of Peace and Conflict. *Politics*, 36 (3), 308–323.

Mach, Z. 1993. *Symbols, Conflict and Identity: Essays in Political Anthropology*. New York: State University of New York Press.

Mann, S., and Derleth, J. 2011. UNSCHOOLED: How to Better Train Our Nation Builders. *World Affairs*, 173 (6), 81–87.

Meernik, J. 2005. Justice and Peace? How the International Criminal Tribunal Affects Societal Peace in Bosnia. *Journal of Peace Research*, 42 (3), 271–289.

Miller, B. 2009. Between the Revisionist and the Frontier State: Regional Variations in State War-Propensity. *Review of International Studies*, 35, 85–119.

Multinational Capability Development Campaign. 2014. Understand to Prevent: The Military Contribution to the Prevention of Violent Conflict. https://assets.publishing.service.gov.uk/government/uploads/system/uploads/attachment_data/file/518617/20150430-U2P_Main_Web_B5.pdf. Accessed 4 April 2018.

Nathan, L., and Toft, M. 2011. Civil War Settlements and the Prospects for Peace. *International Security*, 36 (1), 202–210.

Olaifa, T. 2012. Corruption and Sustainable Peace in Nigeria: Equipping Youth for Reconstruction. *International Journal on World Peace*, 29 (3), 85–101.

Palanisami, K., Meinzen-Dick, R., and Giordano, M. 2010. Climate Change and Water Supplies: Options for Sustaining Tank Irrigation Potential in India. *Economic and Political Weekly*, 45 (26/27), 183–190.

Paris, R., and Sisk, T. D. 2009. *The Dilemmas of Statebuilding: Confronting the Contradictions of Postwar Peace Operations*. London: Routledge.

Paris, R. 2002. International Peacebuilding and the 'Mission Civilisatrice'. *Review of International Studies*, 28 (4), 637–656.

Paris, R. 2010. Saving Liberal Peacebuilding. *Review of International Studies*, 36 (2), 337–365.

Pearce, J. 1998. From Civil War to 'Civil Society': Has the End of the Cold War Brought Peace to Central America? *International Affairs*, 74 (3), 587–615.

Phillips, J., and Phillips, P. 2016. *Handbook of Training Evaluation and Measurement Methods*. London: Routledge.
Pogodda, S., Richmond, O., and Mac Ginty, R. 2015. The Great Disconnect: Global Governance and Localised Conflict in the Casesof India and the EU. *Global Society*, 29 (4), 551–573.
Power, D. 2013. From the Congo to Mali: Changing Perspectives on Peacekeeping in Africa. *Irish Studies in International Affairs*, 24, 121–136.
Prosterman, R. L., Riedinger, J., and Temple, M. 1981. Land Reform and the El Salvador Crisis. *International Security*, 6 (1), 53–74.
Pugh, M., Cooper, N., and Turner, M. 2008. *Whose Peace? Critical Perspectives on the Political Economy of Peacebuilding*. New York and Basingstoke: Palgrave.
Rath, S. N. 1964. National Sovereignty in the Present Day World. *The Indian Journal of Political Science*, 25 (3), 22–31.
Richter, S. 2005. Frieden schaffen mit den waffen der demokratie? Theorie und praxis von demokratisierung als friedensstrategie. *Zeitschrift für internationale Beziehungen*, 12 (H. 1), 77–116.
Ritchie, N. 2011. Rethinking Security: A Critical Analysis of the [UK] Strategic Defence and Security Review. *International Affairs*, 87 (2), 355–376.
Robbin, A. 2010. *Iraq at a Distance: What Anthropology Can Teach Us About the War*. Philadelphia: University of Pennsylvania Press.
Rogers, P. 2011. The 'War on Terror' and International Security. *Irish Studies in International Affairs*, 22, 15–23.
Ruggeri, A., Gizelis, T., and Dorussen, H. 2013. Managing Mistrust: An Analysis of Cooperation with UN Peacekeeping in Africa. *The Journal of Conflict Resolution*, 57 (3), 387–409.
Rundell, P. 2015. Experiences and Lessons from the Helmand Provincial Reconstruction Team. In R. Johnson and T. Clack, eds. *At the End of Military Intervention*. Oxford: Oxford University Press, pp. 295–303.
Rynhold, J. 2011. The German Question in Central and Eastern Europe and the Long Peace in Europe After 1945: An Integrated Theoretical Explanation. *Review of International Studies*, 37 (1), 249–275.
Sandbrook, R. 1986. Hobbled Leviathans: Constraints on State Formation in Africa. *International Journal*, 41 (4), 707–733.
Schnabel, A., and Erhart, H. 2005. *Security Sector Reform and Post-Conflict Peacebulding*. Tokyo: United Nations University Press.
Shapiro, J. N., and Fair, C. 2009. Understanding Support for Islamist Militancy in Pakistan. *International Security*, 34 (3), 79–118.
Shepherd, A. 2009. 'A Milestone in the History of the EU': Kosovo and the EU's International Role. *International Affairs*, 85 (3), 513–530.
Shepherd, L. J. 2008. 'To Save Succeeding Generations from the Scourge of War': The US, UN and the Violence of Security. *Review of International Studies*, 34 (2), 293–311.

Shields, V. E., and Baldwin, N. D. 2008. *Beyond Settlement: Making Peace Last After Civil Conflict*. London: Fairleigh Dickenson Press.
Slaughter, A. M. 2000. Governing the Economy Through Government Networks. In M. Byers, ed. *The Role of Law in International Politics*. Oxford: Oxford University Press, pp. 177–205.
Snyder, R., and Bhavnani. R. 2005. Diamonds, Blood, and Taxes: A Revenue-Centered Framework for Explaining Political Order. *Conflict Resolution*, 49 (4), 563–597.
Sørensen, M. L., and Vienjo-Rose, D., eds. 2015. *War and Cultural Heritage*. Cambridge: Cambridge University Press.
Sovacool, B., and Halfon, S. 2007. Reconstructing Iraq: Merging Discourses of Security and Development. *Review of International Studies*, 33 (2), 223–243.
Toft, M. D. 2009. *Securing the Peace: The Durable Settlement of Civil Wars*. Princeton, NJ: Princeton University Press.
Torsti, P. 2009. Segregated Education and Texts: A Challenge to Peace in Bosnia and Herzegovina. *International Journal on World Peace*, 26 (2), 65–82.
Tropp, J. 2003. Displaced People, Replaced Narratives: Forest Conflicts and Historical Perspectives in the Tsolo District, Transkei. *Journal of Southern African Studies*, 29 (1), 207–233.
Turku, H. 2017. *The Destruction of Cultural Property as a Weapon of War: ISIS in Syria and Iraq*. Basingstoke: Palgrave.
United Nations. 2014. *Unmanned Vehicles in Humanitarian Relief*. https://docs.unocha.org/sites/dms/Documents/Unmanned%20Aerial%20Vehicles%20in%20Humanitarian%20Response%20OCHA%20July%202014.pdf. Accessed 22 August 2017.
Unruh, J. D. 2001. Postwar Land Dispute Resolution: Land Tenure and the Peace Process in Mozambique. *International Journal on World Peace*, 18 (3), 3–29.
Varden, H. 2011. A Kantian Conception of Global Justice. *Review of International Studies*, 37 (5), 2043–2057.
Ward, T. J. 2007. The Political Economy of NGOs and Human Security. *International Journal on World Peace*, 24 (1), 43–64.
Weiss, T. G. 2001. Researching Humanitarian Intervention: Some Lessons. *Journal of Peace Research*, 38 (4), 419–428.
Welasek, H. 2018. *Bosnia and the Destruction of Cultural Heritage*. London: Palgrave.

CHAPTER 2

The Discreet Indispensability of Unpiloted Assistance? Remote Aerial Capabilities in Upstream Preventative Stabilisation Interventions

Paul Schulte

Assessments of the role of remote airpower in low-intensity conflicts are often either classified or impressionistic. There has been little incentive for rigorous public examination how far discreetly, and sometimes confidentially, provided American RPAS (including underreported Intelligence, Surveillance, Target Acquisition, and Reconnaissance (ISTAR) models), together with SF and precision munitions, have helped defeat indigenous terrorists in Violent Extremist Organisations (VEOs) fighting to overthrow friendly governments. Current efforts against Daesh in Libya, Tunisia, and the Sahel, are still more instructive. Here, limited, deliberately low profile, "light footprint", intervention combines RPAS with SF to facilitate partnership with friendly local forces, Commentators, however, disagree sharply about how far this "discreet new normal" can achieve the long-term systemic changes in governance and Security

P. Schulte (✉)
University of Birmingham, Birmingham, UK

T. Clack and R. Johnson (eds.), *Before Military Intervention*,
https://doi.org/10.1007/978-3-319-98437-7_2

Sector Reform (SSR), conventionally specified as essential for enduring "structural stability". This article consequently touches on some of the wider issues which arise in judging the "the use and targeting of … air operations and measures of success", currently under consideration by the UK Parliamentary Committee on Defence (Commons Defence Committee 2018). Without convincing methodologies to analyse net effectiveness, controversy will continue, deriving from divergent underlying assumptions about the utility of force in the twenty-first century, the attainability of different kinds of "stabilisation", uncertainly anticipated overspill and delayed effects, sources of violent Islamism, alternative futures of fragile states, the feasibility of reform options, and the moral weighting of different costs of intervention or abstention. "Drones" and "stabilisation" each remain unusually contentious; combining them multiplies dispute.

The Obama Doctrine

By 2012, the US and its allies, had tried and abandoned transformative "nation-building" interventions. Announcing America's strategic response to the eruption of Daesh, President Obama publicly stressed that Americans should:

> understand how this effort will be different from the wars in Iraq and Afghanistan. It will not involve American combat troops fighting on foreign soil. This counterterrorism campaign will be waged through a steady, relentless effort to take out ISIL wherever they exist, using our air power and our support for partner forces on the ground. This strategy of taking out terrorists who threaten us, while supporting partners on the front lines, is one that we have successfully pursued in Yemen and Somalia for years…to use force against anyone who threatens America's core interests, but to mobilize partners wherever possible to address broader challenges to international order. (Obama 2014)

The resultant "Obama Doctrine" remains the background to contemporary thinking on stabilisation operations, which, according to Krieg (2016), has been a grand strategy of delegation amounting to surrogate war.

Western loss of confidence about achieving acceptably stable end states after large-scale military intervention has contributed to international inaction over the Syrian Civil War, and various worldwide refugee crises. One recent commentator, Christopher Tuck (2016), has summed up the situation as a prolonged failure to develop any reliable theory of victory for complex "liberal state-building". He therefore criticises residual "planning-school" doctrinal approaches to stability operations, expecting to rebuild weak states through some universally applicable technique. Michael Mandelbaum (2016) locates strategic pessimism, or paralysis, about interventions in the crumbling of America's unprecedented predominance during immediate post-Cold War years, which had encouraged grandiose transformative visions to extend Western values rather than defend US security interests. In his election campaign, President Trump repeatedly rejected nation building as a basis for future US involvements. Interventions will therefore be limited, seeking, at most, to foster stability by incremental reform and internal political settlements. But in countries facing urgent threats from fiercely destabilising VEOs, non-reformative interventions are being improvised without expecting early political settlements or improved governance. Since taking office, revelations about American counter-terrorism in Niger, Afghanistan, Yemen, Somalia and Syria have confirmed Trump's predicted preference for military operations with low US footprint focused on killing terrorists.

US Presidential Global "Drone Warfare"

The "Drone Warfare" dominating media and legal attention since 2001 is an apparently endless succession of targeted killings by US Medium Altitude Long Endurance (MALE) RPAS types such as the Predator and the more potent Reaper, using missiles, or guided bombs, against otherwise unreachable VEO leaderships, without (at least publicly acknowledged) acceptance or invitation, from governments unwilling or unable to act against them. This unprecedented global counterterrorist decapitation strategy has been enabled by RPASs' newly developed range, persistence and precision, indispensably supported by America's worldwide air basing, intelligence, and communications networks—with unobtrusive, though still controversial, allied assistance. It has largely averted attempted arrest or targeted killing by commandos which would more severely affront local pride and risk capture or death. US government figures for Drone Strikes against Terrorist Targets Outside Areas of Active Hostilities (US DNI 2016) of Iraq, Afghanistan and Syria between 2009 and 2015, claim drones caused 2372–2581 combatant and 64,116 non-combatant deaths. Disputes over such figures merge with the widespread and legal moral objections which have conditioned aversive international attitudes to RPASs.

Modalities of Interventionary Air Power in Reformative Stabilisation Interventions

Basing, Symbolic Signalling, and Operating Options

Given the negative reputation of "drones" the presence and visibility of interventionary air power will have intrinsic signalling effects, and will be technically constrained by territorial restrictions, operational ranges and airspace coordination. Deployments can be publicised for reassurance to allies, influence over their approach to stabilisation, or warning to hostile groups and states. Symbolically salient "manhunting" MALE types of RPASs might be openly revealed and publicised within the supported state, as in Afghanistan, or set up within clandestine bases, as US Predators initially were in Pakistan. They may be discreetly admitted, as with the US in Djibouti and Niger, or kept out entirely of local public discussion, as with UK Reapers flying against Daesh in Iraq and Syria whose basing locations are confidential. Additional decisions arise about badging and national control. These might be shared, denied, faked or kept deliberately opaque. RPAS types can be funded by intervening countries, and then largely turned over to various indigenous forces. But they will often need foreigners to operate them, who might be more acceptable if Loan Service Personnel or contracted employees of private military companies.

Specific RPAS Roles in Upstream Reformative Stabilisation

Ideally, judiciously controlled and well-balanced commitments of remote airpower will improve a supported government's ability to resist armed groups, or to negotiate (whether sequentially or continuously) with them from strength. It might also be conditionally limited or even withdrawn to nudge reluctant local allies towards responsible behaviour.

Adapting and extending Beck's (2008) typology, the following uses of remote interventionist airpower in these scenarios can be distinguished:

1. **Strategic and Operational ISTAR**

Huge streams of intelligence information from remotely operated aerial platforms (especially High Altitude Long Endurance (HALE) types like Global Hawk), fused with other sources, will increasingly be analysed by continually updated algorithms, using machine learning to improve interrogation ("mining") of flows of Big Data. Foreseeable composite ISTAR/Artificial Intelligence capabilities could not substitute for the deep cultural understanding lacking in interventions in Afghanistan, Iraq, and Libya. But they would further increase certain kinds of cognitive advantage enjoyed by advanced interventionist militaries. With appropriate resourcing of predictive AI, especially in areas covered by their aerial surveillance, those states will simply come to know not only more and more about key aspects of what is operationally occurring, but also what is (probabilistically) about to happen, than the supported government or faction. This discrepancy may increase the leverage of interventionist forces over local partners—conceivably at the cost of increased resentment and friction. The degree of sharing or trading of information with local partners, and arrangements for intelligence fusion will be highly sensitive in almost any intervention scenario.

Although RPAS have the same formal legal status as manned aircraft, their overflights seem in practice (like movements of their frequent SF ground partners) to constitute a lesser, practically unenforceable, category of transgression against sovereign national boundaries. Invariably, sensitive negotiations on basing and access may reduce legal constraints. Gaining, and selectively sharing, situational awareness delivered by remote aerial ISTAR across unstable regions offers clear-cut advantage for both interventionist forces and apprehensive governments concerned to improve local resilience against terrorist threats. It can enable a range of responses including RPAS strikes, manned aerial attack (which may seem indistinguishable to survivors from RPAS attack), CT activities by ground forces, police interception and the continuously updated protection of vulnerable national boundaries

2. **Counterterrorism**

Killing or capturing irreconcilable high-value opponents would be most efficiently achieved by moving towards a high tempo CT complex developed by the US Joint Special Forces Command (JSOC) in Iraq after 2003, involving RPASs less to conduct strikes but as ISTAR assets for manned aircraft and ground forces. Each interrogation or exploitation of captured written or electronic records adds to the knowledge base supporting the CT campaign. The infrastructure and human resources needed to run such a complex would exceed the capabilities of threatened host states, implying high levels of external assistance, including intelligence input. Targeted killing of individual insurgent or terrorist leaders by foreign RPAS attack will be dependent on host government attitudes-though frictions may be less over reluctance than excessive enthusiasm for eliminating rivals. Political costs need to be understood and minimised, both for the host state, whose population will view RPAS as the embodiment of outside interference, dispensing life or death, and to interventionist nations through reputational risks (and Information War vulnerabilities) from mistargeting or misrepresentation. Nevertheless, states like Nigeria, Iraq, and Pakistan, combating terrorists and insurgents are proudly broadcasting combat imagery from their own, less advanced but still lethal (mostly Chinese) MALE RPAS. Local partners will increasingly make their own targeting decisions. As an officer in the West Point Combating Terrorism Centre warned, "I'm very hesitant on backing foreign militaries or paramilitary forces or militias. … You can't control them, and you don't have transparency over what they do, and it blows up in your face the same way that a bad drone strike does (Scahill 2013)." In these situations, there could be serious political objections and legal challenges for international military personnel or assets involved in the kill chain. Conversely, eliminating individual terrorist targets as part of the US global counterterrorism campaign may conflict with stabilisation efforts, if actions are perceived as unconnected with local interests, as with the 2014 seizure of Abu Khattala in Libya discussed below. Even if they could be convincingly measured, there is little reason to assume that balances between destruction, degradation, and disruption of VEOs by targeted killing and incitement of supporters will be the same in every theatre, with similar effects on relevant groups over time. But decapitation strategies will generally be more effective against primarily terrorist groups with centralised leaderships than with dispersed insurgencies. The more that visible kinetic use of RPAS could be integrated into popular narratives supporting the intervention's local partners, stressing national control or physical ownership of remote aerial assets, and reducing resentment of foreign forces (ideally amplified by an integrated communications strategy) the greater their likely net benefit.

3. **Tactical ISTAR**

Here remote airpower capabilities offered by intervention forces could very obviously increase direct situational awareness, survivability, and combat power of at least some friendly units, especially when assisted by outside trainers or SF. Commercially available systems, such as Black Hornet, as with so many aspects of remote airpower, will grow exponentially without foreseeable limit to models and capabilities.

4. **Organic Close Air Support (CAS)**

Combat power and confidence might similarly be augmented by issuing man-portable models, like the Switchblade "Flying Shotgun" loitering munition, at favoured small unit level. Whatever their specifications, the real battlefield effectiveness of small RPASs depends upon trainers or mentors. In the longer term, advanced armies are moving towards mixed teams of humans and remote robotic systems plus swarms of autonomously self-choreographing RPASs. Heavy pressures can be expected to make new capabilities available to assist local allies, though there will be financial, security and technical limits accommodating such demands.

5. **Force Protection**

RPAS operating persistently above friendly units, able to warn or conduct kinetic attacks themselves, have shown considerable effectiveness in reducing casualties from Improvised Explosive Devices (IEDs) or ambush in Afghanistan, Iraq and presumably Libya, can reduce risks to exposed small units which risk disastrous strategic effects on public opinion such as the isolation and murder of the British RMP patrol near Basra in 2003, the ambush of French paratroopers near Kabul in 2008, the near overrun of the US Army position at Wanat in Afghanistan in 2008 and the loss of the AFRICOM SF team in Niger in February 2018. For British forces around Basra in February 2005, facing a classic stabilisation predicament, with too few troops to protect a large population, lack of ISTAR resources was judged the most significant capability shortfall in a long list (Clarke 2016). And. In a widely-quoted interview, General McChrystal (2013) while criticising America's overuse of "hated" "drone strikes", emphasised that protective RPAS allowed more flexible and audacious deployments of smaller groups of SF.

Discreet RPAS force protection has intangible, repeatedly confirmed, benefits, permitting wider options for "tailored engagement", limited direct action by SF and intelligence specialists, assisting partnered forces, ensuring military progress is sustained, and building the capacity of local partners to retake territory from VEOs. Mentoring or embedding arrangements are a persistent interventionist success story. Their continuing effectiveness was reconfirmed in the 2016 RAND study (Jones et al. 2016) of US Africa Command (AFRICOM)'s assistance to the African Union Mission in Somalia (AMISOM)'s campaign against al Shabaab. US advisers plan missions, provide aerial surveillance and conduct air-strikes to protect partner forces. According to Congressional testimony, "demand for drones by SF units outpaces that of any conventional military unit by orders of magnitude … ongoing SF missions require 44 drone combat air patrols—each consists of four drones and hundreds of personnel" (Gettinger 2015). In general, supported local forces "know Americans are not going to be left out to dry… so if things go badly, we're a security blanket for them". While AFRICOM is notoriously secretive, protective RPAS strikes may be included in totals reported by the US, without explanation, outside the three recognised American operational theatres. Remote aerial force protection also limits insurgents' offensive tactical options—or else inflicts disproportionate losses. But high bandwidth requirements, problems of access to sensitive C3I arrangements, and the skilled manpower and training required to operate and maintain advanced MALE RPAS mean that they are unlikely to be widely or reliably available to protect host nation units.

6. **Interdiction**

Movements of terrorists and supplies can be threatened or attacked, beyond national frontiers (especially against hostile proxy state action), in border zones, at sea or against internal routes. RPASs' role might well be to detection, and coordination of local or interventionist troops or police. Aerial surveillance will be particularly effective in sea or desert environments and Tunisia has demonstrated how even wary governments, anxious to keep their distance, will accept American ISTAR RPAS on their territory when facing threats from chaotic neighbours.

7. **Strategic or Coercive Bombardment**

Whether conducted by manned or remotely piloted aircraft, this would run counter to reformative stabilisation and risk international opprobrium. Moreover, terrorists or insurgents in an early stage of a campaign are unlikely to offer strategically tempting centres of gravity.

8. **Air Transport**

This is not yet practicable or cost-effective for RPASs, even for frontline medical evacuation. If a contested aerial environment of this kind develops, the overall situation is unlikely to be described as upstream. But calculations may change as advanced countries begin to use RPASs for transport to increase flexibility, speed of distribution and immunity from terrestrial impediments, much like non-military commercial equivalents, but with additional, non-economic, incentives.

9. **Propaganda and Information**

Russia's heavy aerial bombardment of civilian targets in Syria has been assisted by ISTAR RPASs, mostly purchased from Israel. An additional aspect, in support of Information Warfare, was Russian screening of selected video footage to try to exonerate its forces from bombarding an aid convoy in September 2016. RPAS footage of disputed engagements and their aftermath, as in Aleppo, is an increasingly important output of strategic communications directorates.

RPAS in Peacekeeping Operations

The UN now uses ISTAR RPAS routinely and successfully in peacekeeping missions in the Democratic Republic of Congo, the Central African Republic and Mali (where 118 UN troops have, nevertheless been killed by VEOs), protecting soldiers by warning of enemy ambush or attack, and increasing civilian security and confidence (Sieff 2017). This has not, however, assured the overall success of those missions.

Remote Aerial CT Assistance to Protect Reform: The Tunisian Case

Since initiating the Arab Spring of 2011, Tunisia has sought to modernise and reform itself while maintaining stability against violent internal and external extremists. It has successfully managed an electoral transfer of power from an Islamist party, and cautiously accepted considerable Western aid and security support. As in many intervention situations, this must be kept carefully discreet in view of public suspicion of Western intentions. But Tunisia's Armed Forces are at least partially receptive to technical improvement and SSR. Tunisia therefore provides an excellent, though necessarily unobtrusive example of a "reformative stabilisation intervention". CT expertise and advice, with wide-ranging intelligence support, including from RPAS, seems to have been an important feature. Tunisia's small Air Force successfully supported a short counterinsurgency campaign against indigenous Islamists in 2013. There are suggestions that Western aerial intelligence was provided (Cooper 2016) and, since then, it has certainly been reported that foreign reconnaissance aircraft and drones overfly Tunisian territory. With other NATO allies, America has provided Tunisia with unobtrusive military advice and assistance, including cheap and internationally underestimated Scan Eagle ISTAR RPAS.

Libya's neighbouring tragedy deepens Tunisia's problems. In March 2015, 3 Libyan trained militants murdered 22 people in the Bardo National Museum in Tunis. Later that month, AFRICOM SF, and an American surveillance aircraft (very possibly an RPAS) circling overhead, were reportedly crucial to a successful, widely publicised, and intentionally lethal ambush of an Islamist terror group by elite Tunisian security personnel at Gafsa, helping to restore national morale. This could not prevent a mass shooting of tourists on a beach near Sousse in June 2015 by the exceptionally difficult intelligence target of a single radicalised gunmen, again trained in Libya. In May 2016, Islamists were still able to kill 50 people in the border town of Ben Guerdan, though they themselves suffered 40 killed and wounded. The balance would have been worse if government forces had not been alerted (Mekhennet and Ryan 2016).

In July 2016, NATO announced the establishment of an intelligence fusion centre to improve transfer of information from all sources and platforms to assist Tunisia's SF and the US supplied Tunisia with another Scan Eagle (Cordall 2016).

In mid-2016 Tunisia confidentially agreed to base unarmed US Reapers on its territory, to facilitate ISTAR around Sirte. Distances from AFRICOM bases in Niger, and Mediterranean clouds impeding operations from Sicily have been cited to require this concession, traded for increased aerial intelligence on Tunisia's own vulnerable areas, once the focus on Sirte could be relaxed. Intelligence would be shared with Tunisia to improve border security. The Reapers might later be armed if the Tunisian government overcame its concerns about open support for Western military operations against a neighbour (Entous and Ryan 2016).

Libya: RPAS—Assisted Regime Change and After

Libya is the best current example of an urgent non-reformative upstream intervention. RPAS have already been significant in the country's history. The NATO aerial bombardment of 2011 was rare in that it was not described as intended to achieve stability but justified to protect the Libyan people. UNSCR 1973 authorised all necessary means except for a "foreign occupation force". This restriction was not taken to apply to SF, whose involvement on the ground was admitted, especially in the training and aerial targeting role, during the NATO campaign by the US, UK, France, Qatar, and Jordan and possibly others. Mark Urban, the BBC defence correspondent, reported in 2012 that "the architects of the UK involvement judge that Western SF may have turned the military tide in favour of the rebels. Against "Gaddafi's military, NATO largely relied on US JSTARS surveillance aircraft, flying offshore... when... needed... the U.S. flew Predator drones to relay a block-by-block picture." Gaddafi was killed near his hometown of Sirte in October 2011 after his escape convoy was struck by a US Predator RPAS and a French or British fighter-bomber (Barry 2011). Anti-Gaddafi forces had also privately obtained, and rapidly mastered, small commercially available surveillance RPASs before the end of the Civil War. Western SF have since remained, largely unpublicised, in Libya.

Subsequent Western military involvements have been therefore limited and clandestine. Attempts at reformative stabilisation, led by UN diplomats, have clearly failed. This been extensively criticised. But no international force could have gained local acceptance in imposing order, even if troops could have been found, funded, and kept in place after they began taking casualties. Like many fragile states, Libya has a painful and resented history: occupation, bombardment and raids from the sea and air by Christian Europe and America. During the Italian invasion of 1911, which led to an unusually brutal colonial occupation, Libyan fighters were the first in the world to suffer air attack. Libyans show especially acute sensitivity to any suggestion of control or manipulation by the West. Early engagement leading to reformative stabilisation would obviously have been a better outcome for everyone except warlords and VEOs. But, given tribalism, local fragmentation self-interested leaders and atomisation after decades of tyranny, it simply could not be brought about. Libya is not alone in this predicament. Subsequent civil strife has created innumerable additional combative militias, and, at present, three contending national governments. This has provided uniquely favourable opportunities for Daesh, leading to non-reformative Western interventionist expedients, heavily dependent on RPAS.

Remotely Piloted Wings Over a Libya in Chaos

RPASs have been used over Libya in sporadic CT raids, and from August 2016, openly, alongside fixed wing aircraft and cruise missiles for optimum military effect in the prolonged air campaign supporting the ejection of Daesh from Sirte. It is unlikely that intelligence gathering RPAS flights over Libyan territory ever ceased after the 2011 Civil War. In 2012, after the burning of the US Consulate, US Predator RPASs were deployed over Benghazi, forcing the closure of its airport (Associated Press, 2012). In 2014 US commandos seized a pro-Islamist leader, Abu Khattala, for the Consulate attack, and brought him back to the US for trial. Their action seems to have been enabled by over 500 hours of overland reconnaissance by small Fire Scout MQ 8 RPASs flown from an American frigate, "developing [a] pattern of life for US Africa Command's number-one target" (Trevithick, 2016). The arrest was reported as widely unpopular within Libya. Following manned airstrikes against other Daesh leaders, in February 2016, US aircraft and RPAS destroyed the Daesh camp at Sabratha, probably after ground reconnaissance by AFRICOM SF, killing Noureddine Chouchane, a Daesh leader involved in the Bardo Museum and Sousse attacks, and in funnelling 1500 fighters to Iraq and Syria. There were protests from Libyan factions about the lack of advance notification.

Operations al-Bunyan al-Marsus and Odyssey Lightning

Amid deepening nationwide chaos, Daesh moved to occupy large areas of Libya. In eventual response, the UN-backed Government of National Accord (GNA), launched a campaign dubbed "al-Bunyan al-Marsus", (BaM or Solid Foundation) against Daesh in Sirte in May 2016. BaM seem throughout to have enjoyed semi-covert Western assistance, increasingly evidently by mid-2016. Small contingents of SF, certainly from the US, UK, and France, and possibly also Italy, have been active, though carefully unpublicised or even denied. (A US SF group, photographed arriving in civilian clothes, immediately left the country.) According to the London Times, by April 2016 after an intermittent presence of several years, British SF in Libya included up to 40 SAS and SBS personnel and members of the Special Reconnaissance Regiment, experts in covert surveillance, and military intelligence officers, linguists and bomb disposal experts. Their roles included protecting local leaders, mentoring "friendly" militias, training local fighters to take on Daesh and monitoring its positions and commanders. Western military assistance activities for Libya were commended by Jens Stoltenberg, the NATO Secretary General, as contributions to stability (Hookham and Ripley 2016).

US SF are quite certainly protected and supported by nearby RPAS. This is very probably true for other allied contingents. The US has sold armed Predators to Italy and received the right to base RPASs in Sicily, although Italian government authorisation was stipulated for offensive strikes, apparently for fear of retaliatory terrorism and popular Italian backlash. In August 2016 militia forces associated with the GNA advanced into Sirte, to eliminate the Daesh controlled enclave. They were assisted not only by multinational SF on the ground but open American air support from two aircraft carriers, and bases in Europe. Operation Odyssey Lightning, presidentially authorised and announced on 1 August, dragged out until 19 December after 495 "precision airstrikes," each individually requested by the BaM.

Daesh casualties were large, perhaps in the low thousands, but at least 712 BaM fighters were killed and 3210 wounded in overcoming a probably unwisely determined defence. It is unlikely that the city could have been taken at acceptable cost without assistance, advice, training, and occasional combat intervention from Western SF mentors. Events at Sirte, like those Mosul, suggest that, in contemporary Africa and the Middle East, highly motivated VEOs in fortified urban locations cannot be eliminated by local forces without heavy applications of foreign airpower directed by intervention contingents.

Western involvement in Libya will certainly continue, though no provision has been declared for reconstruction. Bombarding Sirte has been described as 'like hitting mercury with a hammer' because many Daesh fighters exfiltrated, to continue fighting in southern Libya, return to Tunisia, or join Boko Haram in the Sahel, to further destabilise North Africa and Europe. In January 2016, the Pentagon announced a conspicuously complex combined air strike, by RPAS and intercontinental B-2 bombers, to maximise assured casualties on 2 Daesh camps south of Sirte (Joscelyn 2017). RPASs will undoubtedly continue combing the Libyan Desert in flexible cooperation with international air and ground forces.

This may be against a background of intensified civil strife. During the Sirte fighting, General Haftar's Libyan National Army seized oil ports from potential GNA control. This unexpected intensification of complex, largely latent, conflict, driven by personalities and tribal and regional rivalries, entwined with foreign alignments, is a strong indication that, quite apart from the struggle with VEOs, internecine conflict between warlords, militias and rival governments will probably continue within and beyond Libya, despite UN negotiators' efforts to assemble the reformative preconditions for eventual structural stability. Unlike the impoverished countries of the Chad Basin in the Sahel, re-establish Libyan oil revenues would be sufficiently lucrative to motivate external self-interest to combine with internal rivalries.

High Stakes and Replicable Swarmed Responses

The context for Western RPAS over Libya involves geopolitical concerns and overspill consequences extending far beyond Libya's borders, including intensified regional conflict, maritime terrorism, and "migration warfare", allowing unlimited numbers of un-vetted refugees and migrants to cross the Mediterranean, with corrosive effects on EU political solidarity. Potential oil resources, around Sirte and elsewhere, are huge. Prolonged control of territory would also provide a VEO proto-state with taxes and fees, ransoms, looting, extortion, and local populations to be forced to fight. And the impression of God-given momentum would be reinforced

The terrorists who crippled the Tunisian tourist industry, by such methodical killing of Western tourists, at the Bardo Museum and on the beach at Sousse, had been trained at the Daesh camp at Sabratha, subsequently destroyed by the combined strike by US RPAS and manned aircraft. Preventing such widening attacks is therefore seen as one factor in avoiding the destabilisation of the region—although both Algeria and Tunisia are both preparing for the worst case by building defensive barriers on their borders with Libya.

The ramifying risks posed by Daesh in Sirte stimulated rare cooperation not only between Western military and intelligence forces, but, less certainly and less visibly, regional anti-Islamist allies like Jordan, Egypt, and the Gulf states, especially Abu Dhabi. US, Italian, British and French SF were already reported in mid-2016 to be operating in Libya to assist anti-Daesh forces and to prepare for a—still possible—larger (but nevertheless limited) ground intervention by multinational Western forces.

The fusion of Operations Odyssey Lightning and al-Bunyan al-Marsus provides an example of drone-assisted strategic counterterrorist swarming (i.e. "several units conducting a convergent attack on a target from multiple axes"), with local allies and overwhelming air power, to overmatch the swarming of Daesh fighters. This is a potentially replicable and scalable response, like the spread of the Daesh or Al Qaeda Vilayets, Emirates or affiliated groups which it is intended to block or eliminate.

It cannot guarantee international cohesion over Libya's future.

RPASs as Unique Enablers in Semi-Surrogate Warfare

As envisaged under the Obama Doctrine, the overall Western approach to combating VEOs remains to rely upon and enable local allies and partners. In Libya, these turn out to be a mix of militias in shifting informal alliances under conditions of uncertainty about effectiveness, legitimacy, and underlying intentions. RPAS provide ISTAR, though limited by distance, visibility, bandwidth, and analytical capability, and enable continuous protection and instant fire support, reducing risks to small Western units, which, in these chaotic situations, will be greater than in upstream reformative interventions. Diplomatically authorised, or informally tolerated, remote aerial overhead availability will therefore be a precondition for much SF activity in these circumstances. Remote aerial force protection allows deployment of SF teams to help recruit, assist, motivate, train, equip, finance and provide forward air control for local forces willing to drive out VEOs. Protected troops and operators in turn constitute forward intelligence hubs, accumulating targeting information to maximise the impact and precision of aerial bombardment in which remote airpower, with its slow airspeed, relatively light payloads and long loiter times can its play specialist part within integrated air operations. SF teams therefore act as 'accelerants 'for multi domain campaigns. And these conveniently deniable troops can also conduct unreported ground raids or defensive actions in support of their local partners.

RPAS-Enabled Offensive Flexibilities: Tailored Engagement and Operational Advice and Assist

Political and legal concerns have led to a considerable blurring between SF "contact teams", operated by armies, intelligence operatives affiliated to intelligence agencies, military trainers, and targeting specialists for drones and ground attack aircraft. Upstream Western deployments are often referred to as" training missions." This may well be true in countries with strong inhibitions on foreign troops going into combat on the national territory. But, according to the RAND analyst, Linda Robinson, quoted in an illuminating series of interviews in the Washington Post, in situations like Libya "there is still this misunderstanding that we have one mode which is combat, and another mode which is [training]." In fact: "There's this whole spectrum in between, which is operational advise and assist." As an anonymous senior US defence official put it: "These situations offer "opportunities for indirect U.S. action, putting both the risk and the glory on partners' shoulders.... "This enables them to take those responsibilities themselves and reduces what are often very politically sensitive issues," ... "It reduces our footprint, our presence, and it gives credit to the [partner] country" assisting foreign forces to carry out assaults, rather than resorting to a direct U.S. strike, involves a balance between long- and short-term objectives. Another former senior Pentagon official observed that, "It's almost always easier for U.S. forces to do it directly," But "if your wider mission is to build up the capabilities of our partner, you accept some risk to mission and support local forces doing it ... Done right, this becomes a virtuous cycle" (Mekhennet and Ryan 2016).

There is a telling historical resonance here with TE Lawrence's famous "Twenty-Seven Articles" (Lawrence 1917), especially:

> #15. Do not try to do too much with your own hands. Better the Arabs do it tolerably than that you do it perfectly. It is their war, and you are to help them, not to win it for them. Actually, also, under the very odd conditions of Arabia, your practical work will not be as good as, perhaps, you think it is.

Lawrence could today be described as an SF team leader relying upon advanced air support and innovatively tailoring his engagement with local forces. Today, as then, it is also unlikely that host forces "doing it tolerably" and "building up capabilities" will wish to move very far beyond the immediate tactical necessities of Security Sector Stabilisation, (which, in evolving UK doctrine, "seeks to enable essential and minimum security and justice and in doing so protect and promote a legitimate political authority and prepare the foundations for transition to longer-term security sector reform.") (UK Stabilisation Unit 2014) towards the demanding, western influenced, cultural and organisational challenges of Security Sector Reform.

Competing Views on Non-Reformative Offensive Stabilisation in Libya

This operational pattern may prove a noteworthy turn in The Long War, driven by the imperative of avoiding overt Western boots on the ground, and dependent upon newly advanced airpower capabilities. It diverges, at least in the short term, from previous definitions of "stabilisation". It relies neither upon the American military formula of "Clear, Hold and Build" or the UK Stabilisation Unit's developing philosophy of working for inclusive internal political settlements. Non–reformative stabilisation represents the conscious (though perhaps temporary) securitisation of interventionist involvement—the worst humanitarian or development organisation nightmare. It is concerned with Offensive SSS rather than reformative SSR. It suspends the previous, morally comforting, connection asserted between developmental assistance, improvements in governance, and military force through the, "stabilisation agenda" of "integrated" or "comprehensive" missions. It is conducted largely in places which have deteriorated beyond any convincing euphemism of fragile states, and is conceptualised round a CT rather than a COIN framework. It usually implies at least temporary increases in deaths and physical destruction from interventionist firepower and insurgent resistance and retaliation. It can seldom promise any early end to violence. And it raises potential disputes about the legitimacy, humanitarian necessity, or hegemonic self-interest of stabilisation campaigns.

But will it work? Opinions predictably divide—although "success" criteria are seldom stated precisely.

Limited intervention in Libya, and the wider Sahel can undoubtedly be criticised as a strategic half measure. Impeccably realist security analysts, such as Anthony Cordesman, insist that "No campaign can succeed that does not blend military action with some form of effective stability operations bordering on nation building" and "War Four" either must have a clear and credible strategy and a plan that "visibly learns from our past mistakes and has Congressional, public, and allied support or it simply should not take place" (Cordesman 2015, 2016).

The fact that Western forces assisted, and so strengthened, one self-interested group of militias, which was supporting, maybe temporarily, a single faction jockeying for control of a failed quasi-state, to destroy a VEO proto-state, in the absence of any wider political settlement, is seen by some as "hollow victory" (Megerisi 2016) and even perhaps an irrevocable mistake, since the Libyan political crisis should be resolved before removing Daesh. Anthony Dworkin (2016) warns against Europe converging with American military CT in doubtfully legal and inconclusive "Counterterrorist Wars".

Farad Zakaria (2016) takes an exactly opposite view:

> Creating an effective and inclusive political system in places such as Syria [and therefore presumably Libya] seen by all elements within the society as legitimate [is] an almost impossible task for a foreign country. Better to focus U.S. energies on defeating the most dangerous groups, which would then give local regimes a chance to take control of their countries. (Zakaria 2016)

And retired American SF officers point out that "to avoid Libya becoming like Syria" sending small SF groups under RPAS protection "is one of the tools in your toolbox" and that, in any case, resultant gains in local knowledge mean that the US and its allies could better deploy additional personnel if a broader mission were to be agreed (Ryan 2016).

Remote Aerial Interventions in North Africa and Wider Strategy

The carefully intangible mix of assistance offered to Tunisia, and the combination of airpower, local allies and SF observable round Sirte, together seem to constitute the "latest formulation of states grappling to respond to insecurity and poverty at the periphery", a minimalist definition of stabilisation put forward by Zyck and Muggah (2015). This, and other African cases, strongly suggest that remote airpower, organised with careful discretion, can reduce the human and financial costs and risks of intervention, provided it remains limited. Discreet communications strategies can keep the salience low, both in the theatre of operations and the interventionist countries. Positively, this can minimise the risk of locally xenophobic dynamics which might frustrate or negate the purpose of the mission. Low profile arrangements such as "operational advise or assist" and "tailored engagement", may also eke out scarce and depleted strategic determination in Western states, while minimising chances of imbroglio through commitment traps. That would facilitate protracted or repeated engagement in the different theatres of a global and generational struggle. Structural stability, flowing from internal political settlements, may eventually be reached in at least some of these theatres after prolonged engagements, even if initial circumstances look discouragingly disintegrative. In the best outcome for Libya, what Dworkin might label a Counterterrorist War would become the indispensable, initial offensive stage of progressive stabilisation of the security sector. Diminished threats from VEOs could in turn support the slow, undoubtedly messy, emergence of some good-enough political compromise (which would need to be acceptable to various interested external actors who might otherwise act as spoilers), effective development aid and the progressive attainment of structural stability. Patient progress of that kind, together with similar, interlocking, RPAS-facilitated efforts elsewhere by AFRICOM, could fit within an intelligently coordinated overall strategy of "aggressive containment" (Fromson and Simon 2015) involving "training, weapons, intelligence work, special forces and targeted air strikes to support local forces on the ground" together with "new deals for Sunnis, changes of regime, ideological counter arguments on and off-line, support for countries struggling with refugees, and active conflict prevention."

Like many issues related to CT and COIN, Libya remains a continuing uncontrolled experiment. Its unique features may in fact frustrate any political settlement. But even this would not necessarily mean that the latest improvised light footprint of SF, integrated airpower and local allies could not be attempted elsewhere. And serious interpretation of intervention lessons cannot avoid the counterfactual question: could it really have been better to have left an expanding Daesh proto-State to grow in fighters, resources, and credibility, and, if not, what alternative means were possible?

Remote Airpower in Attritional "Raiding" Interventions?

One pessimistic answer to that is moving towards the "Raiding Strategy "recently proposed by two Israeli defence intellectuals (Inbar and Shamir 2016): successive assaults against dangerous nonstate actors, to limit their ability to inflict external harm. Western "raiding" forces, if necessary, openly using heavily armed ground units and acting without local allies, could temporarily destroy, disrupt and degrade VEO capabilities before withdrawing—and, thus, less certainly, influence their resolve to commit ambitious future attacks, by threatening further intense punishments. This would be done without expectation of finally eliminating the adversaries—though that planning assumption might not be admitted, and it would almost always be possible to point to some advantage for local forces or movements seeking a permanent victory over their national VEO antagonists. The proposed strategy emerges from the pessimistic Israeli experience of endlessly "mowing the grass" of a largely hostile strategic neighbourhood, and recurrent Israeli actions against regional terrorist groups, intended to achieve "cumulative deterrence", are offered as a provocatively tough-minded model.

Within the categories discussed here, this approach might be called "non-reformative attritional security sector mitigation". It is a sobering thought experiment, based on the uncomfortable assumption that the only feasible form of "stabilisation "in relevant conflict zones is now "patient attrition." A turn towards strategic raiding is imaginable after successfully provocative series of terrorist outrages. It might lead to some lethally virtuoso operations in which remote airpower would be an efficient way of mowing the (probably fast-growing) hostile human grass—and as a force multiplier for technology, firepower, and mobility. But the strategy would be internationally divisive, and legally questionable. One extremely negative, collateral outcome might of course be intensified and widened incitement: Hegghammer fears "a vicious cycle whereby terrorist attacks in the West directed by jihadi groups in the Muslim world prompt Western military action against those groups, which in turn fuels radicalization in the West" (Hegghammer 2016). "Strategic Raiding" represents a far-reaching, high-risk but not completely inconceivable, strategic temptation, which might easily become confused with all non-reformative intervention. The article's appearance in a respected international journal indicates how unpromising prospects for more traditional stabilisation now seem.

Stabilisation and Remote Airpower: Prospects and Conclusions

The endgame challenge of "stabilisation" overhangs irregular conflict and terrorism. The term has turned out to have little reliable or fixed meaning. Yet the less violent end state it implies cannot be abandoned as an international goal. Future interventions and stabilisation operations will, however, have to appear practically achievable with available tools and political determination, and judged worth the risks and costs. Given the discouraging lack of success in more ambitious or emancipatory ventures, discussion of stabilisation will therefore be largely confined to measures aimed against VOEs as hyperactive vectors of destabilisation.

Disputes over remote airpower in such interventions are largely about the utility of military force, in which RPASs are a growing component of almost any operation, already effectively indispensable within sophisticated military organisations. Calls by some Western NGOs to ban all types of remote interventionist airpower therefore amount to a thinly disguised rhetorical objection to any Western military involvement. RPAS cannot compensate for insufficient commitment, flawed understandings of cultural and political dynamics, or adaptive and resilient adversaries. Nor can they replace effective and determined friendly allies (This is especially true for discreet non-reformative campaigns, with few Western SF on the ground). Nor can remote airpower create any general theory of successful interventionism for stabilisation. But, when examined closely, it has already facilitated exceptionally light footprint campaigns, engaged in what might reasonably be labelled Offensive Security Sector Stabilisation. Despite raising complex questions about democratic control (see Knowles and Watson 2017), maintaining minimum visibility about such interventions may be justified, not only in the interests of operational security, but to minimise local xenophobia, postcolonial distrust, religious de-legitimation of local partners, entrapment, or embarrassment of allies, while supplementing Western strategic patience and acceptance of risk.

In judging responsible reporting practice, it is necessary to appreciate that the near monopoly enjoyed by the US and its allies on operating RPASs is breaking down. This momentous, inevitable, change seems to have been signalled by a little noticed report of a "drone strike" near Gardah in south-west Libya on 15 November 2016 (Reuters 2016). The Pentagon explicitly denied responsibility for the attack and NATO allies had no assets in the theatre which could have performed it. There have been plausible suggestions that it may have been conducted by, or on behalf of the forces of General Haftar, a faction leader with Egyptian and Emirati support (including both manned aircraft and armed Chinese MALE RPAS reportedly operated by the UAE in Eastern Libya) (Binnie 2016). Whoever conducted the strike, the small obscure killing, with 7 uncertainly identified casualties, signposts an unavoidably untidy future for RPASs in similar campaigns. Factions and self-designated governments will unquestionably acquire their own RPASs, or host those of supporting states.

Uncertainties will inescapably arise, not only about who should conduct specific remote aerial kinetic operations, against particular target types, but over responsibility for particular strikes and casualties. Answers will probably be lacking or dubious. There is little reason to suppose that RPAS attacks will always be launched only by coherently coordinated allied forces for a single set of campaign objectives. The availability, flexibility, economy, and potential anonymity of remote airpower will be a major temptation to chaotic overuse, with RPAS deployed and flown for clashing objectives, conducting uncertainly attributable attacks, compounding suspicions and compromising political settlements. VEOs, too, will actively complicate such future conflict. Hezbollah and Daesh have already publicised their own very aggressive efforts to acquire and operate ISTAR and armed RPASs in Syria and round Mosul. Metastasising nonstate actor capabilities such as "flying IEDs" will particularly add to the operational problems facing Western intervention forces.

RPAS will therefore increasingly provide additional cards for all sides in complex multiplayer politico military conflicts. These might of course be used badly, in narrowly kinetic repertoires, for misconceived intervention scenarios, whose full human costs will never be paid by outside combatants. But the risk of clumsy employment cannot reasonably mean that remote aerial capabilities should not be fully exploited by responsible governments. An overall strategic pattern, approximating to the model of "aggressive containment", using various forms of tailored engagement with local allies, supported by RPAS, alongside other technical assets, may be emerging, with intentionally little publicity, as the least bad available option. Much might be built on that, through parallel diplomatic engagement, patiently brokering political settlements backed by generous development assistance. But the development resources required for numerous national theatres are likely to exceed the capacities and political appetites of individual interventionist states. Sufficiently effective and sustained political engagement to maximise chances of stabilisation will also be hard to ensure. These scarcities of civilian commitment argue even more loudly for coordination among interventionist states than purely military capabilities. But it is simply unclear, from public sources, how, and in what geometries, any such comprehensive coordination is to be achieved. Decisions about ultralight footprint intervention in Africa are not openly discussed in either NATO or EU, although whatever informal consultations are de-conflicting multinational Western operations in Libya or the Sahel might conceivably be expanded into a wider directing process. Even so, Hazelton (2017) warns that each nation's decisions over RPAS (and SF) should be consistent with its overall Grand Strategy. And this may create wide differences in allied assessments of priorities, risks and costs-especially, perhaps, over the realistic danger which specific terrorist groups in remote impoverished areas are ever likely to pose to Western homelands.

Nevertheless, the special contemporary significance of remote aerial capabilities may be to offer one of the few currently usable forms of hard Western military power in irregular conflicts, which can also potentiate other capabilities in the limited, shadowy intervention campaigns which now seem the only politically sustainable option. However discreet, these interventions will still provoke passionately opposed, ideologically inflected opinions about the prudence and moral acceptability of the mixed and fluctuating outcomes of military involvement or abstention. Conflicting judgements of the effectiveness of AFRICOM—the largest and longest consistent user of remote airpower in upstream stabilisation—illustrate this (Turse 2016). There will undoubtedly be many opportunities for mistaken, mistargeted or misconceived employment of RPAS. It still remains true that, without modern remote aerial capabilities, some feasible interventions might not be made in a timely upstream stage before instabilities have irrevocably intensified, might be tried and then abandoned when they might have succeeded, or could only be carried through at unnecessary cost, in resources and military and civilian lives. The coming proliferation of remote aerial capabilities in numerous roles for all sides in almost every conflict will painfully demonstrate this.

References

Associated Press. 2012. U.S. Drones Behind Airport Closure. *Associated Press*, September 15. Available from http://blog.al.com/wire/2012/09/libyan_officials_us_drones_beh.html. Accessed 20 February 2017.

Barry, J. 2011. America's Secret Libya War. *Daily Beast*, August 30. Available from http://www.thedailybeast.com/articles/2011/08/30/america-s-secret-libya-war-u-s-spent-1-billion-on-covert-ops-helping-nato.html. Accessed 20 February 2017.

Beck, G. 2008. *Offensive Air Power in Counter-Insurgency Operations: Putting Theory Into Practice*. Royal Australian Air Force Air Power Development Centre, ACT, Australia, Working Paper 26.

Binnie, J. 2016. UAE's Forward Operating Base in Libya Revealed. *IHS Jane's Defence Weekly*, October 28.

Clarke, M. 2016. Planning and Fighting a War: The Iraq Inquiry's Judgements on the Armed Forces. *RUSI Journal*, December 21. Available from https://rusi.org/publication/rusi-journal/planning-and-fighting-war-iraq-inquirys-judgements-armed-forces. Accessed 20 February 2017.

Cooper, T. 2016. *Tunisia Waged a Successful Air War Against Militants—And No One Noticed War Is Boring*. Available from https://warisboring.com/tunisia-waged-a-successful-air-war-against-militants-and-no-one-noticed-bb-f1a73ff39a#.dbqpcs6vx. Accessed 20 February 2017.

Cordall, Simon. 2016. NATO to Establish Tunisian Intelligence Fusion Centre. *Tunisialive*, July 11. Available from http://www.tunisia-live.net/strategy/. Accessed 20 February 2017.

Cordesman, A. 2015. Yemen and Warfare in Failed States. *CSIS Commentary*, April 22. Available from https://www.csis.org/analysis/yemen-and-warfare-failed-states. Accessed 20 February 2017.

Cordesman, A. 2016. Poking the Hornet's Nest in Libya: "War Four" and This Time We Get It Right? *CSIS Commentary*, March 14. Available from https://www.csis.org/analysis/poking-hornet%E2%80%99s-nest-libya-%E2%80%9Cwar-four%E2%80%9D-and-time-we-get-it-right. Accessed 20 February 2017.

Dworkin, A. 2016. *Europe's New Counterterrorism Wars*. London: European Council on Foreign Relations.

Entous, A., and Ryan, M. 2016. U.S. Has Secretly Expanded Its Global Network of Drone Bases to North Africa. *Washington Post*, October 26.

Fromson, J., and Simon, S., 2015. ISIS: The Dubious Paradise of Apocalypse Now. *Survival: Global Politics and Strategy*, 57, 7–56.

Gettinger, D. 2015. *Diaries from the Shadows: Drones and Special Forces in the War on Terror*. Center for the Study of the Drone at Bard College. Available from http://dronecenter.bard.edu/diaries-from-the-shadows-drones-and-special-forces-in-the-war-on-terror/. Accessed 20 February 2017.

Hazelton, L. 2017. Drone Strikes and Grand Strategy: Toward a Political Understanding of the Uses of Unmanned Aerial Vehicle Attacks in US Security Policy. *Journal of Strategic Studies*, 40 (1–2).

Hegghammer, T. 2016. The Future of Jihadism in Europe: A Pessimistic View. *Perspectives on Terrorism*, 10 (6), 156–170.

Hookham, M., and Ripley, T. 2016. SAS Adds Steel to Libya's Anti-Isis Militias. *London Times*, April 17.

House of Commons Defence Committee. 2018. *UK Military Operations in Mosul and Raqqa Inquiry*. Available from https://www.parliament.uk/business/committees/committees-a-z/commons-select/defence-committee/inquiries/parliament-2017/inquiry11/. Accessed 20 February 2017.

Inbar, E., and Shamir, E. 2016. What After Counterinsurgency? *International Affairs*, 92 (6), 1427–1441.

Jones, S. G., et al. 2016. *Counterterrorism and Counterinsurgency in Somalia: Assessing the Campaign against Al Shabaab*. Santa Monica, CA: RAND Corporation.

Joscelyn, T. 2017. US bombs 2 Islamic State camps south of Sirte. *Long War Journal*, January 19. Available from http://www.longwarjournal.org/archives/2017/01/us-bombs-two-islamic-state-camps-south-of-sirte-libya.php. Accessed 20 February 2017.

Knowles, E., and Watson, A. 2017. *All Quiet on the Isis Front: British Secret Warfare in an Information Age*. Remote Control Project. London. Available from http://www.oxfordresearchgroup.org.uk/publications/briefing_papers_and_reports/remote_control_project_report_all_quiet_isis_front_british_. Accessed 20 February 2017.

Krieg, A. 2016. Externalizing the Burden of War: The Obama Doctrine and US Foreign Policy in the Middle East. *International Affairs*, 92 (1).

Lawrence, T. E. 1917. Twenty-Seven Articles. *The Arab Bulletin*, August 20, 1917. Available from https://wwi.lib.byu.edu/index.php/The_27_Articles_of_T.E._Lawrence. Accessed 20 February 2017.

Mandelbaum, M. 2016. *Mission Failure: America and the World in the Post-Cold War Era*. Oxford: Oxford University Press.

McChrystal, S. 2013. Retired General Cautions Against Overuse of Hated Drones. Available from http://uk.reuters.com/article/us-usa-afghanistan-mcchrystal-idUSBRE90608O20130107. Accessed 20 February 2017.

Megerisi, T. 2016. Libya's Hollow Victory Over the Islamic State. *Foreign Policy*, November 28. Available from http://foreignpolicy.com/2016/11/28/libyas-hollow-victory-over-the-islamic-state/. Accessed 20 February 2017.

Mekhennet, S., and Ryan, M. 2016. Outside the Wire: How U.S. Special Operations Troops Secretly Help Foreign Forces Target Terrorists. *Washington Post*, April 16.

Obama, B. 2014. *President Obama's Statement on ISIL*. Available from https://www.whitehouse.gov/the-press-office/2014/09/10/statement-president-isil-1. Accessed 20 February 2017.

Reuters. 2016. Air Strike Targeting Militants Kills Seven in Southern Libya—Official. *Reuters*, November 16. Available from http://www.reuters.com/article/us-libya-security-idUSKBN13A2FU. Accessed 20 February 2017.

Ryan, M. 2016. U.S. Establishes Libyan Outposts with Eye Toward Offensive Against Islamic State. *Washington Post*, May 12.

Scahill, J. 2013. *Dirty Wars: The World Is a Battlefield*. London: Serpents Tail, p. 145.

Sieff, K. 2017. The World's Deadliest UN Mission. *Washington Post*, February 17.

Trevithick, J. 2016. U.S. Navy Drone Choppers Hunted a Top Terrorist in Africa. *War Is Boring*, Jun 23. Available from https://warisboring.com/u-s-navy-drone-choppers-hunted-a-top-terrorist-in-africa-a4e6e5746431#.w8tye-3fyn. Accessed 20 February 2017.

Tuck, C. 2016. *The 'Practice' Problem: Peacebuilding and Doctrine*. Parameters U.S. Army War College. Available from http://www.strategicstudiesinstitute.army.mil/pubs/Parameters/issues/Summer_2016/Vol46No2.pdf. Accessed 20 February 2017.

Turse, N. 2016. Even AFRICOM's Own Commander Admits Its Strategy Is Not Working. *The Nation*, August 2. Available from https://www.thenation.com/article/even-africoms-own-commander-admits-their-strategy-is-not-working/. Accessed 20 February 2017.

UK Stabilisation Unit. 2014. *Security Sector Stabilisation: Issues Note*, March. Available online (no URL given).

Urban, M. 2012. SAS on Ground During Libya Crisis. *BBC News*, January 19. Available from http://www.bbc.co.uk/news/world-africa-16624401. Accessed 20 February 2017.

Zakaria, F. 2016. Obama's Whack-A-Mole Strategy. *Washington Post*, July 14.

Zyck, S. A., and Muggah, R. 2015. Preparing Stabilisation for 21st Century Security Challenges. *Stability: International Journal of Security and Development*, 4 (1). Available from http://www.stabilityjournal.org/articles/10.5334/sta.gs/. Accessed 20 February 2017.

CHAPTER 3

The Dilemmas of Security Assistance to a Failed State: Lessons from Somalia

William Reno

Somalia's government hosts foreign security assistance programmes that are intended to build police and military forces that support the rule of law and can protect the government and its citizens. "Adhering to the rule of law and respecting human rights, while assisting the Somali National Security Forces to counter terrorism, is paramount to gain Somali citizen support for their security forces," said US General Thomas Waldhauser (United States Africa Command 2017). Foreign assistance typically involves helping Somali security forces increase intelligence and reconnaissance capabilities to fight extremist groups to bring stability and security to their country. In contrast, a pragmatic version of security assistance to Somalia recognises that Somalia's government, or at least large parts of it, lacks the capability and more importantly, does not possess the political will to build effective security forces. Foreign trainers frequently encounter members of Somali security forces who are implicated in terrorist and criminal networks that their own security forces are supposed to counter. Foreign security assistance providers often discover that they have to engage in pragmatic adjustments and even openly

W. Reno (✉)
Department of Political Science, Northwestern University,
Evanston, IL, USA

T. Clack and R. Johnson (eds.), *Before Military Intervention*,
https://doi.org/10.1007/978-3-319-98437-7_3

defy the local officials whom security assistance is officially intended to support.

The gap between official statements and the realities of security assistance in Somalia highlight problems facing security assistance to states that lack effective central governments. Problems include commanders who recruit foreign-trained soldiers and police into their own private security companies and who double as heads of clan militias. Some of these security forces engage in criminal activities, even in collusion with insurgents that they are supposed to fight. Providing more security force assistance to these government officials and commanders often simply augments these activities. These realities in so-called failed and fragile states like Somalia make these countries particularly resistant to the objective of security force assistance. In Somalia, the evolution of state collapse that occurred under the rule of President Siad Barre (1969–1991) involved the president's intentional transformation of otherwise purely local tensions into armed struggle between clan militias that he carefully supported to maintain a balance of conflict. This political strategy enabled the president to keep communities from cooperating to oppose his authority. His officials came to rely upon various dubious forms of commerce, including in illicit goods, and their control over militias and youth gangs to pursue their private interests. This political evolution weakened the social bonds that previously held together communities, leaving most Somalis dependent upon competing armed strongman-politicians for protection (Simons 1995). When the central government collapsed in 1991, these deep and persistent societal antagonisms impeded the construction of new institutions. Security assistance shares in this dilemma, since it operates in this fragmented social context. Its key local partners are deeply embedded in the networks of dissolution, forced to hedge their bets and play as many sides as possible. The only groups that have imposed modestly sustained order in this context, at least in Somalia's southern core, are armed Islamist groups like Al-Shabaab that security force assistance is meant to eradicate.

Somaliland and Puntland, two fairly stable regions in the northern half of Somalia, appear to be successful institution-builders. Somaliland has maintained a considerable degree of political stability, particularly since 1997, and regularly holds competitive multiparty elections (Bradbury 2008; Renders and Terlinden 2010). But this political system remains susceptible to centrifugal clan-based political competition, with key actors constantly hedging their bets and playing multiple sides. Ken

Menkhaus notes that as a consequence these "local governance arrangements are quite complex, in a constant state of flux, and hence very challenging for Somalis to navigate," requiting 'a level of political acumen that outsiders often fail to appreciate' (Menkhaus 2014: 146).

This chapter explores an official narrative of the success of a conventional model of foreign security force assistance. Then it turns to the record of Somalia's security environment to illustrate the substantial failure of these policies. This evidence then sets the stage for a critical examination of the flawed assumptions that underpin conventional security sector assistance and security force reform in Somalia since Al-Shabaab was driven from Mogadishu in 2012. The chapter then turns to the pragmatic adjustments and compromises that foreign providers of security assistance make as it becomes apparent that the conventional strategy is likely to fail in this environment. This record, set alongside the promises of official policies, points to important underlying dilemmas of security force assistance in so-called failed states beyond Somalia.

The Rhetoric

By August 2011, soldiers of the African Union Mission in Somalia (AMISOM) drove Al-Shabaab fighters from Mogadishu. This advance enabled the Transitional Federal Government to move back to the capital. Then in London in February 2012, representatives of more than 50 governments and international organisations, alongside major Somali political groups agreed to work together to support a new national government. The final communique focused on promises to reconstruct security and judicial institutions and provide social services to citizens. Foreign governments reiterated promises to security assistance for AMISOM and received pledges from Somali leaders to elect a new legislature and write a new constitution (Foreign and Commonwealth Office 2012). By the end of 2012, a legislature convened in the capital and its 135 members selected Hassan Sheikh Mohamud, a former professor, as president. The mandate of this new Federal Government of Somalia (FGS) was to build security institutions and provide social service provision in time for elections in 2016. The "election" actually occurred on 8 February 2017 in a hangar at Aden Adde International Airport under AMISON guard amidst Al-Shabaab mortar attacks. Again, only members of Somalia's legislature, themselves elected by clan elder appointed delegates, actually voted. Former Prime Minister Mohamed

Abdullah Mohamed "Farmago" was selected as Somalia's next president. Michael Keating, the UN's Special Representative for Somalia, described this as a "political process with electoral features" (Burke 2017). The US Department of State welcomed the results: "We commend the Somali Security Forces and the African Union Mission in Somalia for their efforts over the past six months to allow the electoral process to unfold in a relatively safe and secure environment" (Department of State 2017).

The inability to hold one-person, one-vote elections exposed the incapacity of the Somali National Army (SNA) and other security forces to provide a basic level of security, even in the country's capital city. Nevertheless, a series of meetings in London prior to the 2017 election and the arrival of European and American training missions established the framework for long-term security assistance geared specifically towards improving Somali forces so that they could take over from AMISOM troops to fight and defeat insurgents. A London Conference in April 2015 set out a plan for a 10,900 strong core of the SNA to conduct joint operations with AMISON and provide the basis to further build the SNA to about 17,000 soldiers. Another London conference, in May 2017, produced a pledge from the Somali government to implement a National Security Architecture, integrate fighters from various militias into the SNA, and complete an Operational Readiness Assessment to reform the SNA and police (DfID et al. 2017). This security sector reform took place simultaneously with political reform designed to create a federal system that supports local self-government to give citizens a sense of 'ownership' of an evolving democracy, and set a path to one-person, one-vote elections in 2020.

Since 2012, Somalia has relied upon significant external financing and training support, due in part to very low levels of domestic revenues available to the Somali government. Support includes payments of 'stipends' to SNA troops by the US and other governments (Hogendoorn 2018: 3). Somalia absorbed 38% of US Defense and State Department Africa programme expenditures, or about $742 million for 2016 (Security Assistance Monitor 2015). The US provided about $900 million to AMISOM for logistics, equipment and training from 2007 to 2016, more than $400 million to support Somali forces, and an additional $720 million to the UN's Support Office in Somalia (UNSOM) from 2009 (Williams 2018). EU support for AMISOM and related security initiatives amounted to about €1.1 billion from AMISOM's inception in 2007–2015 (African Peace Facility 2016: 15). In addition, international aid to Somalia totalled $1.3 billion in 2016 (Office of the Prime Minister 2017: 5). This foreign role in Somalia's security sector reform and political development overshadows actual Somali capacities. Nevertheless, Nicholas Kay, the former Special Representative of the Secretary-General and head of UNSOM asked: 'Why is it coming together and why is it being successful? Because it is firstly a Somali-led and owned process and the result of a unique partnership between the African Union, UN, and the Federal Government' (United Nations 2015b).

Foreign providers of assistance were not uncritical of Somali government performance. In January 2017, the US Department of Defense announced it would scrutinise security assistance generally, calling for more serious attention to actual political and social conditions and the real interests of potential partners (Office of the Under Secretary of Defense for Policy 2015). In December 2017, the United States temporarily suspended aid to the SNA over frustration that the Somali government could not account for missing food supplies (Babb 2017). Aid was briefly suspended again in April 2018. But foreign officials are often caught between their frustrations that security force assistance and other aid to Somalia produce poor results and the necessity of working with the government of Somalia as it actually is, rather than the Somali government that they wished it would be. This problem points to the underlying dilemma of security force assistance to failed and failing states: State failure produces a distinct social context that undermines efforts to create effective state institutions, and those that are built often lack the political will or capability to benefit from security force assistance. This often leaves foreigners engaged in training programmes to wonder if their mission can ever succeed under conventional policies. A closer look at developments on the ground since and the roles of Somali officials in them since Al-Shabaab's apparent expulsion from Mogadishu and the arrival of the SFG in 2012 points to the sources of this frustration and the context of a more pragmatic approach to security force assistance.

Meanwhile, on the Ground

The real record of the security situation in Somalia, including in the capital Mogadishu, tells not just a story of security assistance failure. Close examination of specific incidences of violence illuminates the extent to which Somalia's situation is less one of a government versus insurgents, as it is of personal, kinship and commercial networks that infiltrate the government and particularly its security forces. These networks are susceptible to Al-Shabaab influence, perhaps less out of ideological or programmatic appeals as out of the interests of people to hedge their bets in the complex social environment of a collapsed state that is constantly in flux. Thus even officials who cooperate with foreign security assistance experts have to apply considerable acumen to managing their relations with Al-Shabaab and various militias as a matter of personal security and out of obligation to kin and their immediate communities. This means that these officials can be simultaneously embedded in official security forces, private security companies, and at times, in collusion with armed Islamist groups. These personal ties that cut across state and non-state organisations facilitate flows of information in ways that frustrate efforts to defeat insurgents and build state institutions. The shortcomings of security force assistance and the poor security situation overall are due as much to this failure to control flows of information as they are to the difficulties of building capable institutions in the failed state's social environment.

Developments on the ground in Somalia since 2011 stand at odds with the official narrative of security sector reforms. Somalia's government exercises tenuous control even in the capital city and its officials are frequent targets of Al-Shabaab attacks. As Table 3.1 (ACLED 2018) shows, the pace of violent incidents and associated fatalities highlights the extent to which Somali's security forces (in conjunction with AMISOM) have failed to provide Somali citizens with a secure environment.

Al-Shabaab attacks in Mogadishu, particularly on hotels, point to the particular character of the poor security environment. Hotels are favoured targets because of their important informal role in Somali politics. Many hotel proprietors are political players in their own rights.

Table 3.1 Table of violent incidents and fatalities in Mogadishu

	Violent incidents	*Fatalities*
2011	1399	1975
2012	2152	3341
2013	3129	3153
2014	2944	4457
2015	2356	4104
2016	2661	5641
2017	3034	5934

Some proprietors were notable warlords who earlier were members of the Alliance for the Restoration of Peace and Counter-Terrorism (ARPCT). Up to the ARPCT's defeat in 2006 by militias loyal to the Islamic Courts Union, some ARPCT members received American support to capture or kill extremists suspected of links to Al-Qaeda (Lacey 2006). Ten years later, some warlords served in Parliament or occupied other official positions, including ones who retained personal control over militias. This combination of political, military and commercial roles was ideal for launching ventures in Somalia's hospitality industry that requires armed protection for guests. Even though a successful hotelier must maintain an expensive armed force, hotels are a lucrative business because proprietors can collect stipends from international organisations to house and protect Somalia's legislators. Providing protection to these politicians improves the proprietor's commercial and political standing and connections, while in many cases also fulfilling kinship obligations to protect fellow clan members. Hotels thus become prime locations for deal-making and trading information: an ideal target.

Insurgent attacks on hotels make sense in light of this particular feature of Somalia's political scene. These attacks on Mogadishu hotels are a key element of Al-Shabaab's strategy of destabilisation through frequent deadly attacks on government officials. A steady pace of attacks also communicates to Somali observers that their government cannot even protect its own officials, much less average citizens. Even though AMISOM supposedly pushed Al-Shabaab out of Mogadishu by 2012, years later the group was able to launch numerous deadly attacks on hotels in the heart of the capital city. In January 2015, a car bomb targeted FGS officials and a Turkish delegation at the SYL Hotel. A month later, Al-Shabaab suicide bombers and gunmen killed 28 people at Central Hotel, including two legislators and Mogadishu's deputy mayor. In March, Al-Shabaab's attack on Maka Al-Mukarama Hotel, its fourth, killed Somalia's representative to the UN office in Geneva and thirteen others. In April, a car bomber and gunmen attacked the ministries of education and natural resources, killing eight people. The next day, a car bomb attack on a restaurant killed ten. In May a legislator was shot and three transportation ministry workers were killed in drive-by shootings. At least a dozen died in a July truck bomb attack on the Jazeera Hotel, host to the embassies of China, Qatar and Egypt. A November attack on the Sahafi Hotel, situated at a central crossroad of the capital, killed a legislator, a general and at least 13 others. Attacks in 2016 included two more strikes on SYL Hotel (killing nine, then 13), and in July, on Naso Hotel, killing 15, and Ambassador Hotel that killed two legislators. An attack the same month on the Criminal Investigations Department headquarters killed ten, and an attack at the main gate to the AMISOM zone killed thirteen. A car bomb in November killed 20 people in the Beerta market. In December, a truck bomb at the port killed 29 people.

Then in early January 2017, an explosion at Peace Hotel near a checkpoint to the international airport killed seven. Twenty-eight people were killed later that month in an attack on Dayah Hotel, close to Somalia's parliament. In February, 39 people were killed in a car bomb explosion near Wadajir market. A car bomber intending to target Weheliye Hotel killed 13. A week later, an explosion near the presidential palace killed 10. April attacks included a car bombing of a restaurant that killed seven, and a car bomb outside the Ministry of Defence that killed 15, an attack on an SNA facility that killed nine soldiers. After numerous smaller attacks in May, a June attack on a restaurant killed 31 and 15 more were killed a week later in an attack on the Wadajir neighbourhood government office. After a period of relative calm, the 14 October truck bomb attack killed at least 587 people. The suspected target was the heavily guarded airport compound that houses UN offices and embassies. In terms of fatalities, this was one of the world's largest terrorist attacks after the 11 September 2001 attacks on New York and Washington, DC. Later that month, a bombing near the National Theatre claimed 25 lives. A December attack in a police training camp killed 18 police officers. In February 2018 suicide car bombers killed 45 near the president's residence and Fiyad Hotel. The Weheliye Hotel was attacked yet again in March, with 14 people killed. Four days later a blast near Parliament killed four. In April, a car bomber killed 17 at Nasahablod Two Hotel, 600 metres from the presidential palace. Later in the month, an attacker in a suicide vest killed three security officials and two soldiers at a restaurant.

Alongside these larger attacks in the capital, Al-Shabaab has maintained a campaign of targeted killings of security forces and government officials. Some of these attacks may be connected to disputes over Al-Shabaab demands for monthly 'tax' payments from Mogadishu businesses, market associations and wealthy individuals, ranging from \$10 for market traders to \$70,000 for large companies (UN 2017: 13; UN 2017 Security Pact). Despite optimistic official pronouncements from Somali and foreign officials about reform processes and progress in the fight against Al-Shabaab, attacks in Mogadishu convey an image of an insurgency that is able to operate fairly effectively at the centre of state authority, despite the considerable resources, instruction and advice delivered through foreign security assistance to the Somali government.

Beyond Mogadishu, Al-Shabaab has demonstrated its capacity to overrun AMISOM's forward bases. The intent of these attacks is to force AMISOM contingents to remain in defensive positions in their bases, and thus limiting AMISOM's contacts with local communities and ultimately hasten the departure of AMISOM from Somalia. Suspicions that local Somalis collude with Al-Shabaab attackers also undermine AMISOM's capacity to develop intelligence networks among these people. Complex attacks do suggest that Al-Shabaab maintains a presence in nearby communities to plan operations and assemble fighters. This capability was demonstrated when Al-Shabaab fighters overran AMISOM's Janale base in southern Somalia in September 2015, killing more than 50 Ugandan soldiers. In another notable operation two months earlier, attackers killed at least 50 Burundian AMISOM soldiers at their Leego base. In January 2016, Al-Shabaab fighters attacked a Kenyan AMISOM base in El Adde. All but a few of approximately 150 Kenyan soldiers were killed or taken prisoner. In June 2016, Al-Shabaab attacked an Ethiopian base. In January 2017, Al-Shabaab fighters overran another Kenyan base near Kulbiyow, killing an estimated 68 soldiers (Anon 2017: 12). Forty-six Ugandan soldiers were killed in May 2018 in the course of an Al-Shabaab attack on their base at Bulamarer. Later in the month, AMISOM forces attacked a Burundian base on the outskirts of Mogadishu.

Attacks on AMISOM bases and Somali military positions and links to armed groups in Yemen's conflict provide Al-Shabaab with munitions that they are able to use to manufacture their own explosive devices (UN 2016a: 39). This development has led to an Improvised Explosive Device (IED) capacity that grew to 395 such incidents in 2016, double the number of incidents in the previous year (Muibu and Nickels 2017: 33). Hit-and-run attacks and assassinations of Somali officials reinforce the narrative that Al-Shabaab can operate anywhere in Somalia with relative ease. These attacks also enable Al-Shabaab units to move into areas abandoned by AMISOM or the government. Targeting takes into account intricacies of local political infighting, and is designed to graft pursuits of local community and personal agendas to Al-Shabaab's fate. While such strategies are typical of insurgents across many conflicts, this 'social strategy' in Somalia's failed state environment is particularly useful for drawing into Al-Shabaab's orbit the complex networks of self-protection and hedging that people develop to manage persistent insecurity and uncertainty.

Numerous operations highlight Al-Shabaab's success at infiltrating the Somali security and intelligence agencies that are beneficiaries of foreign assistance. The 2013 French attempt to rescue a hostage who had been held captive since 2009 when he and a compatriot were kidnapped from the Sahafi Hotel illustrates how insurgents are able to use the 'networks of dissolution' (and how these networks can undermine their cohesion) in the course of conflict. One of the hostages supposedly escaped his captors after a few days, but more likely was sold back to the French. But to rescue the remaining hostage the French intelligence agency Direction générale de la sécurité extérieure needed information to determine where the hostage was held. They enlisted the help of Somali government's National Intelligence and Security Agency (NISA), which was built in part with assistance from the US Central Intelligence Agency (Gettleman et al. 2011). But members of the intelligence service, some of whom were integrated into the agency in the course of regular government amnesties for insurgent fighters, led the French force into a trap, and the French Defence Minister alleged that Al-Shabaab fighters were forewarned of the French attack (Agence France Presse 2013; Anon 2013: 11). Al-Shabaab fighters fought the rescuers, killing two French soldiers (Le Drian 2013). Several days later Al-Shabaab announced on Twitter that they had killed the hostage (Roggio 2015).

Other attacks point to infiltration into security services. The January 2013 suicide bomb attack on the Prime Minister's home and multiple subsequent attacks near the presidential palace required that the attacker first get inside the compound that houses the offices and residences of high officials, a heavily fortified position as observed by the author. Again in 2013, an attack on the vehicle of the Somali intelligence chief, Khalif Ahmed Ilig, killed ten people while the intelligence chief received minor injuries (BBC News 2013). This attack followed successful attacks on two senior intelligence officers. Repeated instances of attackers wearing security force uniforms and carrying official IDs raises questions over whether members of Al-Shabaab are able to infiltrate security agencies (Mohamed and Freytas-Tamura 2017). Closer investigation of these attacks points to layers of possible motives beyond the general aim of attackers to promote instability. The intermingling of insurgent agendas with the politics of the fragmented social scene, for example, can recruit fighters who seek personal and family desires for vengeance for regular killings of Al-Shabaab kin at the hands of security force agents.

UN investigators determined that Al-Shabaab infiltration 'includes sensitive Government agencies, such as the NISA and various levels within the Presidential Palace' (United Nations 2014: 64). UN experts also pointed to Al-Shabaab infiltration of the police force and NISA that played a role in the hotel bombings. When suspects were arrested, they were released later without charge (United Nations 2015a: 185; Anon 2016: 9–10). Infiltration and flows of information across networks also appeared to play a role in the February 2016 bombing of Daallo Airlines flight 159. The attacker prematurely detonated a laptop bomb and was sucked out of the hole that he created in the airplane fuselage. The other passengers were unhurt and the airline returned to Mogadishu's airport. Events prior to the flight point to how information flows and personal networks intersect in Somalia's political and social context. Some of the passengers on flight 159 were on board because their Turkish Airlines flight was cancelled due to weather problems. Though Somalia is rife with conspiracy theories, this decision raised particular suspicions on a day of ordinary weather conditions. The Daallo Airlines pilot explained: "We found out that Turkish had cancelled their flight and that they had received a warning from somebody before about a bomb two days before" and after the bombing claimed that they cancelled their flight due to weather (Baum 2017: 23). It was suspected that several airport workers facilitated the operation and a Mogadishu businessman managed logistics for the operation, connections that raised (unproven) allegations that Al-Shabaab was able to get access to information and assistance from within Somali government offices (Anzalone 2016: 13).

Insurgent attacks do not appear to stimulate SFG officials to build their state's institutions, and in 2017, Somalia appeared as the world's most corrupt country in Transparency International's perceptions of corruption index (TI 2016). After Al-Shabaab's apparent expulsion from Mogadishu, UN observers concluded that "the systematic misappropriation, embezzlement and outright theft of public resources have essentially become a system of governance," as private individuals, inside and outside the government, made personal demands on state resources that officials cannot resist, due to obligations of kinship or political clientage (United Nations 2012: 12). This mode of politics extends to elections. European Union election monitors team noted of legislative and presidential elections in 2016–2017: "The open circulation of candidate money in the polling process appeared to be widespread. Interlocutors informed the EEM of instances when delegates openly compared how much money they received from candidates and political brokers present with cash to distribute as needed" (Election Expert Mission to Somalia 2017: 22). An expert estimated that in the decade to 2013, 88% of Central Bank payments were made to private individuals (Fartaag 2013), while UN investigators concluded in 2014 that this figure stood between 70 and 80% (United Nations 2014: 28–30). A World Bank report observed that "although a Central Bank was in existence, with a main building in Mogadishu… it apparently was (and continues to be) largely circumvented by the TFG executive branch and their key staff" (World Bank 2012: iv). Civil servants regularly go unpaid, while seats were reported to have sold for $1 million in the 2016 parliamentary election (Gettleman 2017).

The SNA's actual strength is difficult to determine. Official statements and documents cite figures of about 22,000 soldiers, while the real force may be closer to 10,000 solders of questionable effectiveness (United Nations 2016: 6). Many SNA units remain under the control of the clan to which they belong, and in Mogadishu, soldiers double as private sector security guards. Determining actual SNA strength also is complicated by reports that some soldiers defect and rejoin clan militias, and in some instances, Al-Shabaab (World Bank 2017: 30). Sometimes politicians and commanders collude to harvest salaries of non-existent 'ghost soldiers.' Soldiers provide other rent-seeking opportunities too: Somalia's politicians agreed to allow the United Arab Emirates to recruit real Somali soldiers to fight Houthi rebels in Yemen, for which UAE's government allegedly paid Somalia's government $2500 per soldier per month (Anon 2015: 11). As noted above, foreign governments that provide security assistance had to include "stipends" to otherwise unpaid "ghost" and real soldiers. Despite this assistance, many Somalis are familiar with the experience of being robbed at gunpoint by people dressed in SNA and security force uniforms (Marqaati 2017: 9).

Flawed Assumptions and Basic Realities

The international effort to build a capable central government in Somalia suffers from two critical problems. First, Somalia's government does not exhibit a consistent political will or capacity to engage in institution-building measures. Second, despite years of foreign assistance, Somalia's army and police lack the command structure and discipline to fight insurgents effectively. These failures challenge conventional models of security assistance premised upon the condition that a recipient government controls an armed force that has the potential capacity and legitimacy to protect government officials and the country's citizens. State collapse in Somalia, as elsewhere, turns out to be a long-term condition. In place of a conventional state, Somalia's political authorities operate in an environment in which armed groups infiltrate one another and their members make selective deals with people that they fight. Even in Mogadishu is can be difficult to define 'rebel control' or 'government control,' or boundaries between 'licit' and 'illicit' behaviour as political actors operate across numerous networks well beyond the institutions and practices of conventional state-building and security force assistance.

Insurgents face the same challenges as counterinsurgents in this environment. Like security assistance providers, Al-Shabaab also pursues elements of a conventional state-building agenda. This group's agenda includes replacing the existing state (or what there is of it) with what Al-Shabaab considers to be a more efficient and appropriate alternative. Indeed, Al-Shabaab and the other armed Islamist groups that preceded it prove to be Somalia's most proficient state-builders. Unlike conventional security assistance providers, Al-Shabaab is much more adept at turning elements of the failed state social environment such as the constant hedging, side-switching and sharing of information. These competitive responses to persistent insecurity reflect the pre-collapse dictatorship's exploitation of parochial rivalries and conflicts to undermine collective action can, if insurgents can harness them in particular ways, become powerful tools for infiltrating and hollowing out efforts to build state institutions, including state security forces. The constant targeted assassinations and bomb attacks convince onlookers that their government is ineffective. Many wonder whether attackers benefit from insider assistance. This equips insurgents to insinuate themselves into myriad parochial disputes and to take sides and offer protection to gain tactical advantage. Thus tapping into networks of kinship obligations, commerce and protection, insurgents make deals with key individuals, even in the security forces. The overall effect is to push large elements of the security forces to fall apart through desertions, deal-making and migration into commercial security companies (possibly in collusion with insurgents), and opportunistic side-switching.

These developments leave many foreigners, including security assistance providers, with an impression that Somalia's government is in a continuous freefall, perpetually dependent on AMISOM and other foreign military forces to prop up a façade of a national government. A reconsideration of the story of the kidnapped French agents reveals how this militarisation of kinship networks can create a situation that at first glance seems like constant turmoil. A relative of the Interior Minister and a deputy leader of the Islamic Courts Union (ICU) allegedly mastermind the operation (Mareeg 2013). The ICU's previous leader, Sharif Sheikh Ahmed, had become the president of the TFG in January 2009 as a result of a political pact, which gave the ICU opportunities to position their members in the government security services, including the intelligence agency. Illustrating how information sharing and collaborations work, Hizbul Islamiyya emerged as a separate faction that rejected the power-sharing deal with the TFG. But given the multiple layers of political calculation in this failed state, at the time of the 2009 kidnapping, ICU and Hizbul Islamiyya members fought together against the TFG in Mogadishu and against each other in Kismayo (Filiu 2009).

Kinship ties provide a more consistent logic with which to interpret the French hostage situation. Hizbul Islamiyya's capture of the French hostages discredited the feeble government and a foreign backer while asserting a sub-clan's place within both insurgent and government camps in the wake of the recent political reshuffling. Seen through the lens of political jockeying, this kidnapping looked like an inside job rather than a strike against a foe. But then Al-Shabaab operatives appeared soon after the kidnapping to demand one of the hostages, leaving Hizbul Islamiyya with only the other hostage to sell to the French (Campbell 2016). Now the situation looked more like a power-play by a hard-line faction. Or it was related to a settling of scores between kinship groups following the struggle to control territory and assert clan interests in Kismayo in southern Somalia in the preceding months. Complicating the situation further, the receipt of the ransom activated quarrels between the original kidnappers and the recipients of the ransom over how the seizure and the distribution of the ransom would affect the power of factions within the larger collection of Islamist groups and the complexities of local clan politics. This was further related to the multifaceted nature of the Islamists' participation in the TFG and anxieties of individuals to smooth over kinship relations while personally benefiting from the ransom. After that, one will appreciate that the situation became even more complex.

Pragmatic Security Assistance

Conventional foreign security assistance and state-building efforts permit only limited recognition of the political realities in places like Somalia. Shortcomings are discussed within a narrative of incremental progress through international cooperation and local resolve. This narrative does not hide the fact that foreign officials that provide security assistance harbour anxieties about the real situation. They worry that failure will mean that terrorists will continue to use Somalia as a base to launch attacks in other countries, or that Somalia's extremist groups will make common cause with groups such as al-Qaeda or Islamic State. Foreign officials who have to take consequences most seriously tend to be more interested in Somalia's real political environment. Their urgency thus pushed them towards more pragmatic approaches. Pragmatism thus shifts security assistance closer to counterterrorism. It is somewhat more ambitious than just identifying and killing enemies, as doing this in the Somali context means building an effective local proxy force that prevents its members from sharing information, switching sides and hedging in collusion with other armed groups. In practical terms, this means insulating the local proxy from the host government and its security services that are supposed to be the critical partner and eventual guarantor of security.

In contrast to the conventional paradigm's attention to the incremental strengthening of a legitimate state with an effective security force that protects citizens, pragmatic security assistance in failed states necessitates a somewhat looser approach to issues of sovereignty and the opinions of the Somali people. The aim of local security forces is to collect (and protect) information to learn about and disrupt plots, and to target specific individuals. Success requires thinking in specific terms about how the failed state environment shapes the relationship of coercion and authority, rather than engaging in futile state-building exercises. The primary focus of the pragmatic expert is to understand how the failed state environment affects how people fight. It is difficult, for example, to expect a member of conventional security forces to focus on a single mission and carefully guard information. The soldier himself may reflect a typical family strategy that attempts to place kinsmen in as many networks as possible to collect information and play roles in complex political calculations. Thus the solider may have a brother in Al-Shabaab, another who works for foreigners, another embedded in a local business (illicit or otherwise) and one in politics. This is a sensible strategy for a family in an insecurity environment, while also contributing to the difficulties of building institutions able to act consistently in the interest of a state, much less a security force that is able to do so.

Pragmatism is not a new feature in foreign security assistance in Somalia. An earlier example appeared in after the 7 August 1998 simultaneous bombings of US embassies in Kenya and Tanzania that killed 224 people, including 12 Americans. The bombers were connected to local members of the Egyptian Islamic Jihad group, and ultimately to Al Qaeda. The architect of the attacks, Fazul Abdullah Mohammed, took refuge in Somalia, where he evaded foreign efforts to kill him. As it turned out, he was killed at a Mogadishu checkpoint in 2011. His death was the result of a chance encounter in a chaotic environment, not the collective acumen of Somali security forces. Indeed, several days earlier, Somalia's interior minister was killed at his home in the small area of Mogadishu under government control. Somali officials said that a female suicide bomber, possibly the minister's niece, operated as an Al-Shabaab agent (Gettleman 2011). Events of this kind alerted US officials to the dangers that the absence of an effective Somali government posed to US interests. 'We need to recognize that Somalia is a front line in the broader fight against terrorism,' said US Senator Russell Feingold, 'and that it needs more than just intermittent attention' (Subcommittee on African Affairs 2006).

A pragmatic approach to these dangers in the context of a failed state materialised from 2004 in American recruitment of Somali businessmen in Kenya and beyond to return to Somalia. Once back in Somalia, these businessmen were encouraged to use their armed security details (some of which later guarded their commanders' hotels) to collect information and to target individuals in coordination with US advisors (Mazetti 2006). Announced in February 2006, the Alliance for the Restoration of Peace and Counter-Terrorism (ARPCT) brought these armed businessmen together to fight the Islamic Courts Union (ICU) in Mogadishu and capture or kill suspected al Qaeda members. US State Department officials described a 'parallel Somalia policy' in which the group allegedly received CIA assistance (Anon 2006b: 8). Nevertheless, this approach produced poor results. Several ARPCT members colluded with Islamist groups along the lines of shared kinship networks. These violent and predatory warlords also convinced many Somalis that they were better off under Islamist rule. The 'parallel Somalia policy' also highlighted the tendency for pragmatic approaches to exacerbate bureaucratic tensions, as in this case between the CIA, the State Department and Pentagon officials over which agency would define a strategy for dealing with political instability in Somalia.

Poor coordination in Washington led to some particularly unproductive initiatives. For example, head of a private security firm boasted of connections to the CIA and to British security experts and presented a plan to organise Somalis to fight the ICU (Anon 2006a). Somehow she sold various officials and journalists on an extravagant plan to control piracy and undertake economic development projects through a non-profit foundation and a variety of other entities. 'It's pretty sad when a horse-country socialite has more sway in Somalia than the whole U.S. government,' said a US official (Kloor 2013). This plan exposed an apparent lack of policy focus on the part of the US government. A more coherent plan appeared with the creation of security agencies and armed forces that would appear on official organisational charts, but were capable of autonomous operation vis-à-vis the relevant Somali officials. From 2008 NISA received assistance from US advisors, and has operated in spite of a variety of Somali governments and Islamist armed groups that have struggled to control Mogadishu (Gettleman et al. 2011). From 2013, a small team of US military advisors, the Mogadishu Coordination Cell, has assisted this and other agencies. Foreign advisors and private firms help to maintain budgeting, staff and command structures in an effort to insulate them from the rest of Somalia's government and the social pressures that individuals face to share information. This autonomy provides conditions to develop a local cadre of local operational and analytical security expert who are at ease and are effective when working with foreign advisors.

This approach partially reflects a 'bottom-up' tactic of adapting to local conditions and grows out of critiques among analysts in the military and intelligence communities of shortcomings of American counterinsurgency in Iraq and Afghanistan. Karl Eikenberry, the former Commander of Combined Forces in Afghanistan (2005–2007) and then US ambassador to Afghanistan (2009–2011) acknowledged that the Afghan government did little to improve the effectiveness of their government institutions and security forces, despite (or in fact, because of) the willingness of the United States and its allies to cover 90% of the Afghan government's public expenditures. Counterinsurgency as it was practised in Afghanistan and Iraq, he wrote, 'unwittingly tried to achieve revolutionary aims through semicolonial means' (Eikenberry 2013: 74). The alternative to this ambitious goal of transforming countries like Somalia into capable states is a 'light footprint' approach that relies on airpower, including drones, and pairs Special Operations Forces (SOF) with local armed groups to target insurgents. The aim of this approach is to refocus the mission on degrading the operational capacity of Al-Shabaab with relatively few personnel and at a lower cost in financial terms, while ensuring that the Somali government can continue to present the semblance of governing despite its weaknesses. Conventional counterinsurgency through state-building thus is refocused in a pragmatic approach on the core security problem in foreigners' eyes: transnational terrorism (Metz 2017).

The pragmatic use of organisations like NISA uses sovereignty as a façade, while creating conditions for at least tactical proficiency. During AMISOM's 2011 offensive against Al-Shabaab in Mogadishu, some local residents reported proficient fighters who stood out: "We initially thought that Alphas were foreign soldiers," reported a business operator. "Even when we discovered that definitely they were Somalis, we can't tell where they came from. They are completely covered so you can't see their faces and they don't interact with army or AMISOM" (Interview: Dagmada Shangaani, Mogadishu, 1 July 2012). A US official acknowledged support for special units to fight Al-Shabaab. 'The aid we provide includes training support for the Somali advanced infantry company, also known as "Danab" – the Lighting Force. This is a 150-person unit we believe can become a source of future leadership for the entire army' (Sherman 2014). These fighters are trained separately from other Somali forces (McCormick 2015). Some Somali officials reported that their contact with this group was limited. For example, a former deputy minister's aide reported that his boss was prevented from entering a compound housing private security forces near the Alpha compound. He speculated that "Americans there hesitate because they aren't confident about the Somali government's reliability" to guard information from Al-Shabaab (Interview with informants, Dagmada Waaberi, Mogadishu, 17 August 2013). An observer of the July 2014 Al-Shabaab attack on government offices attributed the efficient response of Somali special units to US training and specifically to their segregation from the influence of Somali government officials (Interview, Villa Somalia, 13 August 2014).

Private firms play important roles in pragmatic security force assistance, particularly in filling in for missing government capacity or willingness to take on more responsibility for security and domestic order. The selection of private firms offers another point of discrimination through which planners can insulate Somali special forces from the surrounding political and social environment. An example of a poor choice appeared in a UN report that noted an advisor to the president who was also a fellow kinsman and former logistics facilitator for Al-Shabaab, maintained close relations with the army chief of logistics while also running a private security company in Mogadishu that was implicated in the "leakage" of government weapons to Al-Shabaab (United Nations 2014: 32). Bancroft Global Development provides a good contrast. This organisation is registered in the United States as a charity, but is considered a private security firm by UN experts who are charged with examining the flows of foreign assistance to Somalia's armed forces. Their report notes that the firm was active in Mogadishu from 2007, and was involved in a variety of projects involving AMISOM and Somali armed forces (United Nations 2013: 11–14). These arrangements, put alongside the start US Special Forces operations in 2003 and drone strikes in 2011 against Al-Shabaab targets and other groups, typifies a "light footprint" counterterrorism approach. Alongside the disappointing performance of Somalia's government noted above, the increase of drone strikes in 2016 to nine, more than double those of a year earlier, and 21 strikes in 2017 point to an intensification of this strategy (International Security 2018).

Coordination between Somali armed groups and foreign advisors adapts to Somalia's social system in the collapsed state context. The discipline of members is critical for collecting accurate information, preventing its sharing with others, and controlling direct infiltration of insurgents that occur in other Somali armed forces, partly as a result of poorly managed periodic government amnesties for insurgents. The pragmatic attention to social structure and behaviour in Somalia can influence how people fight, a concern that is central to accurately targeting insurgents and protecting Somalia's weak government at low cost. Private security firms and foreign special units are effective not only for the training that they provide to recruits as for insulating special units from the influence of state officials. This insulation leaves units with the capacity to provide the deterrence that individual fighters need when they have to deal with the family members of the Al-Shabaab fighters that they have killed or captured. Family members typically want to revenge these acts, but free-standing forces are able to protect their members from attacks, thus freeing members from the immediate burdens of having to weigh the interests of insurgents and others when launching an attack. This capacity to focus on a single purpose reduces incidences of hedging through side deals and trading information, directly or indirectly, with the people that they are supposed to fight.

AMISOM contingents also have exhibited a pragmatic understanding of Somalia's politics, albeit in a more ad hoc fashion. For example, the Ugandan People's Defence Force before 2012 used the militia of Omar Mohamud Mohamad "Finish," a former member of the ARPCT, as a buffer between AMISOM forces and Al-Shabaab controlled areas of the city (Oloya 2016). Interviews with AMISOM officers in 2012 and 2013 revealed that this approach required careful attention to selecting a partner that was better than most at mastering the capacity to prevent reprisals from family members against its members for acts of violence committed against their kin. This arrangement, however, consists of identifying a cohesive local force, providing them with logistical and financial support in return for a degree of coordination. Groups such as Danab are more effective partners because they can be insulated to a greater extent from obligations of clan politics and the need to play various sides in political games in return for protection in an uncertain future. As a proxy of a foreign military, their primary protection comes from one source.

The SNA and other Somali security forces become less desirable partners if one's focus narrows from a state-building/counterinsurgency approach to the pragmatic approach's counterterrorism. The pragmatic approach can be less concerned with SNA predation at impromptu checkpoints, or instances when soldiers masquerade as Al-Shabaab to prey on communities, or pursue kinship/sub-clan agendas and fight their fellow SNA soldiers (United Nations 2016b: 161). Journalists regularly report shootouts among soldiers (Reuters 2018). Meanwhile, Somali security guards seized $9.8 million from a UAE aircraft at the Mogadishu airport that was intended for security force assistance. Shortly after, soldiers looted the UAE training facility and sold stolen weapons to local arms dealers (Maruf 2018). Years after AMISOM supposedly drove Al-Shabaab from Mogadishu, one might wonder if an army and a government exist, at least as these organisations are conventionally conceived.

Tactics and Strategy

Security assistance to Somalia's military forces and its government face the harsh realities of politics in a failed state. Key domestic actors appear to lack the capacity and the political will to carry out basic tasks necessary to build their own state. The conventional mode of security assistance also shows that some international actors also lack the political will and the capacity to carry out the state-building tasks associated with conventional counterinsurgency strategies. Yet concerns remain that Somali extremist groups will launch terrorist attacks in the region and beyond. This conundrum drives foreign governments, particularly the US, to consider pragmatic adaptations to Somalia's failed state context. Some adaptations are controversial, even if they are logical responses to the need to insulate security forces from the local political context as a necessary condition to maintain a sustained focus on counterterrorism goals and to avoid sharing information with potential foes. Using children as fighters, for example, can aid NISA in identifying insurgents (Sieff 2016). Children in such contexts, especially ones captured from areas under Al-Shabaab control, may be enticed or coerced into identifying insurgents. As among insurgents in numerous conflicts across time, this practice provides recruits who are released from constraints of the wider social system and are forced to rely exclusively on the armed group for protection. This can be an effective way to collect valid information but can be politically counterproductive when they clash with core values of security assistance providers.

In any event, after years of seemingly fruitless pursuit of a conventional strategy of security assistance in Somalia, as in other failed and failing states, a pragmatic approach has come to look more attractive. Relatively inexpensive, more limited in their political aims, and reliant on existing structures of authority on the ground, this approach suggests several key considerations for security assistance in any failed state.

- Above all, local political context matters, particularly as politics in failed states directly undermines the essential preconditions of a conventional security assistance strategy: domestic political will and capacity to build state institutions.
- The objective of security assistance in failed states should be clear and measurable: most likely it will focus on counterterrorism.
- The operation of security assistance in failed states should be more discriminating in the choice of local partners on the basis of capacity and will to pursue common objectives.

Pragmatic approaches to security assistance have pitfalls as well. Thus general prescriptive advice needs to come with caveats.

- Counterterrorism in failed states is likely to involve an open-ended tactical pursuit of key individuals with the aim of suppressing an armed group's capacity to launch foreign attacks and to provide protection for the façade of a minimally functional government.
- Devoted proxy forces have a tendency to manipulate their patrons for their own interests. This tendency can generate domestic conflicts that implicate the security assistance providers in the eyes of local people.
- A bunch of tactics do not amount to a strategy. Tactics in place of a strategy leave even proficient operators exposed to blame by the political leaders when things go wrong, even though it was political leaders who failed to articulate a strategy.

In sum, security force assistance to Somalia, especially after the experiences of the United States and its partners in Iraq and Afghanistan, signals the demise of security force assistance premised on classic foundational assumptions of counterinsurgency, at least in failed states. Counterterrorism comes as a kind of relief, as it seems to rescue security assistance from its pathologies in failed states. But retreat from strategy brings its own problems.

References

African Peace Facility. 2016. *Annual Report 2015*. Brussels: Européen Commission.

Agence France Presse. 2013. France defends failed Somali raid as toll mounts, 13 January.

Anon. 2006a. Mission Mogadishu. *Africa Confidential*. 47 (18), 8 September.

Anon. 2006b. Foreign funds. *Africa Confidential*. 47 (8), 14 April.

Anon. 2013. French Somalia raid 'was a trap'. *Africa Confidential*. 54 (2), 18 January.

Anon. 2015. AMISOM loses friends. *Africa Confidential*. 56 (20), 9 October.

Anon. 2016. Somalia: Amisom struggles. *Africa Confidential*. 57 (5), 4 March.

Anon. 2017. Somalia: Another Kenya army base hit. *Africa Confidential*. 58 (3), 3 February.

Anzalone, C., 2016. The resilience of Al-Shabaab. *CTC Sentinel*. 9 (4), April, pp. 13–20.

Armed Conflict Location & Event Data Project (ACLED). 2018. Data.

Babb, C., 2017. 'US Suspends Aid to Much of Somalia Military'. VOA, December 15. https://www.voanews.com/a/us-suspends-aid-somalia-military/4164892.html. Accessed August 2018.

Baum, P. 2017. Daalli Airlines Bombing: Interview with Captain Vladimir Vodopivec. *Aviation Security International*, 23 (1), February, pp. 22–29.

BBC News. 2013. Somalia's capital Mogadishu hit by deadly car bomb, 18 March.

Bradbury, M. 2008. *Becoming Somaliland*. Oxford: James Currey.

Burke, J. 2017. 'Somalis greet 'New Dawn' as US dual national wins presidency.' *The Guardian*, 8 February.

Campbell, M. 2016. 'French agent Marc Aubriere's amazing barefoot escape through Mogadishu.' *The Australian*, 31 August.

Department for International Development, Foreign & Commonwealth office, and Ministry of Defence. 2017. 'London Somalia Conference 2017: Security pact,' 11 May.

Department of State (US). 2017. The United States congratulates Somalia on the conclusion of its electoral process, 8 February.

Eikenberry, K. 2013. 'The limits of counterinsurgency doctrine in Afghanistan: The other side of the COIN.' *Foreign Affairs*, September/October, pp. 59–74.

Election Expert Mission to Somalia. 2017. *Somalia 2016–2017 limited election process: EU Election Expert Mission final report*. Brussels: European Union.

Fartaag, A. 2013. *Reconstructing Somalia and the politics of public sector finance*. London School of Economics.

Filiu, J.-P. 2009. 'Lesson from Kismayo.' *Jihadica*, 6 October.

Foreign and Commonwealth Office. 2012. London Conference on Somalia Communique. London (23 February).

Gettleman, J. 2011. 'Somalis kill mastermind of 2 U.S. embassy bombings.' *New York Times*, 11 June.

Gettleman, J. 2017. 'Cash flows freely as Somalis hold "fraudulent" election.' *New York Times*, 7 February.

Gettleman, J., Mazzetti, M., and Schmitt, E., 2011. 'US relies on contractors in Somalia conflict.' *New York Times*, 10 August.

Hogendoorn, E.J. 2018 'Somalia's current security and stability status' [Testimony before US Senate Foreign Relations Committee], 14 March.

International Security. 2018. Drone wars Somalia: Analysis. http://securitydata.newamerica.net/drones/somalia-analysis.html. Accessed January 2018.

Kloor, K. 2013. 'Pirates and warlords aside, Michele Ballarin believes she can turn Somalia around.' *Washington Post*, 4 October.

Lacey, M. 2006. 'Efforts by C.I.A. fail in Somalia, officials charge.' *New York Times*, 8 June.

Le Drian, J.-Y. 2013. 'Soldat français tué en Somalie: publient des photos.' *Le Monde*, 14 January.

Mareeg. 2013. 'Somalia: The abduction of French agents well planned, sources.' 15 April.

Marqaati. 2017. '2016 State of Accountability in Somalia'. Available at: https://marqaati.org/wp-content/uploads/2017/02/Marqaati-2016-Corruption-Report.pdf. Accessed August 2018.

Maruf, H. 2018. 'Somalia seizes nearly $10m from UAE plane in Mogadishu,' *VOA*, 8 April.

Mazetti, M. 2006. 'Efforts by C.I.A. fail in Somalia, officials charge.' *New York Times*, 8 June.

McCormick, T. 2015. 'U.S. operates drones from secret bases in Somalia.' *Foreign Policy*, 2 July.

Menkhaus, K. 2014. 'State collapse and local responses in Somalia.' Trauschweizer, I & Miner, S., eds. *Failed states and fragile societies: A new world disorder?* Athens: Ohio University Press, pp. 142–150.

Metz, S. 2017. Abandoning counterinsurgency: Revising antiterrorism strategy. *Parameters*, 47 (3), Autumn, pp. 51–64.

Mohamed, H., and Freytas-Tamura, K. 2017. 'Somalia blasts expose security failings and possible Shabab infiltration.' *New York Times*, 16 October.

Muibu, D., and Nickels, B. 2017. Foreign technology or local expertise? Al-Shabaab's IED capability. *CTC Sentinel* 10 (10), November, pp. 33–37.

Office of the Prime Minister. 2017. *Aid flows in Somalia: Analysis of aid flow data*. Mogadishu: Federal Republic of Somalia.

Office of the Under Secretary of Defense for Policy. 2015. *DoD instruction 5132.14: Assessment, monitoring, and evaluation policy for the security cooperation enterprise*. Washington, DC: Department of Defense.

Oloya, O. 2016. *Black Hawks rising: The story of AMISOM's successful war against Somali insurgents, 2007–2014.* Birmingham: Helion and Company.

Renders, M., & Terlinden, U. 2010. Negotiating statehood in a hybrid political order: the case of Somaliland. *Development & Change*, 41 (4), pp. 723–746.

Reuters. 2018. Rival groups from Somali army clash at former UAE training facility, 23 April.

Roggio, B. 2015. Shabaab executes French hostage Denis Allex. *Long War Journal*, 16 January.

Security Assistance Monitor. 2015. 4 Charts on spike in U.S. Military and police aid to Africa. Available from http://securityassistance.org/blog/4-charts-spike-us-military-and-police-aid-africa. Accessed December 2017.

Sherman, W. 2014. *U.S. foreign policy in Somalia*. Washington, DC: United States Institute of Peace (3 June).

Sieff, K., 2016. 'Exclusive: U.S.—funded somali intelligence agency has been using kids as spies.' *Washington Post*, 7 May.

Simons, A. 1995. *Networks of dissolution: Somalia undone*. Boulder, CO: Westview Press.

Subcommittee on African Affairs. 2006. *Somalia: U.S. government policy and challenges, S. Hrg. 109-874.* Washington, DC: US Senate.

Transparency International. 2016. Corruption Perceptions Index 2016.

United Nations. 2012. *Security Council, Report of the Monitoring Group on Somalia and Eritrea pursuant to Security Council Resolution 2002 (2011), S/2012/544.* New York: UN Security Council.

United Nations. 2013. *Report of the working group on the use of mercenaries as a means of violating human rights and impeding the exercise of the rights of peoples to self-determination, A/HRC/24/45/Add.2.* New York: UN General Assembly.

United Nations. 2014. *Report of the Monitoring Group on Somalia and Eritrea pursuant to Security Council Resolution 2111 (2013): Somalia, S/2014/726.* New York: UN Security Council.

United Nations. 2015a. *Report of the Monitoring Group on Somalia and Eritrea pursuant to Security Council Resolution 2182 (2014): Somalia, S/2015/802.* New York: UN Security Council.

United Nations. 2015b. *Somalia: UN envoy applauds successes as country 'comes together'.* New York: UN News Centre.

United Nations. 2016a. *Report of the Secretary-General on Somalia, S/2016/27.* New York: UN Security Council.

United Nations. 2016b. *Report of the Monitoring Group on Somalia and Eritrea pursuant to Security Council Resolution 2244 (2015).* New York: UN (October).

United Nations. 2017. Somalia Report of the Monitoring Group on Somalia and Eritrea submitted in accordance with resolution 2317 (2016), 8 November.

United Nations Mission in Somalia 2017. Security Pact, 11 May.

United States Africa Command. 2017. U.S. support to the Federal Government of Somalia continues to make a positive impact, 27 December.

Williams, P. 2018. *Fighting for peace in Somalia.* New York: Oxford University Press.

World Bank. 2012. *World Bank summary of financial diagnostic assessment of audit investigative financial report 2009–2010.* Washington, DC: World Bank.

World Bank. 2017. *Federal Republic of Somalia: Somalia security and justice sector PER.* Washington, DC: World Bank.

CHAPTER 4

'Fighting Out Its Own Complex and Fatal Destiny'? On the Limitations on the Use of Force in Yemen

Aaron Edwards

In the Spring of 2015 civil war once again returned to Yemen. Operation Decision Storm, the major military offensive launched by a coalition of Arab states led by Saudi Arabia, sought to "eliminate the threats" posed by Ansar Allah (known popularly as the Houthi militia), which had seized territory across Yemen, including the capital city Sanaa in September 2014. In a press conference in Washington on 22 April 2015, the Saudi Ambassador to the United States, Abdel bin Ahmed Al-Jubeir, announced that, within a few weeks, the coalition had "degraded… [Houthi] capabilities substantially and thereby eliminated the threat that they pose to the Kingdom of Saudi Arabia." The Saudis stated that their military campaign was primarily undertaken to preserve 'the safety of our borders, our territory and our citizens,' while also acknowledging that it served a secondary objective of bolstering the position of Yemen's new president, "Abd Rabbu Mansour Hadi. 'Those objectives have been achieved," claimed Al-Jubeir, "so now we enter a new phase." With their

A. Edwards (✉)
Department of Defence and International Affairs,
Royal Military Academy Sandhurst, Sandhurst, UK

T. Clack and R. Johnson (eds.), *Before Military Intervention*,
https://doi.org/10.1007/978-3-319-98437-7_4

objectives apparently met, the Saudi Ministry of Defense announced that the end of its military campaign would pave the way for a new "political" phase, Operation Renewal of Hope, in which the protection of civilians and the continuing frustration of the Houthi militia within the country would take priority.

In switching focus to give the diplomatic and aid instruments a more enhanced role in their attempts to resolve the Yemen crisis before it got any worse, the Saudis refused to rule out a complementary 'military component' to the operation. Soon afterwards, however, the coalition spokesman, Brigadier-General Ahmed al-Asiri, informed a press conference that the end of Operation Decisive Storm would not necessarily mean the end of air strikes or the lifting of a naval blockade (Al Jazeera 2015). In the months that followed, the Saudi-led coalition kept its word to use force by deploying hundreds of ground troops, to dislodge an increasingly resilient Houthi insurgency. Nonetheless, the intervention in Yemen would have serious repercussions, including prompting the rejuvenation of a nascent threat from Al Qaeda in the Arabian Peninsula (AQAP) and facilitating the growth of Islamic State in Iraq and al-Sham (ISIS, known as Daesh by the Arabs). The Islamist threat manifested itself in new and more deadly ways, ranging from the targeted assassinations of senior Yemeni military officers and politicians to the bombing of mosques, all of which were aimed at accentuating sectarian and tribal tensions.[1] Furthermore, the failure by the Saudi-led coalition to protect civilians caught up in both terrorist attacks and in coalition air strikes, served to alienate ordinary Yemenis from the Hadi government, which had by now fled to Jeddah and, later, to Aden in the south. Political instability inevitably followed, enabling the southern secessionist movement to continue to lobby for the division of the country along north–south lines, which existed prior to unification in 1990 (ICG 2011; Carapico 2014: 38).

On 15 June 2017, the United Nations Security Council issued a Presidential Statement highlighting the deep humanitarian crisis that had

[1] The deadliest attacks occurred in the Badr mosque on the south side of Sanaa in March 2015. Almost 150 people were killed and twice as many injured after one explosion inside the mosque and another at the gates as worshippers fled. Another attack took place at the al-Hashahush mosque in the north of the city. The attacks were claimed by the Yemeni branch of Daesh. See "Yemen: over 100 dead in suicide bombings at Houthi mosques in Sanaa", *The Guardian*, 22 March 2015.

befallen Yemen over two years since the outbreak of civil war. They called on all parties to return to cease hostilities and return to the negotiating table (UNSC 2017). Ironically, they had little to say about negative consequences of the Saudi-led intervention, which have been truly catastrophic for Yemen. Apart from the deaths of 10,000 people and the injuries sustained by an untold number, well over half of Yemen's population of 26 million have become dependent on food aid. Additionally, over one million people have been affected by the spread of cholera and diphtheria. In Yemen, communicable diseases have combined with manmade security challenges—including external intervention, war, economic instability, and an absence of a functioning government—to ensure the country languishes at the top five of the Failed States Index.

This chapter is not an in-depth study of the Yemeni situation, which has grown more complex and precarious since 2015. Instead, it analyses the Saudi intervention through a strategic lens, arguing that it should be viewed more scientifically in terms of why Riyadh has found it difficult to balance the means with its stated ends. Far more important a concern is the lingering persistence of the view held by international state actors that the military instrument holds the promise of bringing a swift and decisive end to complex disputes. If the Saudi intervention tells us anything it is this: Launching a military campaign without an appreciation of the changing sociopolitical dynamics of the society in which state actors seek to modify the behaviour of persons or groups (Rosenau 1969: 159) is likely to make matters worse. The chapter, therefore, argues that if intervention is chosen as a course of action, the intervening party must have a more thorough understanding of the context within which force is deployed and employed in service of stated end goals.

Defeating the Houthi? The Challenge of Asymmetric Security Threats

The stated objective in Saudi Arabia's intervention in Yemen's internal affairs has been twofold: One, to defeat the Houthi militia, and two, to bolster the government of President Hadi. If we consider the first element of this objective, it is worth conceptualising the challenge posed by non-state armed actors utilising more generally, especially those employing asymmetric strategies. Defined simply, asymmetry in a given security environment is all about how an opponent opts to fight 'unfairly'. Rod

Thornton uses the example of the hijackers on 9/11 as an example of how low tech, synchronised terrorist cells can have a significant impact well beyond their actual power and influence. Thornton informs us that asymmetry is primarily about exploiting the weaknesses of one's opponent as a means of stretching their physical and intellectual resources (Thornton 2007). Asymmetric conflict is interpreted in this chapter primarily, though not exclusively, as the armed confrontation between a state and a non-state challenger in the form of an insurgent group (Mack 1975; Neumann and Smith 2007). In this kind of strategic contest, there is often a considerable power disparity between the belligerents, with non-state actors usually accepting that they are operating from a disadvantage. Thus, asymmetric threats tend to be irregular in character and aimed at employing sometimes innovative or hybrid capabilities (see Hoffman 2007) to secure leverage over a much more powerful and resource-rich opponent.

In the Yemeni context, the Houthi militia has combined close quarter fighting with small arms and light weapons with the firing of Scud Missiles into Saudi territory and the use of tanks against coalition forces. Asymmetric threats can prove difficult to deter, especially if they have been utilised in ways that are mindful of likely conventional responses (Gray 1999: 5–6). According to Andrew Mack, this kind of strategic contest is also based on an objective reading of the situation, which sees insurgents, in particular, recognising how they "can only achieve their ends if their opponents' political capability to wage war is destroyed" (Mack 1975: 179).

States have, therefore, responded in a variety of ways to the challenge posed by asymmetric threats. In some cases, they have sought to employ conventional force against non-state opponents using asymmetric means in ways which have failed to bring about a decisive outcome. For instance, in the early Twentieth Century, Britain responded "coercively" to the IRA's guerrilla campaign and ultimately hastened its own disengagement from Southern Ireland. Similarly, French counter-insurgency operations in Algeria in the 1950s were based on the application of disproportionate 'brute force' that alienated a wider constituency and led ultimately to the failure of its military campaign against the National Liberation Front (FLN). Both these cases reflect a tendency by states to reach for the military instrument when faced with asymmetric threats they do not fully understand, something that may well jeopardise their political legitimacy (Edwards 2017: 114). By the 1960s, state actors had developed Special Forces capabilities, which afforded them the option of effecting strategic gains against opponents that turned to asymmetric strategies and tactics. What is important to underline here is the fact that states have had to adapt to the challenge issued by asymmetric adversaries or they risk losing the contest. Quantitatively speaking, the odds are not good, as Ivan Arreguín-Toft (2001: 96) has shown in an influential study, for weak actors have tended to win approximately 30% of all asymmetric wars. As Arreguín-Toft convincingly argues, strong actors "lose asymmetric conflicts when they adopt the wrong strategy vis-à-vis their weaker adversaries" (Arreguín-Toft 2001: 121).

By studying the Saudi intervention in Yemen, we may be able to determine whether the current fighting—what the Prussian philosopher of war Carl von Clausewitz referred to as the 'central component in war' (von Clausewitz 1976)—has advanced the goals of those who have committed their troops to battle. The conceptual scaffolding provided by Strategic Studies allows us to also ask whether Saudi grand strategy (i.e. the use of all military and non-military instruments in pursuit of its stated policy objectives) has made the Kingdom safer and brought the reinstatement of centralised government in Yemen any closer.

The civil war in Yemen, like the armed conflicts in Iraq, Syria and Libya, demonstrates the difficulty facing analysts who wish to understand how armed conflict is changing. Over a decade ago, retired British general Sir Rupert Smith argued that the world was littered with 'wars among the people', in which military force no longer offered the promise of a decisive resolution to disputes. Smith painted a rich picture of war that was complex and multilayered and in which there was a "criss-crossing" between crisis and confrontation, more than a "linear" movement from war to peace, and from peace to war. Even though many militaries around the world have recognised this radical transformation in war, there still remains an expectation in some quarters that force will "deliver a definitive military victory in its own right that will resolve the political problem" (Smith 2005: 371).

Another issue falling out of the strategic question of the utility of force is the exponential rise in civilian casualties and structural harm inflicted on societies experiencing war in the early 21st Century.[2] We are well-aware of the step-change in "new wars" where the casualties

[2] For example, it is estimated that, of Yemen's 26.18 million population, approximately 18 million people are dependent on food aid.

are more likely to be innocent bystanders than combatants. This can be readily seen in the new wars of the 1990s, in places as geographically diverse as Bosnia, Rwanda and the Democratic Republic of Congo. In these places, the mass killing of people from a particular ethnic group or religious sect becomes just as important as the occupation of territory, the defeat of armies and the toppling of governments were in "old wars." Mary Kaldor argues that this points to a resurgence in the politics of identity, the decentralisation of violence, and the globalisation of a war economy (Kaldor 2006: 178).

The incubation chamber for many of these security threats has been identified as fragile, failing and failed states.[3] For some commentators, it is these ungoverned spaces that pose the most significant challenges for the use of force in the contemporary world. Most states suffering decline in power terms can continue to exercise authority in abeyance as long as their "monopoly over the legitimate use of violence goes unchallenged," writes Michael T. Klare. "But once substate organizations of a paramilitary nature – ethnic militias, separatist forces, guerrilla groups, warlord armies, and so on – begin to form, the central government must act swiftly to disarm and dissolve these entities or its control over the nation (or the particular regions affected) will rapidly evaporate" (Klare 2004: 117). In the case of Yemen, the central government in Sanaa has, arguably, never enjoyed a monopoly over the legitimate use of force, with armed tribalism particularly strong in the north and in the south (see Jones 2011, for more on this point). On the other hand, there are some commentators who caution us against assessing the strength and vigour of tribal confederations in light of apparent orientalist notions of an idealised type of state (Dingli 2013). This is sensible but it is not the whole story. As rational actors, these tribes are outward manifestations of Yemeni power structures hidden to the naked "orientalist eye."

In the literature on civil wars, it is generally recognised that the strategies of the parties to a conflict have a bearing on the direction which such conflict takes. What experts on the Yemen case have stressed though is the highly cynical nature of repeated external interference (Carapico 2014; Willis 2015; Lackner 2018a, b). It is undeniable that

[3] Due to space constraints, it is impossible to elaborate upon the concept of the 'failed state', or whether or not we should categorise Yemen as a 'failed state', a term that has come to shape US policy towards unstable parts of the world. For a fuller discussion of this point see Wedeen (2010) and Carment et al. (2015).

the strategies of intervening external actors, like Saudi Arabia, have a direct bearing on the duration and character of conflicts which have complex and overlapping endogenous and exogenous sources. As Regan and Abouharb (2002: 44) point out:

> The strategy adopted by the intervener can influence the estimate of the probability of victory held by the parties to the conflict, as well as the costs of continued fighting. An intervention strategy incorporates a number of elements, such as whom to target in the intervention, its timing (when to intervene), and whether or not to use force on behalf of your client. Intervening on behalf of either the government or the opposition has the immediate effect of altering the balance of capabilities. And as costs and estimates of victory will vary with time, the timing of the intervention will contribute to the willingness to settle now versus continuing the fight.

Before delving into the strategic dynamics of the case in greater depth, it is, perhaps, worth considering how previous external interventions have fared in Yemen.

'Yemen's Destruction and Chaos': A Brief History

Sheila Carapico has made the forceful argument that the various conflicts in Yemen cannot be understood in purely endogenous terms. 'Instead,' she argues, 'they reflect the profound contradictions of the Arabian peninsula between the wealth and passivity of the Gulf and Yemen's destruction and chaos' (Carapico 2014: 29). In this respect, we must also pay due attention to the exogenous sources of conflict, including the meddling by more powerful international actors. Yemen is no stranger to intervention. At the turn of the sixteenth century, the Portuguese blockaded the Persian Gulf and laid siege to the ports around the peninsula. When the Ottoman Turks landed in the southwestern port of Aden in 1538, it was a bustling commercial centre with a population of 50–60,000 people. The finest city in Arabia, Aden flourished as a result of passing trade from East Africa, the Gulf and India. Within a year of arriving, the Ottomans established a governor-general in Sanaa who would rule for three hundred years. Ottoman dominance of the peninsula was finally broken when the East India Company seized Aden from the Sultan of Lahij after bombarding his military defences from the sea. In a treaty concluded with him shortly afterwards, the British established themselves as the leading colonial power in the area. For the remainder of the nineteenth century, Aden would be an important waypoint for steamships on route to India, a strategic position that gained considerably more value after the opening of the Suez Canal in 1869. Many of the steamships carried wealthy passengers, commercial trading products and pilgrims on their way to Mecca (Van den Berg 1887).

By the early twentieth century, Yemen was to gain new strategic significance with the outbreak of the First World War, when Ottoman and British troops fought each other across the Arabia peninsula. In a letter to his biographer, the Arabist and British Army officer, TE Lawrence believed that British policy was always aimed at containing the tribal fighting that characterised Arabia. "We decided to put a ring wall around Arabia," wrote Lawrence, "a country which must be reserved as an area of Arab individualism. So long as our fleet keeps its coasts, Arabia should be at leisure to fight out its own complex and fatal destiny" (cited in Graves 1927: 397). The idea of erecting a buffer zone between Britain's imperial interests and the many hundreds of Arab tribes continued to inform British policy throughout the interwar years and beyond. One hundred years later Britain's peace with the tribes in the hinterland continued. In 1937, Britain made Aden a crown colony. The British colonial official Harold Ingrams remarked how the British employed airpower "as a stick with which troublesome tribesmen in difficult countries are licked into submission." For Ingrams and many other colonialists, the Royal Air Force performed 'a police function', which allowed the British to bring 'peace at the cost of so little damage'. Until the British withdrawal from Aden thirty years later, air action was only ever resorted to 'when all other methods have failed' (Ingrams 1936: 383).

By the middle of the twentieth century Britain had also developed a new strategy to protect its interests in Aden by building up a system of indirect rule in the surrounding hinterland (Mawby 2005). Ingrams once again offered an insight into the new British strategy. "If they [the Arabs] had any power they had more or less relied on the British Government to support them in one way or another, generally with gifts of arms, in order to oppress their people and screw financial advantages out of them" (Ingrams 1954: 30). In the 1950s and 1960s the British spent an inordinate amount of time, money and other resources building up the Federal Regular Army (later to become the South Arabian Army) to ensure the continuation of the newly independent South Arabia in their sphere of influence. When it became clear in 1966 that the British had no intention of staying to act as the midwife for the new state, some Federal Army officers opened a dialogue with the NLF, an insurgent group that began a campaign of violence against the British authorities and their federal allies in 1963 (Edwards 2014). The NLF was fiercely nationalist and sought to blend conspiratorial work with mass agitation and support (Halliday 1974: 228). When the British announced their imminent withdrawal in 1967, the vacuum was soon filled by an alliance of Federal Army officers and NLF fighters who quickly set about establishing a Marxist government along Soviet lines.

In October 1978, the NLF became the Yemeni Socialist Party (YSP). For Yemen expert Fred Halliday, the NLF (now renamed the National Front (NF)) had undergone a "double radicalisation", initially, between 1963 and 1969, drawing on Nasserite tendencies within the broad Movement of Arab Nationalism. By 1969 a Marxist-Leninist faction had come to dominant the upper echelons of the NF (Halliday 1979: 12). The formation of the YSP brought with it a deepening of Marxist conviction and the establishment of a Soviet-style Politburo and General Committee. In the aftermath of reorganising the army, the NF purged its officer corps and made a more vigorous attempt made to indoctrinate its ranks. By the mid-1980s around one-third of the YSP were soldiers (Brehony 2014: 126). Although the South had close connections to the Soviet Union, the North did not embrace either East or West (Dresch 2008: 120). For the remainder of the 1980s, most states with an interest in Middle Eastern affairs stayed clear of the two Yemens. In many ways, they were not considered strategically valuable in wider Cold War terms.

Meanwhile, in the separate state of the Yemen Arab Republic, a civil war raged after the overthrow of the old Zayidi Imam in September 1962. Despite the use of chemical weapons by Egyptian aircraft against royalist positions and civilian villages, the UN opted out of seeking to end the violence peacefully and ignored the wishes of the two major powers in the region, Saudi Arabia and Iran. Unsurprisingly the instability favoured the Egyptians who continued to sponsor the Movement for Arab Nationalists and its associated armed groups across the region. The Yemeni civil war ended in 1970, with the military officers still very much still in charge. Over the next twenty years Riyadh would continue to pay stipends to North Yemen, and, after he rose to power in 1978, Ali Abdullah Saleh followed Riyadh's clientelist policy by remaining hostile to the southern Marxists. Conversely, Moscow would continue to back the People's Democratic Republic of Yemen (PDRY), its surrogate in the south, which would be backed by Tehran after the Iranian revolution of 1979. With the collapse of the Soviet Union and the end of the Cold War, the two Yemens were united in 1990. Senior Western diplomats, like the former US ambassador to Sanaa, Charles Dunbar, believed that this was indicative of a new-found eagerness by the people of both Yemens to build a unified, independent country, even if, as Paul Dresch argues, most Yemenis were 'little prepared for unity' (Dresch 2008: 183).

Ironically the unification of Yemen was almost strangled at birth, not through internal politicking or unpreparedness, but by external events elsewhere in the region, with Iraq's invasion of Kuwait on 20th August 1990. Saleh's government abstained from the ensuing vote backing an international coalition under the auspices of the UN Security Council. Although it would be wrong to blame the Yemen government for not foreseeing the hostility it would provoke from the international community, it did little to help itself out of diplomatic isolation. In political terms, Saudi hostility to Yemen's defiance saw Saleh turn inwards to pursue a strategy of managing the inevitable economic challenges facing Yemen. His approach was known as 'dancing on the heads of snakes', which saw him dispense patronage to a variety of different interest groups at local and national level to stave off internal unrest to his independent stance in the face of Saudi and Western pressure. It is the legacy of Saleh's chaotic policies for balancing internal opposition that has contributed to Yemen's continuing instability (Carmet et al. 2015: 1316–1332). It also partly explains why Riyadh is acting in the way it is with respect to its intervention in the country since 2015.

Yemen and the Arab Spring: The Fall of the Ancien Regime

By 2011, Saleh's over-reliance on a network of patronage could not shield him from the outbreak of revolutionary fervour across the Middle East and North Africa. In December 2010 a market vendor set himself on fire in Tunisia in protest against the unjust taxes being levied on him and his family by officers of the Ben Ali regime. This dramatic act of self-sacrifice poured an accelerant onto an open fire of intense resentment that had been building up across the region. In Egypt, Libya, Syria and Iraq, protests broke out, all of which shook these regimes to the core. In Yemen, women and youth groups, deeply ingrained in civil society, began to protest at Saleh's unpopular rule (Alley 2013). One leading protestor, Tawakkol Karman, who went on to win the Nobel Peace Prize, said that the Arab Spring emerged 'as an expression of people's dissatisfaction with the state of corruption, nepotism and bribery' present in the states affected. She believed that the revolution in Yemen, like in other places, was passing through four distinct stages. First, the dictator and his family were toppled. Second, their security networks were crumbling. In Yemen, this manifested itself in the most dramatic of ways when Saleh's key lieutenant, General Ali Mohsen al-Ahmar, refused to back his president's hardline stance against the supporters. Third, a transitional phase was now being entered into. Lastly, she argued that a new state would emerge out of this process that would establish a modern civil and democratic state. In line with many other activists across the region, there was a belief that war and repression were being exchanged for peaceful struggle (Karman 2011).

Yet, as with the revolutions in other parts of the Middle East, this optimism was to prove short lived. While the Tunisian regime fell almost without a shot being fired, Egypt was to enter a period of political instability, only stabilised by the military in what would later amount to a coup, while peaceful protests in Libya and Syria quickly turned violent (see Lister 2015). Both states soon became engulfed in civil war, with the latter seeing the casualties rise as Islamist terrorists flocked to the country to launch an offensive against the government and also the neighbouring state of Iraq.

In Yemen, an end to Saleh's rule was hastened by a bomb attack on his compound, which left him badly injured. After an elite-driven process sponsored by Riyadh, Saleh reluctantly handed over power to his deputy, Mansour Hadi. Although Hadi backed the political transition process, which had as its centre-piece a nominally inclusive National Dialogue Conference (NDC), a question mark remained over how reflective the transition was of the revolutionary change now sweeping Yemen (Carapico 2014). A period of instability followed, due in the main because the Houthis walked away from the process in its closing stages. The Houthis are part of the Zaydi tribal lineage in northern Yemen. They began an insurgency against the Yemeni government in 2004, an offensive that saw their leader Hussein al-Houthi killed by Saleh's troops. For most of the next decade, the Houthis were kept in check by Saleh through a range of strategies, including punitive action in the form of air attacks launched by both Sanaa and Riyadh. After Saleh was eventually pushed from power in 2012, the Houthis could no longer be contained. In January 2015, led by Abdul Malik al-Houthi, the brother of their slain figurehead, they stormed Sanaa and defeated the meagre military forces defending the city. After capturing the presidential palace, they placed President Hadi under house arrest. In his place, they formed a council of representatives twice the size of the NDC. Despite its size, it lacked inclusiveness and was rejected by the broad mass of the Yemeni population. The seizure of power did little to unite the country and in fact endangered regional attempts aimed at national reconciliation.

Reaction to the Houthi seizure of Yemen's capital was swift. The UN condemned the move, demanding that the Houthis 'immediately and unconditionally' engage with the United Nations' brokered negotiations, withdraw their forces from Sanaa, release President Hadi and members of his cabinet, and, importantly, refrain from actions that might undermine the Yemeni political transition (UN OCHA 2015). The calls were ignored. However, the problem ran much deeper than the Houthi's attempts to spoil the process, as Charles Schmitz has argued:

> Since the Arab Spring, the state in Yemen has, in essence, ceased to function. The transitional government is a caretaker government responsible to no one. Backroom negotiations in Riyadh and Sana created the transitional government, and its composition is a compromise between warring factions in Yemen who continue to battle. Government institutions serve not as institutions of government but fields of play in the fierce competition taking place between political factions trying to position themselves for whatever form of government arises in the future. (Schmitz 2014: 11)

The major power-brokers remain the General People's Party, previously headed by Saleh until his death in late 2017, which ejected Mansour Hadi from its higher echelons. Hadi's administration became politically isolated inside Yemen from late 2014 onwards, despite retaining UN recognition.

While UN efforts to persuade the parties to the conflict to call a ceasefire and return to the negotiating, there were signs of an emerging proxy war taking root in Yemen, involving Riyadh and the Islamic Republic of Iran in Tehran. In September 2014, Ali Reza Zakani, a representative of the Iranian Parliament, was quoted as saying that "Three Arab capitals have today ended up in the hands of Iran and belong to the Islamic Iranian revolution." Sanaa, he went on to claim, was the fourth capital now considered to be well on its way to becoming part of Tehran's sphere of influence (Middle East Monitor 2014). At that time it was suggested by supporters of Riyadh that the Iranians had backed the Houthi militia. However, some experts remain sceptical about Iranian designs for Yemen and have even gone as far as to dispute the inference that the Houthis are merely a puppet of Tehran (Juneau 2016). According to Juneau, the Iranians are using the current instability in Yemen as an opportunity to sow confusion and project themselves as a protector of oppressed minorities. For their part, the Saudis have historically also played a spoiler role. As Carapico has observed, "the kingdom has consistently sought to thwart Yemeni nationalism, self-determination, unity, welfare, poverty alleviation, workers' rights, women's empowerment and democratization" (Carapico 2014: 46).

Just as the Iranians have stepped up their provision of capacity building programmes for youth and women's groups and, covertly, by the supplying of arms to the Houthi in northern Yemen. The Houthis do not deny their links to Tehran: "Iran, Hamas, Hezbollah - what unites us is that we are against American imperialism," one of their political leaders told a Rolling Stone reporter. "It's not something that we hide. We're proud of it." However, the Houthis deny that they would allow Iran to use Yemen as a base of overt or covert operations (Aikins 2015). Barry Rubin once suggested that Middle Eastern states were more likely to become involved in the sponsorship engaged in sponsoring proxy armed groups because they could not afford to run the risk of a 'serious and costly inter-state conflict' (Rubin 2002: 139). We know from recent state-based actions by Russia in Eastern Ukraine and non-state actions by Da'esh in Syria and Iraq that hybrid or 'ambiguous' warfare has been utilised by a range of state and non-state actors, including Iran. There may well be some truth to the allegation but it is much more likely that it serves Tehran's purposes in the region to be blamed for such interference, even if there is little evidence to support the allegation (for more on the debate on Iranian involvement, see Junea 2016).

It is generally accepted that Riyadh has also intervened in Yemen to prevent the further spread of Islamist terrorism. However, it is legitimate to ask how far their decision to intervene has actually prompted the spread of this brand of non-state extremism. Islamist extremism has found fertile ground in Yemen, which predates the 2015 intervention. In the 1980s, a number of Yemenis had answered the call to jihad and had gone to fight in Afghanistan. By the early 1990s, they began to return home. Tariq al-Fadhli, the son of the former Sultan of al-Fadhli tribe, which was rooted in the Yemeni towns of Ja'ar and Zingibar in Abyan province, was one of the leading Islamist militants (Clark 2004).

He would emerge as one of the key individuals who remained on the periphery surrounding groups like Al Qaeda. Recognising the challenge Islamists like al-Fadhli posed, President Saleh entered into a pact with him and other jihadis so as to neutralise the armed threat they posed to his authority.[4] In October 2000 al-Qaeda launched its first successful attack on its American enemies when two suicide bombers detonated their payload of explosives alongside the USS Cole, killing 17 sailors and injuring another 49. Al-Fadhli, who had initially hostile to the West, soon came out in support the United States in the wake of the 9/11 attacks, famously hanging a huge American flag outside his house. He began to distance himself from a new generation of jihadis who had spent some time with Osama bin Laden and other leading al-Qaeda operatives in Afghanistan.

Al Qaeda continued to build a small, but ruthless band of followers in Yemen for much of the remainder of the decade. In 2009 the Saudi and Yemeni branches of the organisation amalgamated to form AQAP. It embedded itself deep in the Yemeni south, in towns like Ataq, Jaar and Mukulla, which it was able to do because its operatives told people they represented 'local interests' (Asher-Schapiro 2016). In 2011, a loose affiliate of AQAP and their ideological kinsmen in Ansar al-Sharia declared an emirate when it seized control of part of Abyan Province, which included Mukulla. Twelve months later—and with the support of the US military—Yemen's armed forces managed to clear the province of all Islamist forces. However, with the collapse of central state authority, AQAP bounced back, seizing the ground it had lost a few years earlier. It was to take Saudi-led coalition forces another year before they regained control of the ground.

As history suggests, there is no guarantee that the threat posed by this group has been eliminated for good and there is evidence that they might return again.[5] Yemeni journalist Farea al-Mulsimi acknowledges

[4]Saleh's most trusted general, Ali Mohsen, even married one of al-Fadhli's sisters. Interview with a member of the al-Fadhli family, December 2012.

[5]This point was made in July 2010 when one of the UK's most senior counter-terrorism officers acknowledged at an event in Chatham House how AQAP had come to represent the greatest threat to UK national security. These remarks followed in the wake of the attempted Christmas Day bomb attack in Detroit in 2009. They were to gain more traction in October 2010 when it was discovered that AQAP had attempted to bring down aircraft with a plot to detonate explosives secreted in printer cartridges. For more analysis of the threat posed by AQAP at that time (see Phillips 2011).

that "AQAP has retreated, mostly, to its old strategy of hiding in mountains and hiding before striking again." Al-Muslimini and other informed commentators believe that the only way of decisively ending the challenge posed by AQAP is to end the broader civil war and enable the rebuilding of legitimate political leadership (Gilbert 2016). Clearly, the intervention has not been successful at doing either, which begs the question of whether an earlier, limited intervention—based on clear support for a radical change in politics and security sector reform—might have helped to prevent the relapse into civil war. Arguably, this counterfactual point must be tempered with an awareness of key contractual factors that made such an approach difficult.

It is generally thought that state failure is not necessarily the most permissive environment for the operation of terrorist groups. Terrorists, especially modern ones, need infrastructure, state structures and a government so as to form a symbiotic relationship with their intended target. In short, non-state actors challenge the authority of states but they do so in the full expectation that that challenge will carry them into power at some future date. In such pernicious circumstances, it is unlikely that kinetic operations that seek to dislodge such asymmetric adversaries will bring long-lasting changes, unless the state itself is in a strong position to challenge its non-state actors by utilising a holistic approach that employs non-military instruments of power.

Conclusion

This brief glimpse into the Yemeni case study demonstrates the inherent difficulties facing those states that regard the military instrument as still retaining utility in resolving complex security problems. There have been two context-specific reasons why Saudi Arabia has found it difficult to achieve its stated political objectives in Yemen, even with the vast economic and military resources at its disposal. First, none of the warring factions (which now includes Saudi Arabia) will return to the negotiating table as long as they believe they can achieve their objectives by threatening or employing force. Second, there is the linked question of legitimacy hanging over a third party that has chosen to intervene in Yemeni affairs with the explicit intention of protecting its own national security interests. Although the Saudi-led intervention in Yemen is backed by the GCC, an increasingly security-orientated regional actor, it has also drawn widespread condemnation around the world for its alleged breaches of

International Humanitarian Law (IHL) (UN OCHA 2015). The question of whether IHL has been breached by the parties to the Yemen conflict raises issues relating not only to *jus in bello* but also, inevitably, about jus ad bellum. Without legitimacy, the GCC cannot continue to operate in Yemen without the consent of the Yemeni population (Lackner 2018a). Moreover, an improvement in the security situation will depend on the local dynamics of internal actors perhaps even more than the coercive strategy being followed by external actors. Given that the peaceful support of the international community during the NDC process in Yemen, added legitimacy to the search for peace by local parties, it stands to reason that diplomacy and not force is more likely to yield long-term stability in Yemen.

References

Abel bin Ahmed Al-Jubeir. 2015. Operation Renewal of Hope, Statement by Ambassador, April 22. Archived at http://www.operationrenewalofhope.com/saudi-ambassador-operation-decisive-storm-achieved-its-objectives/#st-hash.CWq3lnbY.dpuf. Accessed 14 March 2016.

Aikins, Matthieu. 2015. Yemen's Hidden War: A Journey Into One of the Most Remote and Dangerous Countries in the World. *Rolling Stone*, July 30. Archived at http://www.rollingstone.com/politics/news/yemens-hidden-war-20150730. Accessed 19 May 2016.

Al Jazeera. 2015. Saudi-Led Coalition Declares End to Yemen Air Strikes. *Al Jazeera*, April 22. Archived at http://www.aljazeera.com/news/2015/04/saudi-led-coalition-begins-phase-yemen-campaign-150421155500641.html. Accessed 9 May 2016.

Alley, April Longley. 2013. Assessing (In)Security After the Arab Spring: The Case of Yemen. *PS, Political Science & Politics*, 46(4): 721–726.

Arreguín-Toft, Ivan. 2001. How the Weak Win Wars: A Theory of Asymmetric Conflict. *International Security*, 26(1): 93–128.

Asher-Schapiro, Avi. 2016. Al Qaeda Is Making Serious Gains amid Chaos of Yemen's Civil War. *Vice News*, February 2. Archived at https://news.vice.com/article/al-qaeda-is-making-serious-gains-amid-chaos-of-yemens-civil-war. Accessed 3 May 2016.

Brehony, Noel. 2014. The Role of the PDRY in Forming a South Yemeni Identity. In Lackner, Helen (ed.), *Why Yemen Matters: A Society in Transition*. London. Saqi.

Carapico, Sheila. 2014. Yemen Between Revolution and Counter-Terrorism. In Lackner, Helen (ed.), *Why Yemen Matters: A Society in Transition*. London: Saqi.

Carment, David, Joe Landry, Yiagadeesen Samy, and Scott Shaw. 2015. Towards a Theory of Fragile State Transitions: Evidence from Yemen, Bangladesh and Laos. *Third World Quarterly*, 36(7): 1316–1332.

Clark, Victoria. 2004. *Yemen: Dancing on the Heads of Snakes*. New Haven, CT: Yale University Press.

Dingli, Sophia. 2013. Is the Failed State Thesis Analytically Useful? The Case of Yemen. *Politics*, 33(2): 91–100.

Dresch, Paul. 2008. *A History of Modern Yemen*. Cambridge: Cambridge University Press.

Edwards, Aaron. 2014. *Mad Mitch's Tribal Law: Aden and the End of Empire*. Edinburgh: Mainstream.

Edwards, Aaron. 2017. *Strategy in War and Peace: A Critical Introduction*. Edinburgh: Edinburgh University Press.

Gilbert, Benjamin. 2016. Al-Qaeda May Have Retreated from Its Yemeni Capital, but Will Likely Return to Fight Another Day. *Vice News*, May 2. Archived at https://news.vice.com/article/al-qaeda-may-have-retreated-from-its-yemeni-capital-but-will-likely-return-to-fight-another-day. Accessed 3 May 2016.

Graves, Robert. 1927. *Lawrence and the Arabs*. London: Jonathan Cape.

Gray, Colin S. 1999. *Modern Strategy*. Oxford: Oxford University Press.

Halliday, Fred. 1974. *Arabia Without Sultans*. London: Penguin.

Halliday, Fred. 1979. Yemen's Unfinished Revolution: Socialism in the South. *MERIP Reports*, 81(October): 3–20.

Hoffman, Frank. 2007. *Conflict in the 21st Century: The Rise of Hybrid Wars*. Arlington, VA: Potomac Institute for Policy Studies. Archived at http://www.potomacinstitute.org/images/stories/publications/potomac_hybridwar_0108.pdf. Accessed 1 June 2018.

Ingrams, W. H. 1936. Unexplored Regions of the Hadhramaut. *Journal of the Royal Central Asian Society*, 23(3): 378–412.

Ingrams, Harold. 1954. The British and South Arabia. *The Arab World*, no. 20, July.

ICG (International Crisis Group). 2011. Breaking Point? Yemen's Southern Question. *Middle East Report*, no. 114, October 20. Archived at http://www.crisisgroup.org/~/media/Files/Middle%20East%20North%20Africa/Iran%20Gulf/Yemen/114%20Breaking%20Point%20-%20Yemens%20Southern%20Question.pdf. Accessed 19 May 2016.

Jones, Clive. 2011. The Tribes that Bind: Yemen and the Paradox of Political Violence. *Studies in Conflict & Terrorism*, 34(12): 902–916.

Juneau, Thomas. 2016. Iran's Policy Towards the Houthis in Yemen: A Limited Return on a Modest Investment. *International Affairs*, 92(3): 647–663.

Kaldor, Mary. 2006. *New and Old Wars* (2nd ed.). Cambridge: Polity.

Karman, Tawakkol. 2011. Nobel Lecture. *Oslo*, December 10. Archived at https://www.nobelprize.org/nobel_prizes/peace/laureates/2011/karman-lecture_en.html. Accessed 18 May 2016.

Klare, Michael T. 2004. The Deadly Connection: Paramilitary Bands, Small Arms Diffusion ad State Failure. In Rotberg, Robert I. (ed.), *When States Fail: Cause and Consequences*. Princeton, NJ: Princeton University Press.

Lackner, Helen. 2018a. On a Wretched Third Anniversary of the International Intervention in Yemen, Is the Rise of the Huthis Irresistible? Part 1. *Open Democracy*, March 23. Archived at https://www.opendemocracy.net/north-africa-west-asia/helen-lackner/on-wretched-third-anniversary-of-international-intervention-in. Accessed 1 June 2018.

Lackner, Helen. 2018b. Wretched Third Anniversary of International Intervention in Yemen: The Saudi-Led Coalition and Humanitarian Disaster. Part 2. *Open Democracy*, March 24. Archived at https://www.opendemocracy.net/north-africa-west-asia/helen-lackner/wretched-third-anniversary-of-international-intervention-in-yem. Accessed 1 June 2018.

Lister, Charles R. 2015. *The Syrian Jihad: Al-Qaeda, the Islamic State and the Evolution of an Insurgency*. London: Hurst and Company.

Mawby, Spencer. 2005. *British Policy in Aden and the Protectorates, 1955–67: Last Outpost of a Middle East Empire*. London: Routledge.

Mack, Andrew. 1975. Why Big Nations Lose Small Wars: The Politics of Asymmetric Conflict. *World Politics*, 27(2): 175–200.

Middle East Monitor. 2014. Sanaa Is the Fourth Arab Capital to Join the Iranian Revolution. *Middle East Monitor*, September 27. Archived at https://www.middleeastmonitor.com/20140927-sanaa-is-the-fourth-arab-capital-to-join-the-iranian-revolution/. Accessed 1 June 2018.

Neumann, Peter R., and M. L. R. Smith. 2007. *The Strategy of Terrorism: How It Works, and Why It Fails*. London: Routledge.

Phillips, Sarah. 2011. Al-Qaeda and the Struggle for Yemen. *Survival*, 53(1): 95–120.

Regan, Patrick, and M. Rodwan Abouharb. 2002. Interventions and Civil Conflicts: Tools of Conflict Management or Simply Another Participant?. *World Affairs*, 165(Summer): 42–54.

Rosenau, James N. 1969. Intervention as a Scientific Concept. *Journal of Conflict Resolution*, 13(2): 149–171.

Rubin, Barry. 2002. *The Tragedy of the Middle East*. Cambridge: Cambridge University Press.

Salisbury, Peter. 2015. Yemen and the Saudi–Iranian 'Cold War'. Middle East and North Africa Programme Research Paper. London: Chatham House. February. Archived at https://www.chathamhouse.org/sites/files/chathamhouse/field/field_document/20150218YemenIranSaudi.pdf. Accessed 15 May 2016.

Schmitz, Charles. 2014. *Yemen's National Dialogue*. Middle East Institute Policy Paper 2014-1. Washington, DC: Middle East Institute.

Smith, General Sir Rupert. 2005. *The Utility of Force: The Art of War in the Modern World*. London: Penguin.

Thornton, Rod. 2007. *Asymmetric Warfare: Threat and Response in the Twenty-First Century*. Cambridge: Polity.

UN OCHA. 2015. *Situation of Human Rights in Yemen*. Report of the United Nations High Commissioner for Human Rights, A/HRC/30/31, 7 September.

UNSC. 2017. Statement by the President of the Security Council, S/PRST/2017/7 (2017), June 15. Archived at http://undocs.org/S/PRST/2017/7. Accessed 1 June 2018.

Van den Berg, L. W. C. 1887. *Hadthramut and the Arab Colonies in the Indian Archipelago*, Translated into English by Major C. W. H. Sealy, Second Assistant Political Resident Aden. Bombay: Government Central Press.

von Clausewitz, Carl. 1976 ed. *On War*, edited and translated by Michael Howard and Peter Paret. Princeton, MA: Princeton University Press.

Wedeen, Lisa. 2010. Don't Call Yemen a "Failed State". *Foreign Policy*, March 30. Archived at http://foreignpolicy.com/2010/03/30/dont-call-yemen-a-failed-state/. Accessed 20 May 2016.

Willis, John M. 2015. *Operation Decisive Storm and the Expanding Counter-Revolution*. Middle East Research and Information Project, 30 March. Archived at https://www.merip.org/operation-decisive-storm-expanding-counter-revolution. Accessed 1 June 2018.

CHAPTER 5

Crisis and Intervention: Combating Terrorism in the Sahel

Susanna D. Wing

France's role in Mali might best be described as a case of "you're damned if you do and damned if you don't". Operation Serval was widely applauded for having stopped the territorial advance of militant Islamic extremists. Serval's narrow mission excluded French involvement in domestic politics in Mali and was a shift from France's more familiar and widespread practice of an *approche globale*, a civilian-military strategy to "win hearts and minds." The French were faced with a conundrum in Mali. To engage both the military campaign against the rebellion in the North and the political governance issues at the root of the instability would very likely result in being criticised for neocolonialism. In addition, it would certainly draw France into a complex political environment in which solutions are far from clear. It seemed that a swift military strike would avoid accusations of meddling in domestic politics of Mali. The French could not go it alone however. They relied on allies such as the United States but it was their reliance on the Chadian military that led some to claim that this constituted a return of the Franco-African neo-colonial war by proxy (Helly and Rocca 2013: 5).

S. D. Wing (✉)
Department of Political Science, Haverford College,
Haverford, PA, USA

T. Clack and R. Johnson (eds.), *Before Military Intervention*,
https://doi.org/10.1007/978-3-319-98437-7_5

By "staying out of politics" the French ignore the critical, ongoing problems lying at the root of instability in the first place. Their presence may even make the problem worse because they are supporting weak states across the region, ones that provide very little in terms of good governance and public goods. These, some argue, are the weaknesses that have led to increased insecurity and have facilitated recruitment to local terrorist groups (Raineri and Strazzari 2017). It may also be the root cause of increasing retaliation against security forces including UN peacekeeping troops and the Malian army. We cannot know what Mali would look like if French and UN forces were not there, so we cannot say whether the presence of these forces have actually caused an increase in violence; however, attacks on Malian army or government outposts are growing more common and insecurity has expanded geographically by extending into southern Mali and across the region.

In the "war on terror" France supports allies in the region regardless of their governance record. This permits governments in the region to continue to act with impunity and ignore human rights. Nathaniel Powell argues that "By bolstering governments that prey on their populations, France's interventions increase the potential for unrest, rebellion, and even jihadist-inspired terrorism" (Powell 2016). This perspective is supported by Malians' claims that good governance is the key to improving security. Local imams believe that it is the weakness of the state and its lack of authority that has led to the rise in support for armed Islamic militant groups that have multiplied and coalesced since 2012. These include: Ansar Dine, Al Qaeda in the Islamic Maghreb (AQIM), al-Mourabitoun, the Macina Liberation Front (MLF) and the umbrella organisation Jama'at Nusrat ul-Islam wal-Muslimin (JNIM) that was created in March 2017 uniting these various organisations.

This article explores the crisis in Mali as it relates to the larger war on terror in the Sahel. The French-led intervention in Mali and subsequent Operation Barkhane mark a shift away from the counter-insurgency strategy of winning hearts and minds. By ignoring governance in Mali and the region while continuing to focus on funding and training security forces the French presence will have long-term negative and destabilising consequences for the region.

The Crisis

In March 2012, a coup d'état overthrew President Amadou Toumani Touré known widely as ATT, who in 1991 famously stepped in to support a popular movement to bring democracy to the country and oust the reviled dictator Moussa Traoré. He earned his reputation as a "soldier for democracy" when he then stepped aside to allow elections. The fall of ATT was a surprise to many who had miscalculated the level of unrest and the state of governance in the country. France did not intervene to stop the coup in March 2012 although they certainly had the capacity to do so. It is likely that France made a choice at that moment to let "African solutions to African problems" work itself out in time. In fact, the international donor community, while in disarray, effectively put a stranglehold on the Sanogo regime through the cessation of budget support and development assistance (Bergamaschi 2017). Neighbouring countries put pressure on Sanogo and made it clear that coups were no longer an acceptable way of doing politics in the region. Despite local support for the coup, it caused irreparable damage and Mali lost control of vast amounts of territory in the north within weeks (Lecocq et al. 2013). The international response was integral to bringing Interim President Traoré to power and facilitating presidential elections in July and August 2013.

In May 2012, the Interim President of Mali, Dioncounda Traoré, lay in a hospital bed in Paris after having been brutally beaten by a mob that had infiltrated Koulouba, the presidential palace in Bamako. While he recovered from his wounds, separatist Tuareg and militant Islamic insurgents who controlled Northern Mali were advancing and securing territory. Traoré impressed upon the French foreign minister Laurent Fabius, as well as presidential advisors to François Hollande, that the conflict was not just another African civil war (Chivvis 2015). However, the roots of the crisis were based, in part, on a failure of the state to respond adequately to Tuareg concerns in northern Mali. In addition, the government did not adequately support the Malian military who were struggling to hold back the growing Tuareg separatist movement led by the National Movement for the Liberation of Azawad (MNLA). This was undeniably a crisis rooted in poor governance.

Locally led Islamic militant groups, including those affiliated with Al Qaeda in the Maghreb (AQIM), rapidly overpowered the MNLA. Mali needed French support against the armed rebellion in order to prevent the entire country from falling into the hands of Islamic militants. Many have claimed that the nature of the threat and the ability of rebels to take Bamako was overstated (Reeve and Peletier 2014: 3) and that the taking of Konna was most likely an attempt to take the strategic towns of Sevaré and Diabali in order to prevent an African peace enforcement mission (Reeve and Peletier 2014: 10). On the other hand, repeated claims have been made that there was intelligence that militants were organising in Bamako and preparing to take the capital.

Traoré insisted that the involvement of AQIM posed an international threat about which the French should be particularly concerned. According to the interim president, the Malian army was weak, decrepit, and "for decades, only an army in name, good for 'parades and coups, but not war'" (Chivvis 2015: 77). While the French were convinced, the United States was apprehensive of military intervention in a politically complex situation (Chivvis 2015: 82). Tensions existed between France and the US on two fronts: firstly, whether the restoration of democracy ought to take precedence over military action and secondly, whether the African forces the French were pushing were able to handle the situation (Chivvis 2015: 84). Embedded in the crisis are two key elements: terrorism and politics. How these are balanced is critical to securing peace. Marc-Antoine Pérouse de Montclos writes:

> The de facto partition of the country has structural roots in problems that are far older. While the media and decision-makers insist on the conjectural role of Al Qaida, the internal causes of the crisis prove to be multiple and fundamentally touch on the question of the state. (Pérouse de Montclos 2013: 27)

Therefore, although the international media focuses on Al Qaeda and other terrorist groups, it is the nature of the Malian state and domestic politics that are at the root of the crisis (Wing 2013a). The French mandate in Mali was driven by the international terrorist threat posed by Al Qaeda and its affiliates. The French-led intervention clearly marked a shift in international law and more permissive views towards the extra-territorial use of force as a response to increased capabilities of non-state actors (Stigall 2015: 36). Operation Serval came to an end on 15 July 2014 and Operation Barkhane was launched in August 2014 with the sole mission of fighting terrorism. The "war on terror" has led to the military support of African allies regardless of their human rights or governance records. This approach, reminiscent of Cold War strategies, is likely to have long-term, negative effects on how local populations perceive of French activity in the region. By partnering with the repressive regimes that have been at the heart of the problem in the first place, France risks doing more harm than good (Powell 2016). The increasing insecurity in southern Mali, and more widely across West Africa, is likely to increase frustration with the French and confusion over their long-term goals in the region.

The unexpected story in Mali is that this country, which was long touted as a model of African democracy, found itself in a position in which the interim head of state was pleading a former colonial power to intervene in its sovereign territory. Both domestic and international actors recognised that the security crisis required immediate action. The fall of Konna on January 11, 2013 triggered Operation Serval led by French airpower, combined with French Special Operations Command (COS). The French-led intervention was effective in removing the looming threat of rebel forces overtaking the critical airbase in Sevaré and, possibly, Bamako. However, underlying this threat was a domestic political crisis that had finally come to a head. France was intent on addressing the former while avoiding the latter.

Operation Serval moved away from "l'approche global," a global approach that focuses on "winning hearts and minds" through the coordination of civil and military strategies. This strategy relies on the integration of multiple actors including international armed forces; the host nation and its institutions; countries in the region; and non-governmental organizations and private enterprise. These actors work together through shared knowledge, consultation, cooperation and collaboration (Centre interarmées de concepts, de doctrines et d'experimentations 2009: 5). The global approach envisions a return to stability in a country, no matter the stage of the crisis, and includes coordinated and coherent action to address governance, security, and economic and social development (Chambefort and Folliot 2011: 18). French General Stéphane Abrial, head of NATO Allied Command Transformation, explained the global approach as "a state of mind. It is a method, not a mission" (Chambefort and Folliot 2011: 16). However, by not using the global approach in Serval the French avoided the broader context of the crisis and its root political and social causes. They also diverged from a military strategy that had been increasingly implemented since the1990s (Centre interarmées de concepts, de doctrines et d'experimentations

2009: 1). It would appear that they believed that by avoiding these issues they would avoid the potential quagmire of a Malian civil war. The French originally focused on "leading from behind," a strategy that emphasised "African solutions to African problems," but this goal was not effective because the local and regional partners on whom such a strategy depended were not prepared to act in an effective and timely manner.

Winning Hearts and Minds No More

UN Security Council Resolution 2085 passed unanimously on 20 December 2012 and authorised the creation of the African-led International Support Mission to Mali (AFISMA). AFISMA was to be an African security force that would work alongside the Malian army to secure Northern Mali. For months prior to the intervention, France pursued diplomacy and supported the use of African forces as a means to resolve the crisis in Mali. This was both a political manoeuver and an economic choice. AFISMA would permit France to operate behind the scenes of an African-led force and diffuse the cost of an intervention among European UN members and the United States. Unfortunately, diplomacy was not effective in mobilising the forces needed at the outset of the Malian crisis. AFISMA was too slow to come to fruition and rebel advances on Konna Mali triggered Operation Serval on 11 January 2013. President Hollande announced the objectives of Operation Serval on the day the mission was launched. These incuded:

1. Stop the terrorist aggression
2. Secure the country, one in which there are many thousand French people
3. Permit Mali to recover its territorial integrity (Shurkin 2014: 8).

Serval sent a signal that President Hollande was not the indecisive leader that his critics claimed (Haski 2013). The intervention is generally considered a success which may be linked to the ability of the French to rapidly regain territory lost to the MNLA and militant Islamists; namely, Ansar Dine and MUJAO (Movement for Oneness and Jihad in West Africa). However, Serval has not stopped terrorist aggression. An attack on 13 February 2016 on the MINUSMA camp in Kidal in Northern

Mali killed five peacekeepers. Ansar Dine claimed the attack and stated that it was "a message to the crusader aggressors and all who support them" (*BBC News* 2016). On 18 January 2017, a suicide attack on a Malian army outpost in Gao killed nearly 80 people. Al Mourabitoun claimed responsibility and AQIM stated that the attack was punishment for working with France (Ahmed 2017; Bavier 2017). In the first three months of 2018, there were over 100 attacks in Mali linked to terrorist groups (Dakono and Maiga 2018).

Serval's objectives were aimed at avoiding the internal political dynamics of Mali and therefore its success in the long-term is questionable. The French had no intention of becoming bogged down in the quagmire of Malian politics that was at the root of the crisis. As Michael Shurkin writes:

> The French military abhors mission creep and want no part in things such as 'nation building.' In Mali, for example, the French military sees itself as good at killing members of a few terrorist groups; that is what they do, and they refuse to get involved in anything else, such as sorting out Mali's political mess or involving themselves in the conflict among Mali's various armed rebel groups and between them and the Malian state. Of course, that means the French military is not doing a lot of what Mali needs, but the French are sticking to their policy. (Shurkin 2015)

In order to avoid becoming involved in the domestic politics of the country France focused solely on the pursuit of the Islamist rebels in the North. Once AQIM and its affiliates were in retreat, the French left the situation in the hands of MINUSMA (United Nations Multidimensional Integrated Stabilisation Mission in Mali) and the Malian army. Operation Serval ended July 2014 and Operation Barkhane was launched in August 2014 as a regional counterterrorism initiative.

Why did the French avoid an "approche globale" and a combined civilian/military action in Mali? French colonial history in the region invites accusations that France is interfering in domestic affairs and infringing on the sovereignty of former colonies. This criticism emanated from French citizens as well as from international sources. As a result, there would be little support at home for sticking around and fighting in Mali, despite the fact that the intervention was prompted by request of the Malian government. In addition, it is likely that by 2013 lessons learned from Iraq and Afghanistan made France skittish about the risk of becoming bogged down in Malian domestic affairs when the first goal of Serval was to fight terrorist aggression. This goal was narrowly conceived of as securing territory overtaken by groups designated as terrorist organizations (e.g. AQIM, Ansar Dine, and MUJAO). This approach, of course, ignores the link between marginalisation, poor governance and terrorism in the first place (Dowd and Raleigh 2013).

Winning hearts and minds was a key component of counter insurgency strategies of interventions in Afghanistan and Iraq and has increasingly come under fire.The US promoted a counterinsurgency (COIN) campaign in earnest in 2007 with the publication of US Army/Marine Counterinsurgency Field Manual FM-324. COIN has been widely criticised as a failure with Iraq and Afghanistan as prime recent examples of this failure (Gurman 2013; Gentile 2013).

> In the popular telling, counterinsurgency aims to win the hearts and minds of local populations by providing security along with economic assistance, bridges, schools, roads, and the elements of infrastructure, and finally good governance. As this is accomplished, the population will ally itself with the government and the counterinsurgent force, thereby forcing the insurgents to fight in the open, where they will be hunted down and killed or captured. (Gentile 2013: 2)

Retired US Army Colonel Gian Gentile argues that counterinsurgency operations focus on the procedure, tactics and logistics of intervention. As a result, underlying motives of intervention (in this case American interventions) are seldom be called into question (Gentile 2013: 7).

The French civilian-military approach is deeply rooted in history. The French military is small so winning over local populations is a tactic designed to be successful with the limited military tools at their disposal. There was a widely held belief that winning hearts and minds should be central to any counterinsurgency strategy. However, failures in Afghanistan and Iraq loomed large and factored into France's decision to pursue a much more targeted strike in Mali. Further, there had been the widespread hope that a regional response would come to fruition, but the money and troops failed to mobilise in a timely manner. It is likely that insurgents in Mali considered the slow-moving international actors to be an advantage for them and went on the offensive. This was perhaps their biggest mistake as it triggered swift, unilateral, French action that abandoned the aforementioned global approach.

Counterterrorism Activities in the Sahel

Operation Serval and its successor Operation Barkhane were framed in the context of fighting terrorists and, more specifically, with the idea that the French were fighting the threat posed by Al Qaeda and its affiliates who controlled Malian territory, destabilised the region, and put France and Europe more broadly at risk to terrorist attacks. While France has had multiple military operations in the region including but not limited to Licorne (Cote d'Ivoire) and Epervier (Chad), Operation Barkhane represents the first counterterrorism effort led by French that spanned across the wider Sahel.

Operation Serval and Operation Barkhane were preceded by extensive counterterrorism operations led by the United States in the region. Indeed, in the wake of September 11, 2001 the United States had the most active counterterrorism programme in West Africa. The US Department of State and the Office of Counterterrorism launched the Pan-Sahel Initiative (PSI) in 2002 to fight terrorism and to increase peace and security there. The Trans-Sahara Counterterrorism Initiative (TSCTI), begun in 2005, replaced PCI and extended the scope of US counterterrorism measures in the region. US Africa Command or AFRICOM was established in 2007. In 2008 TSCTI became the Trans-Sahara Counterterrorism Partnership (TSCTP). The US Department of Defense, US Department of State and US Agency for International Development all participate in the program. The TSCTP is a partnership between the US and African countries; it includes Exercise Flintlock, an annual regional exercise that began in 2005 with the participation of Burkina Faso, Canada, Chad, France, Mauritania, the Netherlands, Niger, Nigeria, Senegal, United Kingdom, and the United States. Flintlock focuses on capacity building and training of regional security forces in counterterrorism and the protection of civilian populations. Flintlock 2018 included nearly 1900 participants from over 20 African and Western nations (Herring 2018).

These US initiatives have generally been considered a failure given the large quantity of money that was thrown into the region with very little success in controlling the problem (Powelson 2013). As Samuel Powelson argues, this lack of success is, in part, because the US relied on episodic training of regional military personnel rather than more enduring engagement. Large quantities of funding for counterterrorism had been flowing into the region for years. From 2005 to 2013 Mauritania,

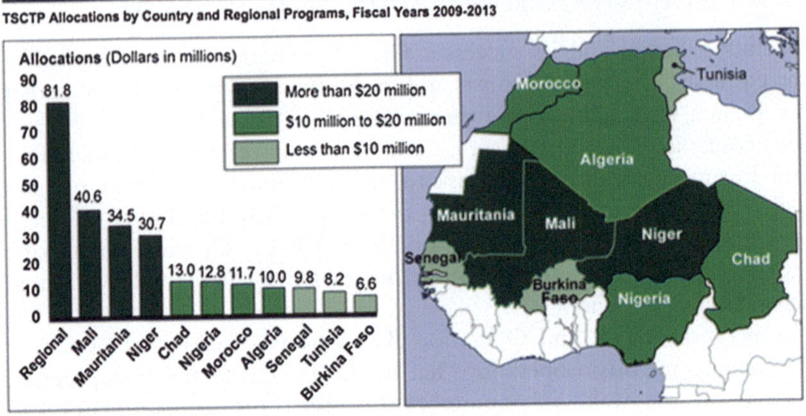

Fig. 5.1 TSCTP allocations by country and regional programmes, fiscal years, 2009–2013 (*Source* GAO analysis of State and USAID data; Map Resource [map])

Chad, Mali and Niger received a large share of the allocated funds, totaling over $600 million. Not only were TSCTP funds allocated but in 2014 Mauritania, Niger and Kenya also received $45 million to purchase and equip three Cessna 208 aircraft with advanced ISR (intelligence, surveillance and reconnaissance) capabilities (Moore and Walker 2016: 702). The GAO allocations from 2009 to 2013 show that, as part of the TSCTP, Mali received more than any other country in the region. This is a noteworthy finding given that the Malian army essentially collapsed in the face of insurgency and that Mali is the country most destabilised by local Islamic militants and AQIM (Fig. 5.1).

Unfortunately, the extensive funding of TSCTP and the militarization of the region connected to counterterrorism initiatives have contributed to undermining governance and human rights. Four countries that AFRICOM has worked very closely with in TSCTP "have experienced successful or attempted military coups in recent years –Mauritania (2005 and 2008), Niger (2010), Mali (2012) and Burkina Faso (2014 and 2015)" (Moore and Walker 2016: 705). Remarkably, Malian military officer Amadou Sanogo, the coup leader in Mali, was a participant in several US training programmes and General Gilbert Diendere, the leader of an attempted coup in Burkina Faso in 2015, was that country's "point person on the US Counterterrorism Partnership"

(Moore and Walker 2016: 705). These examples underscore a disconnect between training of local forces as partners in counterterrorism and the political stability of regional governments.

The US military presence in the Sahel through TSCTP was critical to its ability to assist the French during Operation Serval. During Serval, France relied on allies for 75% of the airlifting; 75% of personnel and equipment used in the first 3 weeks were moved by allies and allies provided 30% of ISR (Shurkin 2014: 2–3). The US ISR support included "satellite images, drones from Niger and Italy, the HALOE mission and manned ISR flights from Burkina Faso, Niger, and several European bases" (Moore and Walker 2016: 703). Because US ISR "... operations were ongoing from long before the French intervention. Intelligence sharing began more or less immediately, and a Global Hawk unmanned aircraft arrived within a week" (Chivvis 2015: 118–119). The September 2012 attack on the US diplomatic facility in Benghazi dramatically altered the US perception of terrorist threats to US interests emanating from the Sahel-Sahara zone (Reeve and Peletier 2014: 7). The US would support the French but not put US military personnel in harm's way by committing soldiers to combat. Despite the events in Benghazi, it was understood that there would likely be significant blowback from US involvement in a region few Americans would consider to be a priority to US security. The death of four special forces operatives in Niger on October 4, 2017 was the largest loss of life of US soldiers in Africa since the 1993 "Blackhawk Down" crisis in Somalia and prompted US congressional representatives to claim that they had no idea the extent to which US soldiers were engaged in the region (Callimachi et al. 2018). In 2012, the US could not engage in Mali without a democratically elected government in place. They could, however, provide essential ISR support. Much like the United States, European Union member states let France take the lead in Mali, and Germany and the United Kingdom refused to put "boots on the ground." They continue to restrict their participation to refuelling, airlift and transport operations (Helly and Rocca 2013: 7).

An analysis of Serval points to three principle problems. First, the French handled the overall situation as a terrorist problem not a domestic political crisis. Second, forces could not hold territory against unconventional tactics and, finally, Serval tried to control transnational armed groups within one country when it was easy for them to move about (Reeve and Peletier 2014: 27). Operation Barkhane operates with continued support from AFRICOM and European allies and the US and France share a number of military facilities (Moore and Walker 2016: 703–704). Two mission goals of Barkhane are (1) to support the armed forces of partner countries in the Sahel-Sahara region in their fight against terrorist and armed groups and (2) to help prevent re-establishment of terrorist safe havens in the region. The US TSCTP has a broader list of goals that include building and enhancing partnerships with counter-terrorism forces in the region, countering terrorist ideology and promoting democratic governance (Reeve and Peletier 2014: 26).

The European Union has pursued programs in the region focused on security and development. EUCAP Sahel Niger (European Union CSDP Civilian Mission) was created in July 2012, at the request of the Niger government, and was extended until July 2016. EUCAP Sahel Mali was established in January 2015 and is "dedicated to supporting the Malian authorities' commitment to restructuring their defense and security forces in 2015" (European External Action Service 2015). These programs are also the targets of criticism. Since Sept 2009, Niger has had a Service central lutte contre terrorisme (Central Counterterrorism Service, SCLCT), linked to the police. The European Scrutiny Committee of the UK House of Commons gave a scathing critique of the EUCAP Sahel Niger. They wrote:

> We concluded that this was shaping up to be a case study in how not to organise a CSDP mission — politically driven by the former colonial power with, because of the rushed launch, little preparatory work with the Nigerien authorities to define their needs properly (House of Commons 2013).

Counterterrorism initiatives can easily fall into the trap of bolstering state security units that then act with impunity and ignore human rights. Most of these initiatives have failed and despite the increased militarization and continued counterterrorism efforts, instability and insecurity are widespread in Mali and across its borders.

Rising Insecurity in the Region

Militarization continues to be the principle approach to addressing the crisis in the Sahel. Despite this, or perhaps because of it, terrorism in West Africa has spread geographically, finding more soft targets. There have been multiple attacks on hotels, restaurants and resorts across the region. These include: March 2015 La Terrace restaurant, Bamako, five killed; August 2015 Byblos Hotel, Sevaré Mali, 13 deaths including five MINUSMA employees; November 2015 20 hostages killed at the Radisson Blu in Bamako; January 2016 Ouagadougou Hotel Splendid and Cappuccino café, 30 killed; March 2016 Cote d'Ivoire 16 killed at the beach resort of Grand Bassam. These attacks are in addition to multiple attacks in Paris: January 7, 2015 the satirical newspaper Charlie Hebdo was attacked killing 11 people; November 15, 2015 multiple attacks occurred around Paris including at the Bataclan killing at least 130 people and July 14, 2016 86 people were killed in Nice.

While these events gained international attention, there have been a number of small-scale attacks in Mali that have taken place farther south than had previously been the case since the crisis began. Several attacks on military outposts or government facilities have been claimed by the Macina Liberation Front (MLF), a branch of Ansar Dine, and have focused on expanding attacks in the Mopti region. Inter-communal violence has been aggravated by the Macina Liberation Front and there have been increasing clashes between Fulani and Bambara in the region. Fulani herders and settlers have traditionally clashed over access to land. In Ténenkou circle in the Mopti region 24 people were killed and five injured during clashes between Bambara and Fulani in early May 2016. Oumar Bathily, mayor of the urban commune of Mopti, argued that the violence is the result of the absence of the state (Studio Tamani 2016). Some residents have killed Fulani, labelling them jihadists, and the presence of the MLF has exacerbated this problem. Violence between Fulani pastoralists and settlers has also increased in Nigeria. Allegedly there are links between this violence and Boko Haram, and Fulani herders have been labelled as a terrorist group. The blurring of terrorist violence and inter-communal violence is evident in Nigeria and Mali with this targeting of the Fulani as terrorists. This is indicative of the challenges in a region in which political and social history is often intertwined with insecurity, producing what becomes a "terrorist" threat (Tayo and Nasrullah 2016; Wing 2016). This situation is complicated by the fact that UN mandates for the French and MINUSMA "effectively authorise an indefinite right of deadly pursuit of groups that France may define as terrorists" (Reeve and Peletier 2014: 3). This is not to argue that terrorist groups are not active but rather that the French and Malian government have great leeway in terms of deciding who is a terrorist. In essence, violence that has roots in complex social and political interactions among communities quite easily becomes simply a “terrorist” problem. This approach does nothing to resolve the problem and so the growing insecurity in Mali and beyond should not come as a surprise.

Reinforcing Local Partners

Since January 2013 France has pursued a military strategy in the Sahel with the support of the European Union, the United States, and other allies, including the G5, an alliance created in February 2014 and composed of Mali, Niger, Burkina Faso, Mauritania and Chad. As the territorial advance of rebels took place in Mali, and prior to launching Serval, the French pursued a strategy of “leading from behind.” By supporting African militaries, the French military hoped they would be able to take a backseat to regional African partners who would then intervene in Mali when it was clear an intervention was needed. President Hollande made it clear that his government would support an African intervention in Mali. Unfortunately, this approach was more of an ideal than a reality. Despite the flood of financial and materiel support, as well as military training to governments in the region, it was insufficient to prepare these militaries to intervene effectively at the time of the Malian crisis.

Unfortunately, governance and human rights are undermined by counterterrorism policies in the Sahel. Chad, with its authoritarian regime, is a key partner in French counterterrorism efforts was viewed by France as “the only reasonable partner for counterterrorism operations in desert environments” (Reeve and Peletier 2014: 6). Mauritania and Algeria, both undemocratic countries, are key partners for counterterrorism initiatives. African allies in the war on terror have benefited from increasing financial and materiel support, and it is well known that African strong men were created in order to achieve geopolitical goals associated with the Cold War. Chadian President Hissène Habré is a good example of a dictator in the region supported by both the US and France as an ally against Muammar Al-Gaddafi of Libya. He received a great deal of military aid that included the training of Chadian secret police notorious for atrocities committed on civilians. On May 30, 2016 Habré was sentenced by a Senegalese court to life in prison for crimes against humanity, war crimes, and torture (Human Rights Watch, no date) History is repeating itself. Although improved governance is a goal of the United States, local partners in the war on terror are strengthened, as are their security forces, with little accounting for their records on governance. Of the four militaries that the US-trained under the Pan-Sahel Initiative, three (Mauritania in 2003, Niger in 2010, Mali in 2012) overthrew democratically elected governments and the fourth (Chad in 2006) split the country in civil war. The most obvious danger is that "... alliances that Washington and Paris have made and must maintain with local strongmen- politicians, military, secret police, and at times, rebel leaders – ... are likely to undermine local confidence in counterterrorism operations" (Reeve and Peletier 2014: 29).

Interestingly, this support has not proven to be a guarantee for leaders to retain power. President Amadou Toumani Touré of Mali was elected in 2002 at the outset of PSI and then the subsequent TSCTP. His government was overthrown in 2012. Blaise Compaoré of Burkina Faso served as a mediator in the Mali conflict in 2012 and was overthrown in 2014. Both leaders were overthrown due to widespread domestic discontent with their rule. Supporters of ousted President Compaoré led an unsuccessful coup in 2015. In each instance coup leaders were individuals trained by the United States. In Mali, ATT lost the support of the green berets responsible for fighting the war in the North. Despite the funds and training going to Mali from training programs such as TSCTP, there were widespread complaints from the army of a lack of adequate food, pay and arms needed to fight the insurgents.

It should be noted that, along with the militarization of the region, multiple donors, including the E.U., the U.S., and France are contributing in other ways to the effort to build the rule of law in the region. However, development assistance designed to achieve these goals has made remarkably little progress and, in some cases, only served to promote instability of the state by increasing opportunities for corruption as well as building resentment among those who see themselves as not benefiting from these significant resources while others grow rich off of them (for a discussion of donor aid strategies see Bergamaschi 2017). The European Union has long focused on improving governance, increasing development and fighting poverty as going hand in hand with increasing security in the Sahel (European External Action Service 2016). Unfortunately, in Mali the key initiative that ATT and the EU promoted was the Special Program for Peace, Security and Development in the North (PSPSDN). This program only served to exacerbate tensions as a result of its top-down approach that ignored the concerns of northern populations while focusing primarily on reinforcing the security apparatus in that region. ATT viewed the program as a way to securitize the North and fight the Northern rebellion whereas donors viewed the project more as a way to implement previous accords (Wing 2013b). More recently, the EU has created PARSEC (Programme d'appui au renforcement de la sécurité) designed to integrate security and development. Tensions exist between regional officials who seek economic integration and the building of infrastructure among the G5 while EU and US officials "are fixated on counter-terrorism and security coordination" (Lebovich 2017: 5).

A Governance Crisis

A quick glance at Freedom House ratings from the 2016 report on Freedom in the World reveals the nature of governance among the G5 countries. On a scale in which 7 is least free, 1 is most free, all of the countries have remarkably low scores, particularly with respect to political rights where no country scores above a 4 (Table 5.1).

These scores are unlikely to improve so long as governments are secure in their reliance on donor funds and their roles as strategic partners to France and the United States. Ironically, Malians living through the crisis in their country see the problem as one that will need to be resolved with improved governance. Deep frustration on the part of the military and many civilians towards the ATT regime led to its collapse in March 2012. According to a survey conducted in 2013 Malians believe that dialogue, negotiation and decreased corruption are the most important factors to improving their current situation and solving the crisis (Bleck et al. 2016). As Table 5.2 illustrates, only 2% believe the reinforcing the military presence in the north is a solution.

As noted above, Serval was never viewed as a solution to state weakness or to the underlying issues that created a welcoming environment

Table 5.1 Freedom of the house ratings 2018

Country	*Designation*	*Civil liberties*	*Political rights*	*Freedom rating*
Mauritania	Not free	5	6	5.5
Mali	Partly free	4	5	4.5
Burkina Faso	Partly free	3	4	3.5
Niger	Partly free	4	4	4
Chad	Not free	6	7	6.5

Table 5.2 Survey: in your opinion, what solutions do you recommend for solving the crisis?

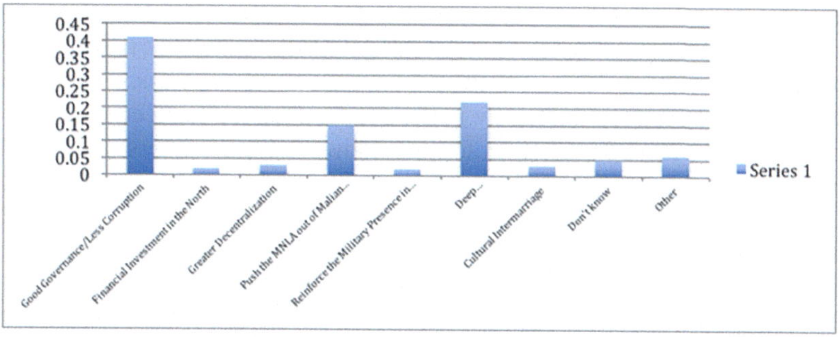

Source Data from Bleck et al. (2016: 9)

for the spread of militant Islamists in the North (Chivvis 2015: 171). Many recognise governance as the crux of the problem in Mali; however, Serval reinforces allies regardless of their governance record. The militarization of counterterrorism has transferred benefits in the region to political and military elites who participate as allies in these counterterrorism programs, thereby altering the political playing field. African elites who work closely with the French or AFRICOM often have their authority reinforced. Just as the participation of authoritarian regimes in AFRICOM's counterterrorism network undermines governance and human rights, the same can be said for those who are allied with the French in Operation Barkhane.

Corrinne Dufka of Human Rights Watch writes in The New York Times that Mali's partners, France and the United States, should insist on the professionalisation and accountability of security forces; support the judiciary and "take concrete action against corruption." These will be the best tactics to fight extremism in the country (Dufka 2016). TSCTP has long focused on professionalization of security forces. The EU tried to reinforce security forces through the failed PSPSDN and they are currently doing so through EUCAP and PARSEC programs. Past efforts have failed and it is unclear what new approaches are being taken to lead to the success of these programs.

One imam interviewed by Dufka argued that young men join jihadists because they "provide a better alternative to the state." In Mali, state interaction with villagers includes bribes at every turn, whether it be for ID cards, animal vaccines or checkpoints. Outright physical abuse of individuals is also widespread. There are few schools or health clinics, and the government has not ensured justice or security when it comes to inter-communal violence (Dufka 2016). Dufka's analysis reveals that, indeed, some Fulani have chosen to join with jihadi movements because of the lack of security. Not only is the state unable to protect them, but their interactions with the state are generally unpleasant, involving bribes or other forms of harassment.

The rise of the Macina Liberation Front, designated as a terrorist organisation with ties to AQIM, plays into the dangerous scenario of confusing inter-communal violence, which has a long history, with terrorism and jihad in the region (Raineri and Strazzari 2017). Macina is the name of a great Fulani empire in the region. When violence erupts between Fulani herders and settler communities it is easy to label the Fulani as terrorists and to rationalise the targeted killing of perpetrators. Obviously, these situations are far more complex and such actions by security forces (either Malian or through Operation Barkhane) may only serve to increase violence. Some Malians have begun to view Fulani more generally with suspicion and consider them to be Salafist insurgents (Ba and Boas 2017: 21). Another imam claims that jihadists, in particular Ansar Dine du Sud or MLF, simply tell residents that they do not need to pay taxes. This makes the MLF a preferable alternative to the state given the lack of public goods provided by the state (Diarra 2016). In the Mopti region, and elsewhere, there is an absence of state administrative structures and state security forces are in retreat. Jean-Hervé Jezequel argues that, in response to the insecurity in the Sahel, "The emphasis should be on providing exactly what's missing – social services, state services. It's a huge project, a long-term project, but it's the central issue" (Anyadike 2016). To date France, the United States and the EU have failed in this regard.

While many make the case for the rise of terrorism as linked to ungoverned territory, it is often the case that the root causes are:

> neither the absence nor the inefficacy of state institutions but the presence of violent and deformed ones. The armed groups that emerge from such areas, such as the National Movement for the Liberation of Azawad (MNLA)… tend to have their roots in local grievances encouraged by these conditions – in the MNLA's case, by Bamako's failure to abide by previous peace agreements with Mali's Tuareg communities and its collusion with criminal networks and smugglers, among other transgressions. (Powell 2016)

The problem lies in the fact that regional authorities use the presence of groups such as the MLF to "conflate broader political opposition with terrorism in order to galvanise international support. By backing such exclusive political systems, the international community, and especially France, contributes to the region's real sources of instability" (Powell 2016).

President Emmanuel Macron visited Mali twice during his first two months in office and displayed France's ongoing commitment to the Sahel. He successfully rallied for increased EU and US support of the G5 Joint Force that was officially launched in June 2017. At the February 2018 meeting in Brussels hosted by the UN, AU, EU and leaders of the G5 nations, €414 million was raised and the EU alone committed €100 million. France's contribution to development and governance increased by 40% thereby promising a total of €1.2 billion over the next five years (Lebovich 2018). Violence targeting the French has spread to Burkina Faso and on March 2, 2018 sixteen people were killed in an attack on the French Embassy and Defense Headquarters underscoring the prevailing insecurity (Monthly Forecast: Security Council Report 2018: 23). Malian presidential elections are scheduled for July 2018. The presidential elections in 2013 were promoted by international actors and considered as evidence that the French-led military intervention was a success (Traoré 2017: 21). Disputes over voter rolls that were prevalent in 2013, remain a concern; nevertheless, timely elections are seen as essential given the current widespread dissatisfaction with Malian President Ibrahim Boubacar Keita (see Dakono and Maiga 2018). The French financial pledge to development and governance, in addition to security, is a step forward. While the Brussels summit marks EU, US and regional commitment to the Sahel it will be ineffectual if it does not result in implementation and engagement of governance and development initiatives at the local level.

The idle repetition of predictable formulas (enhanced military support, showers of external assistance and more regional cooperation) has little prospect of success unless national and international stakeholders accept to bear the cost of addressing key structural aspects of bad local governance, social segregation, corruption and impunity that the jihadists are able to exploit for strategic purposes (Raineri and Strazzari 2017: 4).

Until governance and development are addressed as central to instability in the region it is unlikely that counterterrorism campaigns will result in peace and security in the Sahel or beyond.

References

Ahmed, B. (2017). Attentat: Plusieurs arrestations à Bamako et Gao. *Nordsudjournal*, January 27. Available at http://nordsudjournal.com/2017/01/27/attentant-plusieurs-arrestations-a-bamako-et-gao/. Accessed 30 January 2017.

Anyadike, O. (2016). Briefing: The New Jihadist Strategy in the Sahel. *IRIN*. Available at http://www.irinnews.org/feature/2016/02/04/briefing-new-jihadist-strategy-sahel. Accessed 23 May 2016.

Ba, B., and Boas, M. (2017). *Mali: A Political Economy Analysis*. Research. Oslo, Norway: Norwegian Institution of International Affairs. Available at http://hdl.handle.net/11250/2468085.

Bavier, J. (2017). Al Qaeda Says Mali Bombing Punishment for Working with France. *Reuters*, January 18. Available at http://www.reuters.com/article/us-mali-security-aqim-idUSKBN1522ZG. Accessed 19 January 2017.

BBC News. (2016). Mali Jihadist Mortar Attack Kills Five UN Peacekeepers, *BBC News*. Available at http://www.bbc.com/news/world-africa-35560361. Accessed 26 May 2016.

Bergamaschi, I. (2017). Donors Between a Wake-Up Call and Business as Usual: Talking About Politics, Imagining the State and Revamping Aid in Bamako, 2012–2013. *Mande Studies*, 19: 77.

Bleck, J., Dembele, A., and Guindo, S. (2016). Malian Crisis and the Lingering Problem of Good Governance. *Stability: International Journal of Security and Development*, 5(1): 1–15.

Callimachi, R., et al. (2018). '"An Endless War": Why 4 U.S. Soldiers Died in a Remote African Desert'. *The New York Times*, February 20. Available at https://www.nytimes.com/interactive/2018/02/17/world/africa/niger-ambush-american-soldiers.html.

Centre interarmées de concepts, de doctrines et d'experimentations. (2009). Eléments pour une réflexion doctrinale sur l'approche globale. DEF/CICDE/SEC-CENT/NP.

Chambefort, G., and Folliot, P. (2011). N° 3661—Rapport d'information de MM. Philippe Folliot et Guy Chambefort déposé en application de l'article 145 du règlement, par la commission de la défense nationale et des forces armées, en conclusion des travaux d'une mission d'information sur les actions civilo-militaires. Rapport d'Information 3661. Available at http://www.assemblee-nationale.fr/13/rap-info/i3661.asp. Accessed 11 March 2016.

Chivvis, C. S. (2015). *The French War on Al Qa'ida in Africa*. New York: Cambridge University Press.

Dakono, B., and Maiga, K. (2018). Mali's Problems Are Much Bigger Than July's Presidential Election, *ReliefWeb*. Available at https://reliefweb.int/report/mali/mali-s-problems-are-much-bigger-july-s-presidential-election. Accessed 24 May 2018.

Diarra, S. (2016). Malijet Youwarou-Tenenkou-Macina : L'Etat fout le camp, Ançar Dine s'installe Bamako Mali. May 20. Available at http://malijet.com/actualte_dans_les_regions_du_mali/156131-youwarou_tenenkou_macina_etat_camp.html. Accessed 21 May 2016.

Dowd, C., and Raleigh, C. (2013). The Myth of Global Islamic Terrorism and Local Conflict in Mali and the Sahel. *African Affairs*, 112(448): 498–509. https://doi.org/10.1093/afraf/adt039.

Dufka, C. (2016). Confronting Mali's New Jihadist Threat. *The New York Times*, May 9. Available at http://www.nytimes.com/2016/05/10/opinion/confronting-malis-new-jihadist-threat.html. Accessed 9 May 2016.

European External Action Service. (2015). factsheet_eucap_sahel_mali_en.pdf. Available at http://www.eeas.europa.eu/archives/csdp/missions-and-operations/eucap-sahel-mali/docs/factsheet_eucap_sahel_mali_en.pdf. Accessed 23 May 2016.

European External Action Service. (2016). Sahel Region—EEAS—European Commission, EEAS. Available at https://eeas.europa.eu/headquarters/headquarters-homepage_en/4094/Sahel%20region. Accessed 6 January 2017.

Gentile, G. P. (2013). *Wrong Turn: America's Deadly Embrace of Counterinsurgency*. New York: The New Press.

Gurman, H. (ed.) (2013). *Hearts and Minds: A People's History of Counterinsurgency*. New York: The New Press (New Press People's History).

Haski, P. (2013). Hollande: The "Indecisive" French President Who Intervened in Africa | Pierre Haski. *The Guardian*, January 13. Available at http://www.theguardian.com/commentisfree/2013/jan/13/francois-hollande-french-president-mali. Accessed 24 May 2018.

Helly, D., and Rocca, C. (2013). *The Mali Crisis and Africa-Europe Relations*. Briefing Note 52. European Centre for Development Policy Management. Available at http://ecdpm.org/wp-content/uploads/2013/10/BN-52-Mali-Crisis-Africa-Europe-Relations-2013.pdf. Accessed 7 May 2016.

Herring, N. (2018). Exercise Flintlock 2018 Begins. *DVIDS*. Available at https://www.dvidshub.net/news/272657/exercise-flintlock-2018-begins. Accessed 24 May 2018.

House of Commons. (2013). House of Commons—Documents considered by the Committee on 23 October 2013—European Scrutiny Committee. Available at http://www.publications.parliament.uk/pa/cm201314/cmselect/cmeuleg/83-xviii/8322.htm. Accessed 24 May 2016.

Human Rights Watch. (no date). Hissène Habré | Human Rights Watch. Available at https://www.hrw.org/tag/hissene-habre. Accessed 26 May 2016.

Lebovich, A. (2017). Bringing the Desert Together: How to Advance Sahel-Maghreb Integration. Policy Brief. European Council on Foreign Relations. Available at http://www.ecfr.eu/publications/summary/bringing_the_desert_together_how_to_advance_sahelo_maghreb_integration_7215. Accessed June 2018.

Lebovich, A. (2018). G5 Sahel: Much Done, More to Do. *ECFR*. Available at http://www.ecfr.eu/article/commentary_g5_sahel_much_done_more_to_do. Accessed 24 May 2018.

Lecocq, B., et al. (2013). One Hippopotamus and Eight Blind Analysts: A Multivocal Analysis of the 2012 Political Crisis in the Divided Republic of Mali. *Review of African Political Economy*, 40(137): 343–357.

Monthly Forecast: Security Council Report. (2018). Available at http://www.securitycouncilreport.org/atf/cf/%7B65BFCF9B-6D27-4E9C-8CD3-CF6E4FF96FF9%7D/2018_05_forecast.pdf. Accessed 24 May 2018.

Moore, A., and Walker, J. (2016). Tracing the US Military's Presence in Africa. *Geopolitics*, 21(3): 686–716. https://doi.org/10.1080/14650045.2016.1160060.

Pérouse de Montclos, M.-A. (2013). Dans l'oeil du cyclone. In Gonin, P., Kotlok, N., and Pérouse de Montclos, M.-A. (eds.), *La tragédie malienne*. Paris: Vendémiaire (Géographies): 7–31.

Powell, N. K. (2016). A Flawed Strategy in the Sahel. *Foreign Affairs*, February 2. Available at https://www.foreignaffairs.com/articles/west-africa/2016-02-01/flawed-strategy-sahel. Accessed 12 May 2016.

Powelson, S. J. (2013). *Enduring Engagement Yes, Episodic Engagment No: Lessons for SOF from Mali*. Naval Postgraduate School.

Raineri, L., and Strazzari, F. (2017). Jihadism in Mali and the Sahel: Evolving Dynamics and Patterns | European Union Institute for Security Studies. European Union Institute for Security Studies. Available at https://www.iss.europa.eu/content/jihadism-mali-and-sahel-evolving-dynamics-and-patterns. Accessed 24 May 2018.

Reeve, R., and Peletier, Z. (2014). *From New Frontier to New Normal: Counter-Terrorism Operations in the Sahel-Sahara*. Oxford: Remote Control Project, Oxford Research Groupd. Available at http://www.oxfordresearchgroup.org.uk/publications/briefing_papers_and_reports/sahel_counterterrorism_new_normal. Accessed June 2018.

Shurkin, M. (2014). *France's War in Mali: Lessons for an Expeditionary Army*. Rand Corporation. Available at http://www.rand.org/pubs/research_reports/RR770.html. Accessed June 2018.

Shurkin, M. (2015). The French Way of War. *POLITICO Magazine*. Available at http://politi.co/1QtBCm7. Accessed 6 January 2017.

Stigall, D. E. (2015). The French Military Intervention in Mali, Counter-Terrorism, and the Law of Armed Conflict. *Military Law Review*, 223.

Studio Tamani. (2016). Ténenkou: Calme précaire après les affrontements inter-communautaires Bamako Mali. Malijet.com. Available at http://malijet.com/a_la_une_du_mali/155023-tenenkou-calme-precaire-apres-les-affrontements-inter-communauta.html. Accessed 11 May 2016.

Tayo, S., and Nasrullah, F. (2016). *Nigeria's Government Must Ensure a Balanced Response to the Pastoralist—Settler Crisis*. Chatham House. Available at https://www.chathamhouse.org//node/22288. Accessed 10 May 2016.

Traoré, L. (2017). Beyond Vote-Buying: Personalized Political Ties and Party Activists' Interpretations of Gift-giving in the 2013 Elections in Bamako. *Mande Studies*, 19: 17.

Wing, S. D. (2013a). 'Mali: Politics of a Crisis'. *African Affairs*, 112(448): 476–485.

Wing, S. D. (2013b). Mali's Precarious Democracy and the Causes of Conflict. *USIP*. Available at http://www.usip.org/publications/mali-s-precarious-democracy-and-the-causes-of-conflict. Accessed 23 May 2016.

Wing, S. D. (2016). French Intervention in Mali: Strategic Alliances, Long-Term Regional Presence?. *Small Wars & Insurgencies*, 27(1): 59–80.

CHAPTER 6

Improving Responses to Protracted Conflict: Why Borderlands Matter for Upstream Engagement

Annette Idler

Global security threats today are intrinsically linked to the world's growing interconnectedness. Some of the most protracted contemporary armed conflicts are characterised by their reach across borders and the involvement of transnational networks of criminals, terrorists or other violent non-state groups. Borders do not constitute obstacles to illicit economic exchange and non-state military expansion. Indeed, illicit cross-border flows of money, weapons or ammunitions span entire continents, fuelling instability across the globe. While cross-border movements have long been common, the scope of the activities belonging to the "Other Side of Globalization" is new (Schendel and Abraham 2005). Local entrepreneurs of violence are superseded by global networks, ordinary criminals join transnational terrorists, and chains of illegal drug, human or weapons trafficking expand past regions to extend across continents (Idler 2014a: 56). The easy availability of information, for example, through social media, and the speed with which such information spreads globally, has facilitated human development in some parts of the

A. Idler (✉)
University of Oxford, Oxford, UK

T. Clack and R. Johnson (eds.), *Before Military Intervention*,
https://doi.org/10.1007/978-3-319-98437-7_6

world, yet it has also given rise to new threats to human and national security across the globe. Novel technologies and the increasing relevance of the cyberspace have brought both opportunities and challenges for defence: conflicts far away can easily have repercussions at home, as terrorist attacks in Europe and the massive migrants' crisis attest.

Despite the cross-border nature of contemporary conflicts, borders and boundaries still matter for defence policies, with two reasons standing out. First, global interactions between individuals, groups and other entities continue to be shaped by the state system, whose existence relies on the concept of borders. The concept "border" gained meaning with the Westphalian understanding of the nation-state (Idler 2014a: 57). Interstate conflicts aimed at redrawing borderlines and the deterrence of military incursions through borders characterise the state system's history (Andreas 2003: 81). Borders confer sovereignty and territoriality to nation-states, ideas which have become norms embedded in international law, treaties and resolutions (Idler 2014a: 57). Militarised border disputes have declined and, in line with this, globalists argue that the traditional military function of borders has lost importance. However, power politics and boundary disputes still matter (Klemencic and Schofield 2004: 63–64). Territory remains an important issue to understand the escalation and onset of war (Toft 2014). Interventions in Afghanistan or Georgia demonstrate that neither interstate wars nor military interventions have been banished (cf. Carter and Goemans 2011). Also, more recent events point to the continued relevance of international borders. The Russian intervention in Ukraine, Europe's concern with securing its external border as a result of the so-called "migrants crisis", the British government's emphasis on sovereignty in its demands to take control of its own laws and to leave the European Union's single market in the context of Brexit, and US President Donald Trump's wall plans to fortify the border with Mexico are just some of the most emblematic cases.

Second, the very interconnectedness across borders reinforces other types of boundaries. As Morehouse et al. (2004: 7) argue, the "de-bordering" process of globalisation comes along with strengthened nationalism, economically promoted regionalism and the re-claiming of identities and cultural habits, which reinforces existing borders and also entails new boundaries. In line with this, Kaghram and Levitt (2008: 24) contend that:

> globalist scholarship then, is often not fine-tuned enough to capture cross-border agents, structures, and interactions that are not all worldwide in scope. Furthermore, actors are often depicted as so heavily constrained that they cannot possibly react against these universalistic systemic forces.

Indeed, there is a renewed relevance of identity as a driver of conflict. Boundaries drawn along religious and cultural differences as well as along ethnicity have been characterising human relations ever since. They have been particularly pressing on the agenda of world politics after 9/11 (Andreas 2009: vii–viii), and, in the 2010s, diverse actors on the world stage ranging from the so-called Islamic State to presidents of major world powers have used such boundaries as a (manipulative) tool to gain influence.

While security and defence analysts have been grappling with the tension between an increasingly borderless world on the one hand, and the continued relevance of borders on the other, they have missed to focus on the spaces that are paradigmatic for this tension: transnational borderlands, the spaces that straddle international borders. And yet, reducing the security threats of existing wars and preventing the outbreak of future armed conflict requires accounting for these transnational spaces. Many borderlands of the Global South have been unruly places for decades. From the border area shared by Afghanistan and Pakistan to the Somali-Kenyan border, they have been occupied by insurgent and terrorist groups. The "jungle" in Calais and stranded migrants in Malta show that also border spaces in less vulnerable regions are facing severe governance challenges. And yet, borderlands, rather than borderlines, do not figure prominently in any defence policies.

Similarly, borderlands, especially in the Global South, are often not properly integrated into the national economy. Consequently, the borderlanders' loyalty to the government may yield to self-interested illicit economic cross-border activities with those beyond the borderline. This neglect also explains why what is illegal for the state may be considered legitimate for those involved (Schendel and Abraham 2005: 4). More border control to reduce such illicit cross-border activities may be counterproductive because it makes them even more lucrative. It also alienates the local communities who depend on these activities to sustain their livelihoods. This is relevant for the effectiveness of security policies. Andreas and Nadelmann note that "concerns over transnational law evasions rather than interstate military invasions increasingly drive the security priorities of many states." And after all, while intensified state measures may strengthen the control of the borderline, borderlands, the spaces that surround them, remain neglected (Andreas and Nadelmann 2006: 4).

Against this backdrop, in this chapter I ask how borderlands matter for so-called upstream engagement, which aims to reduce threats to global stability and security that arise from the world's increasing interconnectedness. I argue that upstream operations follow an approach that is ill-equipped to address the security threats that emanate from border areas. As I contend, border areas in vulnerable regions are catalysts of the negative side of global interconnectedness. Violent non-state groups engage in cross-border operations to strengthen transnational networks that undermine global security. They also take advantage of the state's deficient presence in these spaces to impose illicit governance. From this follows that, if defence and security policies account for transnational borderlands in their own right, they are better equipped to deprive rebels, criminals and terrorists of a place to strengthen themselves, thereby reducing threats to international peace and security. This requires overcoming a national security approach centred on the borderline and instead acknowledging transnational security dynamics in borderlands on both sides of the border; and overcoming state-centric perspectives on governance to also consider governance exerted by non-state actors. I will illustrate my argument by drawing on the case of Colombia's borderlands, particularly the border areas shared by Colombia with Venezuela and with Ecuador respectively. Exposed to a particularly protracted conflict, the Colombian one, these areas are paradigmatic for the insecurities that arise in other protracted conflicts around the world, including in the Middle East, Asia and the Horn of Africa.

In order to account for the protracted nature of the Colombian conflict, this chapter is based on longitudinal research. Between 2011 and 2017, I carried out extensive fieldwork in and on those border regions with more than 600 interviews which inform this study. The interviewees included ex-combatants, military and police officials, refugees, civil society leaders, staff members of international organisations, non-governmental organisations and academics. I complemented the data gathered during my fieldwork with comprehensive reviews of the literature on borderland studies and conflict studies more broadly. To adequately address ethical issues that arise with such sensitive research, all interviews were based on informed consent and anonymity.

The chapter is structured as follows: I will start with a discussion of upstream engagement and introduce the concept of borderlands in order to show how these terms intersect. Drawing on the case of Colombia's borderlands, I will then demonstrate how borderlands matter for upstream engagement, focusing on two issues in particular: First, the cross-border operations carried out by violent non-state groups that strengthen transnational networks, and second, illicit governance. I conclude that upstream engagement needs to address these challenges in order.to tackle long-term drivers of protracted conflict and related cross-border challenges—that is, to reduce some of the most serious threats to global security.

Upstream Engagement as Response to Protracted Conflict

The world's increasing interconnectedness that came along with globalisation is relevant to defence. Through transnational networks that facilitate flows of weapons, people, ideas and money, threats seemingly far away can quickly have an impact at home. So-called "upstream engagement" follows this logic: diffuse threats "upstream" are addressed before they arrive "downstream". Put differently, crises and conflicts are prevented, or at least contained, before they erupt or expand.

"Upstream engagement" in defence is an umbrella term that first and foremost highlights activities that place at the root of instability. The term "upstream" is commonly used in the oil and gas industry where it refers to the exploration and production stage of the industry, as opposed to midstream—transport—and downstream—the refining, processing, marketing and distribution of the product. With regard to security and defence issues, there is no clear definition of the concept of upstream engagement. The Ministry of Defence's Joint Doctrine Note 1/15 (2015: 11, 59) specifies that upstream operations include upstream capacity building and upstream conflict prevention. Capacity building can refer to security assistance to local armed forces, military education or training in civilian tasks such as building roads, bridges or participating in other infrastructure projects. Conflict prevention in the form of military operations is less specific and partly overlaps with capacity building. Policy documents such as the UK's Army 2020 brochure (Army 2013: 21) refer to it as "overseas engagement and capacity building" which "if properly targeted and resourced, should deliver benefits to the UK and more widely to global stability by reducing the need to deploy in the future on costly intervention operations." More recently, the 2016–2020 Strategic Defence and Security Review emphasised the importance of "defence engagement", defined as "Ministry of Defence and Armed Forces non-combat activities with international partners which contribute to stability, security and prosperity".

Also, other governments, though not using the term "upstream engagement" explicitly, have adopted the approach of operating "upstream" as an integral part of their security and defence policies. The German White Paper (2016: 39), for example, lists "Fragile States and Poor Governance" as one of the challenges for German Security Policy. It identifies "early recognition, prevention and resolution of crises and conflicts" as one of Germany's strategic priorities. The document states that:

> crises, conflicts, failing states, and humanitarian disasters influence not only directly affected states and regions but also indirectly affected states and regions such as Germany and Europe. The earlier crises and conflicts are countered by preventive measures, the greater the chance of preventing escalation and of achieving stability. Germany must participate in the prevention and stabilisation of crises and conflicts as well as in post-crisis and post-conflict management, depending on the extent to which it is affected and its available options. (Federal Ministry of Defence 2016: 50)

Similar to the British approach, the White Paper (2016: 52) highlights that:

> preventive measures in order to de-escalate conflicts and crises at an early stage [...] in close cooperation with regional and local actors [...] to enable states and regional organisations in fragile environments to independently assume security responsibility in a comprehensive manner. German and international commitment in crisis regions can be adapted and, over the long term, scaled back as regional and local actors establish the rule of law and gain the capacity to take responsibility for themselves.

The North Atlantic Treaty Organization (NATO), an intergovernmental military alliance, is concerned with upstream engagement as well. NATO maintains partnerships with non-member states in order to enhance "international security, peace and stability" among other strategic objectives. These partnerships include capacity building, education and training with a view to preventing crises (NATO 2011: 11).

The high benefits of preventative measures in reducing threats to global security not only underlie increasing upstream engagement efforts in the defence sector, they also underpin change, albeit slow one, in the broader international security architecture. Even though more than forty per cent of conflict prevention interventions fail, the benefits of succeeding are sixteen times higher than what they cost (Picciotto 2007: 16). According to Paul Collier (2008: 32), preventing one intra-state war saves USD 64 billion a year in direct costs. This is because an average internal armed conflict would cost two and a half times the value of the respective state's GDP at the time the conflict begins (Picciotto 2006: 114). Already in 1992 then-UN General-Secretary Boutros Boutros-Ghali (1992) asked for conflict prevention to be intensified and yet it was only until recently that the topic became more "fashionable". In 2012, the United Nations Development Programme's Bureau for Crisis Prevention and Recovery (BCPR) developed a guidance note on "governance for peace" as a major element of conflict prevention (Muggah et al. 2012). Accordingly, governance that is conducive to peace comprises inclusive political processes, responsive and accountable institutions, resilient state–society relationships and strong partnerships across different actors involved in conflict prevention efforts (Muggah et al. 2012: 12). This is in line with the more recently set UN 2030 Agenda for Sustainable Development. In this context, the international community set out Sustainable Development Goal (SDG) 16: "Promote peaceful and inclusive societies for sustainable development, provide access to justice for all and build effective, accountable and inclusive institutions at all levels" (UN 2015).

Neglected Borderlands

Borderlands in vulnerable regions are particularly prone to the convergence of conflict and crime and yet they are largely neglected by upstream operation efforts. Vulnerability arises from fragility and the lack of resilience, features that are particularly prevalent in the so-called Global South. As I will demonstrate below, the transnationality of borderlands makes these spaces prone to cross-border operations by violent non-state groups that allow them to strengthen their transnational networks while undermining local security. Furthermore, weak state governance allows for governance provided by violent non-state actors, and therewith for what I call shadow citizenship: some sort of social contract whereby a state–society relationship is replaced by a mutually reinforcing relationship between a (violent) non-state actor and the local community (Idler 2014b). As a consequence, these spaces lack exactly those elements that are considered to be vital for effective conflict prevention: inclusive politics, responsive institutions and a resilient state–society relationship.

Williams and Godson note that weak states manifest ideal conditions for organised criminals to flourish: Criminals would use weak states as a home bases to extend their operations elsewhere (Williams and Godson 2002: 315–316). Similarly, when discussing the difficulties of tackling violent non-state groups, especially criminal actors, Moises Naím notes that "complicating the fight is that these networks are simultaneously local and global" (Naim 2007: 34). They are entrenched in local power structures and at the same time manifest international mobility. Borderlands not only comprise weak governance structures as do weak states, but due to their transnational nature, this weakness is also little visible since they are located at the periphery anyways, so to speak. They thus not only suffer from insufficient governance—including the coordination between development and military actors interested in enhancing stability—by each of the states they bring together, but also the lack of coordination across the border between the two states, making borderlands convenient sites for the "glocal" operations of criminals and other violent non-state actors. They are hubs for transnational networks that connect fragile regions and facilitate illicit flows of weapons, drugs, people and money. Hence, if upstream engagement is to mitigate one of the biggest threats to global stability and security, namely, increasing economic and/or political power of violent non-state actors, it should address these "glocal" dynamics.

Two characteristics make borderlands a universal concept: their transnationality and their distance to the political and economic state centres (Idler 2014a: 59–63). From the relevance of the transnational nature of borderlands follows that studying borderlands requires a cross-border, or borderland, perspective which considers the area of both sides of the border as one spatial unit of analysis (Baud and van Schendel 1997: 216; Schendel 2005: 44). Understanding borderland dynamics also requires accounting for the relationship between the centres and the borderlands. Borderland dynamics shape state policies that are relevant to territorial sovereignty, a nation's identity and its embedment in the regional context. This approach opposes the conventional view according to which global dynamics shape state centres, and according to which these power centres affect the distant borderlands (Zartman 2010: 9). The power centres would try to expand, militarise their borders in defence or make agreements on cross-border trade which has repercussions on the borderlands (Zartman 2010: 11).

With the following case study, I demonstrate how various violent non-state groups have used the transnationality of Colombia's border areas to engage in cross-border operations while furthering their economic and political agendas through consolidating their transnational networks. I also reveal why borderlands constitute illicitly governed, rather than ungoverned spaces. As I argue, conflict prevention in general, and in the form of upstream engagement in particular, needs to become less state-centric in two regards: first, it needs to move beyond conceptualising borders as borderlines that need to be secured, or defended in line with the idea of national, or external, security. Instead, upstream engagement should address transnational borderlands, and the need for borderlands to be governed peacefully in order to reduce threats to global stability and security. Second, upstream engagement needs to account for governance provided by actors other than the state, especially violent non-state actors. Conflict prevention that is employed in a coordinated approach between development and military actors is necessary to both deprive the violent non-state actors of their illicit authority and hence shadow citizenry, and to foster governance for peace—be it non-state, yet non-violent governance, or indeed governance provided by state actors.

Colombia's Borderlands: Challenges for Upstream Engagement

In Colombia's borderlands, conflict and drug dynamics converge, making them attractive for rebels, paramilitaries, and criminal organisations alike (Idler 2014a). This is a result of their geostrategic location within the global cocaine industry and related forms of transnational organised crime (Clawson and Lee 1996). It is also a consequence of Colombia's decade-long armed internal conflict: they are sites of retreat, reorganisation and operation of the major actors involved in the conflict

(Pécaut 2001). They became the principal war scenes after the shift of the Colombian conflict to the country's peripheries. The financing fronts of Colombia's largest rebel group, the Revolutionary Armed Forces of Colombia—People's Army (FARC) which signed a peace deal with the Colombian government in 2016 operated until recently in the border areas. Being located in border zones allowed them to easily cross over to deal with logistics or supply.

Bogotá's security policies brought Colombia's border areas further to the centre of the country's conflict dynamics. In 2000 the US Congress approved Plan Colombia, a counter-drug and counter-insurgency initiative developed by the Colombian government which later with US assistance became part of former President Uribe's Democratic Security Policy. Uribe's policies brought increased security to urban areas, but moved the conflict's impacts further to the periphery and beyond. The repercussions of military operations and refugee flows were evident both on the Colombian and non-Colombian side of the border. At the same time, criminal and conflict actors expanded their activities in these regions. This was facilitated by the fact that Colombia's borderlands are the places where the states lost, or never had, legitimacy as a result of severe shortcomings in the bilateral border security cooperation.

Cross-Border Operations and Transnational Networks

Borderlands are by definition regulated by several regimes: due to their transnationality, two different jurisdictions and security systems meet in these spaces (Zeller 2013: 194). In regions with low state capacity, multiple forms of regulation make them more prone to impunity: national approaches to border control lack coordination, intelligence exchange is characterised by miscommunication and police cooperation between the two states is undermined by mutual mistrust. Without adequate bilateral cooperation and with the law enforcement agents being tied to their national jurisdictions, crimes are difficult to prosecute. Violent non-state groups legally or illegally cross the border and commit crimes on the other side, but most of the time state forces and prosecutors cannot cross it. In brief, the blurring of two neighbouring jurisdictions offers an advantage for non-state actors in comparison to law enforcement constrained by territorial sovereignty (Donnan and Wilson 1999). Violent non-state actors benefit from cross-border impunity in three ways. First, they can commit crimes one side of the border and flee to the other side.

Due to the lack of intelligence cooperation and the restrictions of state law enforcement officials to their own jurisdiction, these crimes remain without due investigation. Similarly, they can plan the crime on one side, cross the border to commit the crime and return. Finally, they can kill on one side of the border and dump the body of the victim on the other side of the border. In the absence of a body, no homicide is registered and thus homicide rates are lower than actual deaths, rendering violence less visible.

If crimes are committed "across the border" they are less likely to be investigated than within one national territory because the investigation lacks the necessary cooperation. Many incidents of physical violence and other forms of victimisation are often not reported or prosecuted. Violence is invisibilised by the lack of accountability. Officially "inexistent" without figuring in statistics or reports, these crimes fail to attract the attention of the host governments and of the international community: precarious security dynamics in borderlands are neglected or underestimated by policymakers.

In Colombia's border regions, cross-border operations by violent non-state actors contributed to the strengthening of their transnational networks. At the Colombia-Venezuela border, cross-border operations reduced the international community's attention because it kept homicide rates low. Between March and April 2003, for example, the bodies of more than fifty Colombians were dumped on the Venezuelan side close to the border (Fundación Progresar 2010: 86–106). Many of them were buried anonymously on Venezuelan cemeteries close to the borderline. This way they did not count towards the number of homicides occurred in Colombia. More recently, the two main insurgent groups FARC and the National Liberation Army (ELN) used transnational borderlands to their advantage in yet another way: As of 2016, in the Colombian region of Baja Guajira, which borders the Venezuelan state of Zulia, both FARC and ELN controlled vast territories in which they charged taxes to the local population, decided on rules of coexistence, and in return, let the local communities live without any major security issues—as long as they follow the rules. Many rebels had moved their families to the Venezuelan side of the border and had bought properties there. There are reports of violent incidents in the Venezuelan border zone, yet they mostly go unnoticed by the international community. This is because neither the Colombian nor the Venezuelan government recognise the full extent to which those rebels operate on Venezuelan territory.

The Colombians do not consider it their responsibility to address those issues on the Venezuelan side and the Venezuelans downplay the threat—or, as some would argue, may even be complicit (Ramírez 2011: 60–61). As a consequence, while the rebels appear to have lost clout in Colombia, they may in fact use sites of retreat on the Venezuelan side to reorganise and strengthen their transnational networks, not least as this territory is a strategic transit zone on the international drug trafficking route.

As I have demonstrated elsewhere (see, e.g., Idler 2012, 2014c), examples of the FARC's cross-border movement abound. When Colombia tightened cocaine interdiction measures in the Colombian department of Arauca in 2005, the landing strips were moved across the border to the Venezuelan state of Apure. In July 2012 the *New York Times* reported that 121 tracks of illicit drug flights had their starting point in Venezuelan Apure (Neuman 2012). At that time, the FARC coexisted with the ELN and the Bolivarian Liberation Front, a Venezuelan left-wing armed non-state group, in Apure (Idler and Forest 2015). Moving the business across the border therefore allowed them to maintain their income share from the cocaine industry. Similarly, the FARC (and other armed actors) crossed the Colombian-Ecuadorian borderline to pursue their interests and remain unnoticed. They shifted mobile cocaine laboratories from Putumayo to Sucumbíos to evade detection. In other border areas, the FARC charged taxes on illegal mining on the Ecuadorian side of the border. In order to stop these activities, the Ecuadorian military destroyed the excavators, but this had little long-term effects: illegal mining and the FARC's extortion soon continued as usual (Idler 2014c).

If in such contexts upstream conflict prevention stops at the borderline, it misses an important dimension of the security dynamics. Locally, the actual levels of violence are ignored, leaving borderland communities at the mercy of violent non-state actors. Globally, a state-centred approach to upstream engagement means that the strengthening of violent actors across borders is easily overlooked. Similarly, when violent non-state actors move diverse forms of transnational organised crime across the border to evade law enforcement measures, defence actors miss opportunities to cut off their income sources. As I argue, the national security lens that focuses on borderlines as territorial demarcations that need to be defended cannot capture these dynamics. Instead, a more comprehensive view on security that accounts for transnational borderlands proffers opportunities to consider borderlands spaces that need to be regulated adequately in order to thwart illicit cross-border activities of violent non-state actors and promote legal opportunities across the border.

According to the policy documents cited above, upstream conflict prevention involves strengthening the capacities of local communities, making them more resilient and reducing their grievances. Yet cross-border incidents as the ones outlined here, do not fall under any of these preventive activities. Capacity building of local armed forces as one form of upstream engagement is normally designed to tackle security challenges within a national territory or to defend oneself against a threat from outside, yet it does not account for cross-border challenges as the ones described here, due to the state-centric lens, ignoring a wide range of risks that can become major threats if not addressed "upstream".

Borderlands as Illicitly Governed Spaces

In addition to being characterised by transnationality, borderlands distinguish themselves by their distance from the political and economic centres which, especially in vulnerable regions, translates into weak state governance. This marginalisation entails the exclusion from national decision-making processes, as well as from the national economy due to lacking infrastructure and communication channels that connect the periphery with the centres (Clement 2004: 54).

Neglected from central governments, borderlands seldom experience inclusive politics, except on the very local level. Institutions are neither responsive nor accountable, or else borderlanders would be offered basic services, infrastructure and economic opportunities that are available in more central areas of the country's territory. Such shortcomings appear to be in the realm of development cooperation agencies: They can implement programmes to strengthen the capacities of state institutions in such regions. Yet what is often neglected is that border areas are not "ungoverned" spaces where the state can come in to fill a vacuum (Clunan and Trinkunas 2010). Rather, in many vulnerable regions they are "illicitly governed spaces": violent non-state actors operating in these territories exploit state absence and take over governance functions (Kalyvas et al. 2008; cf. Mampilly 2011). They achieve to establish shadow citizenship and thus replace resilient state–society relationships which are essential to effective conflict prevention.

In 2012, during one of my fieldwork trips to the Colombian department of Putumayo in the south of the country, a peasant remembered his life in the 1990s when the FARC were the only ones who "governed" the region: "At least we had our land, our farm and they helped us feed our families". The FARC helped build health centres, roads, and provided what they consider justice (Idler 2014c). Such illicitly governed spaces can exist in any marginalised state territory, but if located in border areas, they are particularly important for upstream engagement which aims to stop security threats from "flowing" downstream. This is because violent non-state groups can use transnational illicit authority in border areas to engage in those illicit cross-border businesses that pose increasing security threats in our interconnected world: drugs, human and wildlife trafficking, which constitute income sources for conflict actors and terrorists; arms and ammunition trafficking to directly fuel conflict; and fomenting a sense of community among the local population that is characterised by being disconnected from the central state because they rely on shared transnational, rather than national identities.

Examples abound. Along the Colombia-Venezuela border, the FARC's Front 33 was known to operate in the Colombian region of Catatumbo in the department of Norte de Santander. Yet when I visited the region south of Venezuelan Machiques on the other side of the border in 2012, locals told me that the Front 33 is likewise present on Venezuelan territory, entering the country via numerous trails that exist across the porous border. They would control the territory, among others, by charging taxes on ranchers and on shop owners, and control everyday life. The porosity of the border and the lack of a sense of belonging to the national citizenry are also evident on the Colombian side. When visiting the homes or offices of Colombians in Catatumbo I saw images of Venezuelan then-president Hugo Chávez on the house walls rather than of Colombian officials. People listened to Venezuelan radio since there was no reception of Colombian channels. I was told that, when a bridge was broken, Chávez would have sent money to get it repaired whereas the Colombian authorities apparently did nothing. Such a situation alienates people from the state and fosters a sense of belonging to a transnational borderland community.

Along the Colombia-Ecuador border things were similar: Ecuadorian farmers in Sucumbíos were regularly called by the FARC to attend meetings on the Colombian side of the border. The FARC informed the Ecuadorian farmers at such meetings about the current rate of the vacuna, the extortion money that they had to pay on the Ecuadorian side, and about regulations regarding what to cultivate at their farms on the Colombian side. Neither Bogotá nor Quito took action to change this situation. Such cases do not fall entirely under the jurisdiction of either Colombia or Ecuador and the exchange of intelligence and other forms of bi-national border security cooperation are insufficient. In the Ecuadorian province of Carchi the rebels' cross-border authority was felt strongly too. When I visited the region in 2012 locals told me that things were calm on the Ecuadorian side, coca cultivation would only be present on the Colombian side.

While this was largely correct, I found that many Ecuadorians regularly crossed the border to work in coca cultivation sites during the day and come home in the evenings to spend the night in Ecuador. People would not tell outsiders about their activities since this would jeopardise their livelihoods. They preferred to adhere to the rebels' rules instead. This attitude confirms the special relationship that borderlanders have with the border. It may turn the state into a greater threat to their livelihoods than any violent non-state actor that operates in those regions. Many borderlanders engage in illicit economic activities themselves, independently, in the service of a non-state group or even in the service of corrupt state officials. When the state criminalises the cross-border trade of certain goods, such as illicit drugs, but does not have the capacity or will to enforce this law, smuggling becomes a lucrative business (Andreas 2009: 22). Those involved in smuggling benefit from this gap between law and its enforcement, yet they also suffer its consequences. Often, small-scale smugglers are extorted by those in whose service they work, they are asked to pay "taxes" on smuggled goods and are threatened in cases of non-compliance. These smugglers cannot turn to the state when those operating against the state inflict or threaten to inflict violence or other harm to them, undermining the state–society relationship even further and fuelling grievances against those who leave them without protection.

Upstream engagement that only engages with state authorities, such as local security forces, misses the reality on the ground: it only captures the deficient state governance yet is not conducive to supporting local community members to escape this dilemma since the very support of outsiders to state authorities only widens the distance between the locals and the state—and risks drawing the local community members closer to the non-state actors who may offer an undemocratic and abusive, yet effective form of protection to them.

The adherence of local community members to a transnational borderland community rather than experiencing a sense of belonging to the national state is not only rooted in illicit economic activities and the protection that the "illicit governors" offer in return. It is also related to economic activities that are licit, yet fuelled by those who govern illicitly. In Ecuadorian Carchi, for example, residents legally sold provisions to Colombians, supposedly including to FARC members in plain clothes. Similarly, as I was told in Machiques in Venezuelan Zulia, there was one small Venezuelan border village which prides itself on selling more beer cans than any other Venezuelan village—the customers being Colombian rebels (Idler 2014c).

Not feeling part of the national community, citizens may find the shadow citizenship imposed by violent non-state groups more in line with and responsive to their everyday life needs than a social contract with an absent state. A resilient state–society relationship, one of the core principles of governance for peace, and therewith of conflict prevention, does not exist. When borderland communities enter a mutually reinforcing relationship with a violent non-state group, they also "exit" the state–society relationship, calling into question the social contract between this part of the citizenry and the state. This contradicts the conventional wisdom of conceiving borderlands as ungoverned or ungovernable spaces (Goodhand 2013: 247–249; Zeller 2013: 193–218). The absence of state governance systems is filled with a governance system provided by other actors, which can either result in institutional pluralism (Zeller 2013: 211), or transform borderlands into illicitly governed spaces.

In conflict prevention efforts including upstream engagement which focus on governance for peace as a major component illicitly governed spaces are often overlooked. The analysis tends to focus on shortcomings of the state, that is, on governance voids that need to be filled. Yet there is hardly any focus on the extent to which such functions have been replaced by violent non-state actors. What is more, state actors and the international community are often not even aware of this. In Colombian Nariño, I learned that in territories controlled by the insurgents people are told not to raise issues related to human rights violations when speaking to officials of humanitarian organisations or otherwise they are punished. Often humanitarian organisations and other "outsiders" are not allowed to enter certain territories thus being unable to verify the actual situation on the ground. As such spaces are often non-violent because the non-state actors have achieved to control the territory, they are invisible to the outside—even more so if these spaces are transnational, for the reasons I have explained earlier. From this follows that a state-centric approach largely prevents upstream engagement from accounting for non-state capacities and how they may be engaged in a constructive way.

Conclusion

In this chapter, I have demonstrated how the transnationality of borderlands and weak state governance in these spaces hamper the elements that lie at the core of effective conflict prevention: inclusive politics, responsive and accountable institutions and resilient state–society relationships. As careful tracing of causal mechanisms demonstrated, this is the outcome of the modus operandi of violent non-state groups: They engage in cross-border operations to consolidate transnational networks and they illicitly govern borderlands where state presence is deficient. As a result, borderlands to become business hubs for organised crime, sites of retreat for conflict actors, and safe havens for terrorists.

This study has contributed theoretically to the literature tackling issues relevant to international peace and security. I have shown that upstream engagement from a defence perspective and conflict prevention from a development and peacebuilding perspective strongly overlap in their emphasis on inclusive politics, responsive institutions and a resilient state–society relationship. I have shown that transnational spaces (in addition to transnational flows such as refugees, or transnational phenomena such as climate change or terrorism) matter to national security issues. The policy implications are clear: if upstream engagement is to mitigate threats to global stability and security, it should address these dynamics in borderlands with a whole-of-government approach to reduce the economic and/or political power of violent non-state actors.

The Andean region sees a paradoxical convergence of peacebuilding efforts after more than five decades of civil war in Colombia, right next to what could be described a situation of state collapse in Venezuela, mostly ignored by the international community. Without appropriate upstream engagement in the spaces where these two divergent dynamics meet, a crisis may unfold whose repercussions could extend well beyond the South American subcontinent. This neglect may backfire, not least due to the alleged penetration of the Venezuelan state by criminal actors and the supposed links of Venezuelan individuals with violent non-state groups in other parts of the world. High-ranking Venezuelan government officials, for example, are accused not only of being involved in the drug trade, but also of having direct links with Hezbollah, also operating in the tri-border area at the junction of Paraguay, Argentina and Brazil. The Peninsula of La Guajira, the region in the north of the Colombia-Venezuela border is home to a sizable Arabic community, mostly involved in commerce. This community has been suffering stigmatisation, especially in the context of the so-called global war on terror due to accusations of links to terrorist cells in the Middle East, even though they mostly distinguish themselves through being honest, hard-working merchants. Yet if the situation deteriorates and Venezuela will face more turmoil, terrorist cells could take advantage of this no mans' land: while the international community focuses on the supposed success of peace deal and what used to be the FARC's strongholds in other parts of Colombia, criminals, terrorists and others, including those linked to Hezbollah, could strengthen their transnational networks and expand illicit governance structures in the region. This would increase the risk of such groups planning criminal activities and orchestrating attacks in Europe, the US or elsewhere in the world.

The cross-border operations and illicit governance by violent non-state groups in Colombia's borderlands, as demonstrated in this case study, also facilitate cross-border migrant flows and constitute an incentive for human trafficking. These borderlands are located on strategic corridors not only for drugs, but also for the movement of people, entering, for example, Venezuela from places such as the Lebanon. These individuals cross into Colombia, and exit Colombia across its border with Panama, often in the hope to make it to the United States. These dynamics already exist, but they may become unmanageable if the Venezuelan situation deteriorates. While some years ago, people fled from brutal violence in Colombia to Venezuela, these flows are now far from unidirectional: we also see a reverse of migrant flows with people fleeing the severe economic and political crisis in Venezuela to Colombia. Such flows could become stronger with borderlands being at the centre of a humanitarian crisis.

Importantly, while I have discussed the case of the Andean region, violent non-state actors have been accumulating power in borderlands across the globe where state capacities are deficient. And yet, they have not received sufficient attention. When armed actors commit violence against civilians, governments and international organisations follow these incidents closely. However, spaces where such violent groups are equally, or more present, yet where they do not necessarily engage in violence, go unnoticed. Yet these are the spaces where violent groups ranging from criminals to insurgents engage in illegal business activities and exert authority over the local population—without the need to resort to violence. In the case of transnational borderlands, even if armed actors do employ violence this modus operandi remains invisible from the outside due to the cross-border nature of their operations, making local communities even more vulnerable. Accounting for transnational borderlands in security and defence policies is necessary to deprive such groups of social support, destroy illegal businesses and resume governance functions that governments have failed to provide.

If governments and international organisations continue to fit their security and defence policies into templates—states—drawn up on the basis of international borderlines, they miss those spaces in-between where upstream engagement would be particularly efficient since they bundle all the deficiencies that conflict prevention aims to address. And if they continue to base decisions on levels of violence rather than the ability of non-state groups to exercise authority and provide governance functions, they react to events rather than taking preventive action. These groups will continue to attract recruits, support, and income necessary to strengthen their organisational structure and implement attacks. Identifying illicitly governed borderlands and offering competitive economic alternatives as well as basic services and goods in these regions would help prevent conflict, curb transnational organised crime, and tackle terrorism from the root rather than combatting its symptoms.

References

Andreas, P. 2003. Redrawing the line: Borders and security in the twenty-first century. *International Security* 28, 78–111.

Andreas, P. 2009. Border games: Policing the U.S.-Mexico Divide, 2nd ed. Cornell University Press, Ithaca.

Andreas, P., and Nadelmann, E.A. 2006. *Policing the globe: Criminalization and crime control in international relations.* Oxford University Press, Oxford.

Army. 2013. *Transforming the British Army. An update July 2013.* Army Headquarters, Andover.

Baud, M., and van Schendel, W. 1997. Toward a comparative history of borderlands. *Journal of World History* 8, 211–242.

Boutros-Ghali, B. 1992. *An agenda for peace: Preventative diplomacy, peacemaking and peace-keeping.* United Nations, New York.

Carter, D.B., and Goemans, H.E., 2011. The making of the territorial order: New borders and the emergence of interstate conflict. *International Organization* 65, 275–309.
Clawson, P., and Lee, R.W. 1996. *The Andean cocaine industry.* Macmillan, Basingstoke.
Clement, N.C., 2004. Economic forces shaping the borderlands, in: Morehouse, B.J., Pavlakovich-Kochi, V., Wastl-Walter, D. (Eds.), *Challenged borderlands: Transcending political and cultural boundaries.* Ashgate, Aldershot: 41–62.
Clunan, A.L., Trinkunas, H.A. (Eds.). 2010. *Ungoverned spaces: Alternatives to state authority in an era of softened sovereignty.* Stanford University Press, Stanford.
Collier, P. 2008. *The bottom billion: Why the poorest countries are failing and what can be done about it.* Oxford University Press, Oxford.
Donnan, H., and Wilson, T.M. 1999. *Borders: Frontiers of identity, nation and state.* Berg, Oxford.
Federal Ministry of Defence. 2016. *White Paper on German security policy and the future of the Bundeswehr.* Federal Ministry of Defence, Berlin, Germany.
Fundación Progresar. 2010. *Tantas Vidas Arrebatadas. La Desaparición Forzada de Personas: una Estrategia Sistemática de Guerra Sucia en Norte de Santander.* Cúcuta, Colombia.
Goodhand, J., 2013. Epilogue: The view from the border, in: Korf, B., and Raeymaekers, T. (Eds.), *Violence on the margins: States, conflict, and borderlands.* Palgrave Macmillan, New York, NY: 247–264.
Idler, A., 2012. Arrangements of convenience in Colombia's borderlands: An invisible threat to citizen security? *St Antonys International Review* 7, 93–119.
Idler, A., 2014a. Arrangements of convenience: Violent non-state actor relationships and citizen security in the shared borderlands of Colombia, Ecuador and Venezuela (Doctoral thesis). University of Oxford, Oxford.
Idler, A. 2014b. *Espacios Invisibilizados: Actores Violentos No-estatales y "Ciudadanía de Sombra" en las Zonas Fronterizas de Colombia.* Estud. Indiana.
Idler, A. 2014c. "The margins at the centre of the FARC's future. A response to Ivan Briscoe's piece on the transition of the FARC in Colombia." DAG-3QD Online Symposia on Peace & Justice. 3 Quarks Dly.
Idler, A., and Forest, J.J.F. 2015. Behavioral patterns among (violent) non-state actors: A study of complementary governance. *Stability: International Journal of Security and Development*, 4.
Kaghram, S., and Levitt, P., 2008. Constructing transnational studies, in: Pries, L. (Ed.), *Rethinking transnationalism: The meso-link of organisations.* Routledge, London and New York: 21–39.
Kalyvas, S.N., Shapiro, I., and Masoud, T. (Eds.). 2008. *Order, conflict, and violence.* Cambridge University Press.
Klemencic, M., and Schofield, C.H. 2004. Contested boundaries and troubled borderlands, in: Morehouse, B.J., Pavlakovich-Kochi, V., and Wastl-Walter,

D. (Eds.), *Challenged borderlands: Transcending political and cultural boundaries*. Ashgate, Aldershot: 63–74.

Mampilly, Z.C. 2011. *Rebel rulers: Insurgent governance and civilian life during war*. Cornell University Press, Ithaca, NY.

Ministry of Defence. 2015. *Joint Doctrine Note 1/15. Defence engagement*. Development, Concepts and Doctrine Centre, Ministry of Defence, Shrivenham.

Morehouse, B.J., Pavlakovich-Kochi, V., and Wastl-Walter, D. 2004. Introduction: Perspectives on borderlands, in: Morehouse, B.J., Pavlakovich-Kochi, V., and Wastl-Walter, D. (Eds.), *Challenged borderlands: Transcending political and cultural boundaries*. Ashgate, Aldershot: 3–11.

Muggah, R., Sisk, T.D., Piza-Lopez, E., Salmon, J., and Keuleers, P. 2012. *Governance for peace. Securing the social contract*. UNDP BCPR, New York.

Naím, M. 2007. *Illicit*. Arrow, London.

NATO. 2011. *Active engagement in cooperative security: A more efficient and flexible partnership policy*. NATO.

Neuman, W. 2012. Venezuela is cocaine hub despite its claims. *New York Times*.

Pécaut, D. 2001. *Guerra Contra la Sociedad*. Espasa, Bogotá, Colombia.

Picciotto, R. 2006. Why the world needs millennium security goals. *Journal of Conflict, Security, and Development* 6, 111–120.

Picciotto, R. 2007. *Global development and human security*. Transaction Publishers, New Brunswick.

Ramírez, S. 2011. Civil society peacebuilding on Colombia's borders, in: Zartman, W., and Ramsbotham, A. (Eds.), *Accord. An international review of peace initiatives, building peace across borders, accord*. Conciliation Resources, London: 60–61.

Schendel, W. van. 2005. Spaces of engagement. How borderlands, illegal flows, and territorial states interlock, in: Schendel, W. van, Abraham, I. (Eds.), *Illicit flows and criminal things: States, borders, and the other side of globalization*. Indiana University Press, Bloomington: 38–68.

Schendel, W. van, and Abraham, I. (Eds.). 2005. *Illicit flows and criminal things: States, borders, and the other side of globalization*. Indiana University Press, Bloomington.

Toft, M.D. 2014. Territory and war. *Journal of Peace Research* 51, 185–198.

UN. 2015. *Sustainable development knowledge platform. Goal 16*.

Williams, P., and Godson, R. 2002. Anticipating organized and transnational crime. *Crime, Law and Social Change* 37: 311–355.

Zartman, I.W. 2010. *Understanding life in the borderlands: Boundaries in depth and in motion*. University of Georgia Press, Athens.

Zeller, W. 2013. Get it while you can: Building business and bureaucracy between wars in the Uganda-Sudan borderland, in: Korf, B., and Raeymaekers, T. (Eds.), *Violence on the margins: States, conflict, and borderlands*. Palgrave Macmillan, New York: 193–218.

CHAPTER 7

Future Stabilisation Strategy and the Changing Upstream Environment

Robert Johnson

There is currently little agreement on how one might define 'upstream' but in its usage there seems to be an intrinsic assumption that the 'upstream environment' of 2020–2035, or beyond, will be much like that which has prevailed in the last twenty years. Yet, while the nature of unstable governments, fragile states and conflict drivers might be recognisable and even measurable, it appears to be a considerable leap of faith to argue that the global environment of the future, not least in geopolitical terms, will be much like today. It is not clear, for example, which countries or entities will be willing or able to intervene in or stabilise, polities that are under threat of collapse or facing significant unrest. The United Nations, a coalition of states, the Western power, Russia and perhaps China, are current or future candidates, but these will not be the only ones. Moreover, there are three fundamental questions we might reasonably ask about specific Western powers regarding stabilisation.

The first question is: '*could* they conduct stabilisation, benignly intervene, or exert influence to prevent conflict by 2035 in the way Western states have done since 2001'? It is by no means certain that the domestic

R. Johnson (✉)
University of Oxford, Oxford, UK
e-mail: robert.johnson@history.ox.ac.uk

T. Clack and R. Johnson (eds.), *Before Military Intervention*,
https://doi.org/10.1007/978-3-319-98437-7_7

will, regional consent or international power will exist then in the way that it did at the beginning of the twenty-first century. Indeed, there is plenty of circumstantial evidence to suggest that there will be severe constraints, even in humanitarian operations or evacuation missions where the case for government action and public support would be clearest. The conflict in Syria from 2011 demonstrated the relative impotence of the UNSC and the West, made reluctant to act by the Iraq and Afghan conflicts, in the face of the assertiveness of Russia, a power which was determined to use force in support of its national interests.

A second question would be: *should* we make some sort of 'upstream intervention'? We may anticipate changes in public expectations on the domestic front and developments in the expectations of allies and partners. Public demands for action can increase rapidly when there is a humanitarian catastrophe, and it is as yet unclear whether the desire to enact the 'Responsibility to Protect' principle, which was championed by the United Nations in 2005, will atrophy or enjoy a new lease of life in the face of mass murder or environmental disaster. Equally, while there is a recognisable 'Iraq syndrome' in British and American policy, that is, a desire to avoid another unpopular, protracted entanglement like that of 2003–2009, both the United Kingdom and the United States conducted limited operations in Libya, Iraq and Syria after 2011, and their armed forces are postured for expeditionary missions.

A third question is: '*where* would this upstream intervention take place'? Would it be a failing, or already collapsed state, or one of the many 'zones of stress' identified in the Ministry of Defence's Global Strategic Trends publication (2014). The difficulty is not only how any intervention, be that by financial, diplomatic or military means, could be measured, but how any one nation could afford the considerable costs of stabilisation. In the Middle East alone, there are many nations that qualify for 'upstream' support, but the numbers are beyond the capacity of, say, the UK and its armed forces to manage, or of the EU.

The chief difficulty of 'upstream' intervention is that 'success' is notoriously difficult to assess. Tragically, failure makes itself more evident. The crucial point is that nations which are the subject of long-term support are not always successful, and it difficult to find evidence that upstream interventions work. That does not mean we should not invest at all in some form of conflict prevention. The UK, for example, possesses and funds embassies and high commissions even though diplomacy does not always succeed, because it improves the chances of success. Not every army that the British armed forces assist will succeed either, but the consequences of failure may be so great that every effort, along every lever of national power, would be worth the exertion in the longer run.

The British use of the term 'upstream' engagement (or 'persistent engagement' as it is sometimes called), is illuminating. In simple terms, it was a semantic device to avoid having to label all defence engagement activities as 'conflict prevention' since not all subjects of engagement were at risk of conflict per se. Yet there is a deeper context. Governments after the Cold War in the Western world assumed that global instability could be 'solved'. Failing states of the 1990s were to be tackled, and, with a somewhat selective interpretation, prevented from descending into the sorts of civil wars that had plagued the former Yugoslavia or which seemed to be unending in Somalia. There was an even greater impetus to this desire when Al Qaeda used first Sudan and then Afghanistan as bases for their murderous brand of mass casualty terrorism against the US; the implication was that failing states fostered terrorism. After '9/11' 2001, there was intense scrutiny of 'ungoverned spaces' which seemed to be generating an international brand of terrorism which was intent on projecting mass casualty violence into the West. Subsequent work nevertheless identified international terrorism emanating from a variety of places, including stable states like Saudi Arabia.

The association of failing states and benign intervention was also driven by the experience of Rwanda in 1994, were mass murders had not been prevented in advance (Melvern 2004). With the distance of time, it is difficult now to appreciate the profound impact this had on institutions like the UN, not least because of the effect it had on humanitarian non-state organisations that believed the UN should assume responsibility for the prevention or amelioration of such events. Today, aid agencies do not wait for the UN to intervene. The civilian agency approach is to be the first to deploy 'emergency aid' as rapidly as possible directly to the point of need regardless of who governs in a particular place and irrespective of UN involvement. Indeed, aid agencies, such as Medicins sans Frontieres, are compelled to work with a variety of governments, violent non-state actors and other agencies in order to gain access to those in distress. Civilian organisations also engage in long term enabling activity. They have moved away from the direct aid model of the twentieth century, which perpetuated dependence, to the training of locals and the fostering of local national leadership. There has also been a preference for micro-projects which go directly to small communities, have immediate and obvious benefits, and which are owned by local actors, rather than governments that might be prone to corrupt practices. The development of land banks, small agricultural loans and community projects has been successful in a number of different locations around the world (https://dfid.blog.gov.uk/, 2016). Nevertheless, the challenge for aid agencies is not just one of 'access', but, against a background of increasing numbers of attacks on humanitarian workers, of their fundamental security.

The military approach to intervention has, much to the frustration of its personnel, was criticised severely in Iraq and Afghanistan. The British army was tasked to find rapid solutions, to deliver emergency aid in insecure and usually hostile environments, and carry out humanitarian work where, as a state actor, it could not be considered 'neutral' by locals and therefore not entirely trusted. This situation arose in Iraq in 2004 because the British government did not possess civilian reconstruction capabilities and that left the armed forces with difficult and unfamiliar work. The armed forces were also stung by the volume of domestic criticism based on the argument that the conflict there constituted an 'unjust war'. Matters deteriorated further over Afghanistan, which the media amplified as a 'defeat'. The armed forces could point to the establishment of a new government and Afghan forces which they had trained, but the critics asserted that Afghanistan remained insecure and the country was financially dependent on the West. When the Western armed forces intervened in Libya in 2011, the perception of the critics was that the British government was exercising a posture of war without responsibility. Unsurprisingly, against this background the British government and the armed forces have been eager to find solutions that are 'upstream' of conflict or, as the soldiers label it, 'left of bang'.

The criticism of the UK armed forces in recent conflicts stems from a perceived lack of enthusiasm for 'nation-building'. The perception is that the UK government and its armed forces have adopted an expeditionary posture but without wanting to commit to an enduring presence. This perception was, however, domestic rather than being international. The media articulated a common view that the UK government had engaged in an 'illegal war' in Iraq in 2003, not least because of the unwillingness of the US and UK to pursue a specific UNSC Resolution to tackle the intransigence of Iraq over possession of Weapons of Mass Destruction (WMD). The suspicion was that the real agenda was regime change, which would be illegal under international law. The Iraq Enquiry was particularly scathing about the government's grounds for intervention (Chilcott 2017). The claim to be protecting populations in the subsequent Libya intervention in 2011 also resulted in regime change and even if that had not been an intended outcome, it reinforced a perception that it was a covert strategic objective. Moreover, there has been a widespread view, reinforced by the *reductio ad absurdum* simplification of the conflict drivers in the media, that the British armed forces were defeated in Afghanistan because the objective—to reduce the ability of international terrorists to strike against Britain—seemed to change into the stabilisation of the new Afghan government. After the military intervention (combat operations were suspended in 2014), Afghanistan remained insecure and its economy dependent on narcotics, despite the establishment of representative government, a peaceful transition of national executives and the handover of security responsibility to new Afghan armed forces and police.

The new policy of Defence Engagement emphasised 'capacity-building' alongside other activities that would facilitate access and influence, in order to fulfil 'UK effects and objectives'. Referring to all activities other than combat operations, defence engagement included visits, liaison and exchanges, loan service, training and education, and affiliations. For capacity building, short-term training missions are designed to work in conjunction with other governments departments such as the Stabilisation Unit (SU), the Foreign and Commonwealth Office (FCO) and the Department for International Development (DfID). 'Persistent engagement' emerged as a specific reference to more precise and selective upstream activity, in support of Defence Engagement, but seemed to emphasise a more limited and realistic degree of intervention.

What has emerged is a clear set of requirements for successful stabilisation, and early intervention (see Chapter 1). These appear to be a comprehensive, cross-government approach; the coordination of effort between government, military and civilian agencies; the careful use of appropriately trained and qualified personnel (with, for example, knowledge of the language, political economy and the context of the engagement); provision of security; the reintegration of antagonised (and perhaps already armed) actors; the implementation of justice; and perhaps access to resources or a redress of grievances. But is there any track record of success in this way of thinking (particularly when cross-referenced with the findings of Chapters 3, 4 and 6 in this volume)? Are the preparations being made more suitable to the 1990s than the twenty-first century? Will the assumptions of today still work in 2025 and 2035?

To analyse ‘upstream stabilisation’ in the environments anticipated in 2035, there are three elements to assess, and they are, for the purpose of clarification, set in hypothetical and generic scenarios. The first of these is to assess how analysts conceived of the future in the 1990s and therefore whether their ‘upstream’ activities or early interventions were effective, which allows us to test the assumptions that prevail. The second is to examine efforts at counter-stabilisation which occur on the cusp of, and especially during the emergent stages of civil wars. The third is to evaluate what might be encountered in the future—the upstream environment—in its geopolitical and economic context.

More insight can of course be gained from the past, where we might derive insights on previous attempts to head off instability, to shore up failing or fragile states, or prevent armed conflict (be that insurrection, insurgency or war). Nevertheless, given the limitations of a short chapter, the purpose here is primarily to evaluate the future operating environment and the relative strength of one country, namely the UK as a medium-sized but influential state, to manage the scale and severity of challenges that can be anticipated.

With this analysis underway we might then test our hypotheses of how stabilisation is conducted ‘upstream’ against a likely case study where a form of intervention is likely, such as Syria some years after the defeat of ISIS, or in the prevention of a civil war or conventional confrontation in the Middle East (a hypothetical evaluation of confronting the ‘next ISIS’). Testing the principles and the theory with examples allows for a more comprehensive assessment of the problems of engaging before conflicts in neighbouring countries, which would be the intended use of the idea of ‘upstream engagement’, or planning for the tasks and assets, that is the ‘upstream preparation’, that might be required for a comprehensive multinational stabilisation mission.

Back to the Future: British Assessments of ‘Upstream’ Intervention in the 1990s

An expeditionary posture for the UK is deeply rooted in its history. During the years of the Royal Navy’s global supremacy, which lasted until 1941, the British benefited from their island security which allowed them to avoid the continental commitment of their European neighbours to focus on global interventions. The British Expeditionary Force that deployed to France at the beginning of the First World War was an exception to the country's global posture. Its usual function was an imperial internal security force. Ministers, like Lord Haldane, the Secretary of State for War in 1906, had predicted that 'our wars ... require an Army wholly different from that of any other nation [whose] possible work may vary between the defence of India to some small war in a Crown Colony.' After returning to the tradition of global expeditionary wars between 1918 and 1940, there was another brief period of continental warfare in 1944–1945. The normative position was reasserted briefly after the war: Britain was able to project itself on land through naval power, that is, until the Suez crisis in 1956 (Guinn 1965). Thereafter, British naval and land power were in relative decline compared with the Superpowers. Yet Britain's close alignment with the United States throughout the Cold War ensured that the former expeditionary posture was retained alongside the new commitment to the defence of Europe. That capability was tested in the Falklands War of 1982, and subsequently in the Gulf War, the intervention in Sierra Leone in 2000, the intervention in Afghanistan (2001–2014), Iraq (2003–2009) and Libya (2011).

Britain had maintained its influence not just through naval power and an expeditionary army, but also through diplomacy and trade. While the British armed forces engaged in a number of engineering tasks that aided stabilisation through enhanced security capabilities (such as the construction of ports and bridges), most of the infrastructural development was conducted by the private sector, and commercial conditions were apt to produce mixed results: some economic changes enriched certain communities and elites, but others could create instability and unrest. Crucially, however, the wealth of the UK was its primary tool of stabilisation, an element that would today be known as its 'prosperity agenda'. Throughout the twentieth century, while Britain's share of global commerce declined relative to other countries and its influence ebbed, diplomatic efforts invariably maintained cordial relations with other states, including those that shed British colonial control through institutions like the Commonwealth. Moreover, the City of London and the financial services sector continued to manage important aspects of the global economy and generate 'invisible earnings' for the UK (Cain and Hopkins 1993).

Nevertheless, there was relatively little success in strategic 'upstream' intervention after 1945. Britain was unable to prevent episodes of armed conflict during the long 'drawdown' of the British Empire. The governments of the day realised that when entire populations had set their heart on liberation, military force was limited in what it could achieve (Darwin 1987). On the other hand, military forces could preserve a state against minorities or separatists, as in the case of Kenya in the 1950s. Moreover, there is one example of early intervention to prevent state failure, namely in Oman between 1970 and 1974 (Hughes 2009; Worrall 2014; Johnson 2016). Other anti-communist struggles required more substantial military commitments, as in Malaya, and therefore were not entirely 'upstream' activities. One might also cite the swift and successful military intervention in Sierra Leone in 2000, followed by a more comprehensive package of support, which did much to re-establish peace and governance after a civil war.

Testing the Idea of Upstream Stabilisation: The Case of Syria

After 2011, the Syrian government was locked in a protracted struggle against much of its population, and both the administration of Bashar al Assad and the various opposition and resistance groups were backed by external agencies. If the West calculated that some form of intervention was required in Syria either to end the conflict, or to re-establish government and reconstruct the economy, how might we assess its 'upstream engagement' that began in the 1990s? Leaving aside for the moment the critical question of whether Syria had become part of the orbit of Russia and that international intervention has been possible, we might still assess this type of environment and expectations against the past record of similar types: In essence, could 'upstream' activity actually work?

In 1997, the European Union concluded a European Cooperation Agreement with Syria, three years before Bashar al Assad succeeded his father as dictator. The new regime was offered a free trade agreement and assistance with transport and infrastructure development as part of an effort to bring Syria 'in from the cold'. Yet hopes for reform, especially amongst intellectuals in Syria, were short-lived. The so-called 'Damascus Spring' in 2000 was suppressed. Nevertheless, in 2008, in spite of Assad's covert assistance to Shia insurgents during the Iraq War, France led a Euro-Mediterranean partnership initiative to make another effort to encourage Assad into the international system. The following year, European Union development targets were set out with Syria on justice reform. There was even an offer by Britain for security sector assistance which included attendance by Syrian officers at the Royal Military Academy Sandhurst and other initiatives on defence cooperation. Nevertheless, while these concessions were being offered, Assad refused to allow the entry of the British Defence Attaché, and there were greater restrictions placed on all Westerners throughout the country.

In fact, Syria's responses to the Western programme were much more negative than they appeared on the surface. Syria continued to supply weapons to Hezbollah, a designated terrorist organisation, to the extent that the US considered imposing sanctions in 2004. Domestically, the same year, the Assad regime erected controls over the internet and suppressed protests by Kurds. Despite the 'upstream' efforts, Syria showed no sign of making any concessions to democracy or international legal standards. With Iraq, its old rival, collapsing into anarchy and under American occupation, the Syrian administration must have viewed the regional situation with some satisfaction.

Nevertheless, all that was about to change. The sudden appearance of public demonstrations on 26 January 2011, and the throughout the weeks that followed, was in part inspired by events in Egypt, but it was also an indication that large sections of the population were exasperated by the ruling elites. Protestors called for Assad to resign and that Baathist rule should be terminated, but there were other drivers. Before 2011, poverty was rising. Fully one-third of the people were categorised as poor and some 11% were below the level of subsistence. To that must be added the blatant inequality of opportunity, and exclusive retention of power by an Alawite minority, both of which fed widespread corruption and abuse of authority. Against the protests, Assad deployed not only his 15 competing intelligence agencies and police but also elements of his 400,000 strong army. The security forces cordoned and besieged the protestors, but resistance became violent. Some soldiers deserted, although any that were caught were shot summarily. Members of the resistance who were captured were beaten, tortured and killed. When fighters subsequently overran government facilities, they discovered gruesome evidence of the emaciated victims of torture. Video footage was also secured and survivors' testimony produced, showing routine brutality by the regime's forces. By 2012, just twelve months into the unrest, some 10,000 civilians were thought to have been killed, and 3000 members of the security forces.

In an attempt to mollify criticism from the West and liken his situation to the one the Americans and their allies had faced in Iraq and Afghanistan, Assad claimed he faced 'armed gangs and terrorists'. The stark difference was that the West had specifically avoided waging war on civilians, whereas Assad was determined to crush all resistance with overwhelming force. The flow of refugees was evidence of how bad things had become inside Syria, and the numbers would reach 4.8 million by 2016. This figure did not include internally displaced persons (UNHCR, Syrian refugees 2016).

Assad continued his deception by offering political concessions. These were little more than window dressing. In 2011, Assad stated that the state security court would be abolished and that conscription would be reduced to 18 months, but, of course, the 'state of emergency' would mean these reforms could not be implemented. In 2012, Assad announced that the Baath Party would no longer have the constitutional right to lead Syria. No one believed that, since, even if there were elections, the Baath would just engineer their victories. Most of the population were outraged by Assad's repression, and even those who had favoured the regime and the security it gave them, such as the people of central Damascus, were more concerned with their own security and had little sympathy for the regime. Assad's response was to increase the pressure. Artillery, mortars, helicopter gunships and air strikes were used against wards of cities where resistance had developed. By 2014, the security forces were dropping 'barrel bombs' into populated neighbourhoods and on more than one occasion, as at Ghouta, chemical agents were deployed. The results were caught on camera and ignited international condemnation (www.gov.uk/government/news/syria-chemical-weapons-attack, 2013). The UN had offered to broker ceasefires, facilitate negotiations and even tried to extract civilians in beleaguered pockets, but the Syrian regime largely ignored it. However, the use of chemical weapons galvanised the reluctant US administration. It protested, asserting that Assad had crossed a 'red line'. Secretary of State, John Kerry, when pressed by journalists, suggested the Assad regime could be spared intervention if it offered to put its chemical arsenal beyond use. Assad seized the opportunity to save his regime, and immediately placed his chemical weapons in the hands of a UN-led technical team.

This was just the beginning of international involvement in Syria's civil war. As a long-standing ally of the Russians, Assad turned to President Vladimir Putin for support. Initially covert, this had become an overt intervention in 2015. Iran also offered assistance and there were volunteers from Hezbollah prepared to fight the resistance in support of their old sponsors. The Iranian and Hezbollah contributions gave the war a more overt sectarian dimension. It also, in something of an irony, gave the Russians and the Iranians the opportunity to condemn the West for advocating regime change, which is illegal under international law. Moscow and Tehran argued that they were actually engaged in the stabilisation of Syria.

Why had upstream engagement with Syria failed? The first factor was inaction by the West in the critical first months of the crisis in 2011. This might be attributed to the 'Iraq syndrome', a reluctance to intervene in any form lest it lead to an unpopular protracted conflict involving Western forces. Nevertheless, once the opportunity passed, the civil war became entrenched. The second factor was the distrust felt by Assad towards the West, despite its overtures. This was based on his observation about dictators who, having aligned themselves to the West, were then deposed, such as Saddam and Gadhafi. There was also insincerity by Assad: he had no intention of relinquishing any powers. The opposition believed he was beyond redemption. Few believed that he should ever be permitted to govern again. Russia, by contrast, insisted in 2015 that Assad must be the interim powerbroker, even if he was not the candidate for the long term, as the means to ensure they retained an allied power in the Middle East.

Subsequent Western intervention was limited to precise air strikes against specific ISIS targets. UN peace proposals were ignored and Russia frequently vetoed UNSC resolutions against further chemical attacks on civilians. Russian intransigence was initially ignored by the Americans, which made missile and air strikes on Syrian airbases and chemical weapons facilities, but exasperation with a Russian-orchestrated attempted assassination with chemical weapons in Britain in 2018 led to a mass, Western deportation of Russian diplomats. Russia clung more closely to its Syrian ally, leaving the conflict unresolved.

The Nature of Civil War and Counter-Stabilisation

The 1990s optimism about stabilisation, and the disappointment of the 2010s, is instructive when considering present and future cases of upstream stabilisation. If the purpose of upstream engagement is to stabilise and influence, it is worth noting there always be elements, if not the majority, who don't want 'stability'; at least, not the *status quo ante bellum*. If the objective is to prevent conflict, then the drivers of civil war will invariably be stronger than any external efforts to stop it. In the case of Syria, this was not limited to the passions of the people or inexorable forces of economics: even governments were not prepared to end the conflict except on their own terms.

Before war, the drivers of conflict might be summarised as a gross inequality and maldistribution of resources; the abuse of privilege and blatant corruption; weak or disputed government; the onset of sudden scarcity; resource expropriation, territorial or political control; religious or ideological antagonism, and, as Thucydides noted famously, a combination of fear, honour and interest. Once armed conflict has broken out, the dynamic of violence means that the thresholds of restraint are reduced. Then, the escalation of force as the sole remaining tool of politics, drives conflict and radicalises the belligerents. The insecurity of conflict generates further polarisation, forcing the protection of particular interests rather than encouraging cooperation. Casualties increase the unwillingness to compromise, and armed conflict tends to distort and inflate war aims. The conditions for peace are far more difficult to obtain than establishing confidence building measures or a negotiation process.

It is not just the nature of war that works against upstream stabilisation but the changing geopolitical environment and developments in the character of war in our age. The boundaries and sovereignty of state power are under threat from new forms of international allegiance, facilitated by electronic tools, which have been exploited by violent transnational Jihadist movements. There are also structural instabilities in the financial and energy sectors which have geopolitical ramifications. Where there are upstream stabilisation efforts, the West is no longer in the lead. In Africa, over 50% of infrastructural development is funded or delivered by China, and it is likely that new spheres of influence will dominate which powers are able to carry out stabilisation missions (Global Researcher 2008).

The changes in the character of war also appear to work against stabilisation in many respects. Modern industrial war tended to be characterised by a definitive end between a limited number of defined actors, but post-industrial war is frequently unending and constant; where industrial war was sustained and high intensity, won by major powers utilising technological supremacy, and with information operations directed towards a well-defined and identifying audience, post-industrial conflicts are of episodic intensity and while major powers possess technological superiority, there are periodic moments where non-state actors have parity especially in urban and remote peripheries. Moreover, information operations are conveyed to a global, critical and sceptical audience. Russia has demonstrated that a barrage of half-truths, propaganda and misinformation can obscure actual intentions.

In the early twenty-first century, there are examples of more distributed warfare, conducted by terrorist movements, but also by proxies and private contractors rather than by states. This development, and other aspects of the changing character of war listed above, militates against upstream stabilisation or conflict prevention. The multiplicity of actors, conflicting agendas and more problematic establishment or acceptance of state control, overlay the bitter nature of civil war. Under these conditions, the historical insight is towards radical solutions that are not acceptable to the Western liberal tradition, since when civil unrest is imminent, it may be far better to act early, to deploy force that is overwhelming, and, if the fighting develops, the fastest route to the restoration of order might be to back one side rather than trying to show an 'even hand'. Nevertheless, in situations of protracted, low-intensity conflict, it seems to be better to contain and de-escalate, to find mechanisms to take the heat out of political grievances, and to deny the fulfilment of strategy by those that threaten order.

The Future Operating Environment

What can Western forces expect of the upstream environment by 2035–2045? Clearly accurate prediction is impossible, but it is possible to identify some themes, test existing modelling, and to construct a scenario where upstream intervention might be envisaged. The Development, Concepts and Doctrine Centre (DCDC) of the UK Ministry of Defence suggest in their work on Global Strategic Trends and the Future Operating Environment that violent non-state actors will continue to make extensive use of global mass communications for recruitment and propaganda, seeking to discredit the efforts of intervening governments. There is also a widespread expectation that insurgent movements will continue to develop links with the criminal underworld for finances, safe locations and licit 'front' organisations. These movements exploit the permeability of international borders. International terrorist organisations are likely to make use of terror attacks to dissuade governments from making interventions. Ideological motivations, playing especially on the sentiments of diaspora, may also be prominent. Cyber attacks are expected to feature as a more common aspect of asymmetrical warfare, blending extremism with apparently legitimate causes and playing on the oscillation of public opinion to discredit or deter government policy.

These information operations would be but a part of a more general attempt to deny access to places and peoples, and would seek to impose severe limits on the ability of Western governments to operate at all. There are several constraints that are even more fundamental. One is cost. The West's ability to project power is dependent on its economic strength, but the increasing prosperity of China and South East Asia will create significant challenges. Moreover, given the number of states that require 'upstream' support today, let alone under conditions that may emerge in the future, the budget for all upstream scenarios may be well beyond the financial means of the Western world. That said, the Middle East is likely to remain within the strategic and national interests of the world's leading states, and the West's responses will be complicated by the presence of countries with their own interests to consider, including Israel, Iran, Saudi Arabia, the GCC nations, and, in light of the Syrian case, Russia too. The implication of this is that all forms of stabilisation activity, engagement, influence or intervention are not only going to require regional ascent, but also dependence on economic conditions and local compliance.

Although it is not currently acknowledged, it is likely that public demands to tackle humanitarian disasters will be a significant driver for governments to intervene, and may occur in an 'upstream' setting, that is, before serious armed conflict breaks out. It is difficult to ascertain how long the 'deterring' effect of operations in Iraq and Afghanistan might last, but the exemplar of Vietnam suggest that a long shadow might be cast. The fear of entanglement, of being trapped in a protracted quagmire of insurgency, with mounting casualties, legal ambiguity, and ebbing popular backing, haunts Western governments and explains why, in Libya (2011) and Iraq and Syria (2014–2017) there was a preference for air operations and small teams deployed in training and facilitation roles. This sentiment may prevail long after its relevance to changed international affairs. The concern to avoid 'boots on the ground' can be maintained despite a well-established situation that requires them: the resolution of conflict often requires ground forces. The political view of 'boots on the ground' is a commentary on our time, and of our future: it is a measure of the West's willingness to project power, and to take risks, over extended periods.

The limitations of air power, when used as the sole instrument of military force, are well-known, but are the preference of political leaders. The risk of collateral damage, especially the accidental bombing of civilian gatherings in Afghanistan which earned the epithet 'wedding party syndrome', or the devastating results of the battle for Kobani (in the autumn of 2014), which destroyed a significant portion of the settlement that the air operations were designed to save, have not deterred leaders from this approach. The Russians and the Syrian government reduced most of eastern Aleppo to ruins, and evacuated the surviving civilian population, to achieve a limited operational victory. In any future upstream intervention, air power may feature as the means to check the onslaught of particular enemy forces, as it did in Libya, but it is dependent on weak air defences and cannot produce a political solution on its own.

New technologies by 2040 may well assist in any upstream intervention, but their effects will be limited by more established constraints. New medical advances will undoubtedly save lives, but getting access to casualties in time, and the injuries caused by more efficient weapon systems would work against this enhancement. Robotics providing armed sentinels, improved surveillance and unmanned vehicles in combat environments will not just be available to Western states, but also to their enemies, including violent non-state actors, as the proliferation of drone technologies has proved in the last ten years. We might also anticipate greater disruption through cyber and electronic warfare, delaying communications and adding to the 'fog' of war. There are strong indications that the use of bio-chemical weapons can be expected. Overall, the general trend suggests that non-state forces will be enabled to a greater extent in communications, weapons, knowledge and the ability to operate in depth. The implication is that Western forces must be able to operate with much greater reach, speed and precision, interdicting the enemy before they have a chance to inflict more damage. Even then, there will be corresponding friction and setbacks to overcome. Mass casualty attacks on the domestic environments of Western countries seems most certain, eroding public confidence in any form of intervention.

If one considers the scenario of Western forces operating in the Middle East sometime in the next twenty years, the 'upstream' environment looks far from the permissive ones envisaged in defence engagement literature. In Syria and parts of Iraq, there has been widespread devastation of urban areas, populations embittered by mass killing and reprisals, millions displaced, who, on their return, would find their livelihoods destroyed. The scale of task of reconstruction is enormous. Future environments may be contaminated, access complicated by mines and improvised ordnance, and there could be residual resistance from ideologically-inspired fighters seasoned in the use of suicide attacks, human shields and other terror tactics.

The future environment looks set to continue to contain a variety of actors, from local state security forces to private contractors. There are likely to be a significant number of ambiguous participants, such as financial opportunists, corrupt officials, antagonistic local civilians and child soldiers. Handling these is always problematic and requires careful judgement and timing. It may be the case that armed criminal elements provide sufficient security and income to local civilians that they continue to be favoured over 'outsiders', be they foreign or just representative of another area or political level. Local knowledge is likely to be crucial in such circumstances, and decisions will have to be made whether to work with the grain of a society or whether to root out the criminal system and have it replaced with legitimate commerce and political activity. The point is that locals do not always know what's best and there may be a majority held in an unequal economic and security environment by a relative minority of armed actors.

Fortunately, there are often strategic vulnerabilities of an adversary that can be exploited. The Daesh movement lacked popular backing. Their murderous campaign produced volunteers seeking to subvert their brutal ideology and exact revenge, and that was in certainly in evidence with regard to Kurdish and minority Syrian groups. At the international level, legal prosecutions for war crimes and crimes against humanity could be brought, indicating that the criminal elements of the regime have no place to hide, even long after the conflict is over. Naming suspects has been known to produce a willingness to abandon an insurgency in order to benefit from providing information or to escape prosecution as an associate. There are countless other vulnerabilities to be utilised, from the economic foundation of their movement to the destruction or surveillance of safe havens.

Any 'upstream' intervention requires identification of strategic tasks and then preparation for them. These will include the deradicalisation of youth, since, in the case of Daesh, children have been used as execution squads, often in the murder of other children, and their education hitherto has been of a violent and radical nature. The lesson from the war in Iraq (2003–2009) was that de-Baathification and demilitarisation was an error, since demobilised troops joined an insurgency against the intervention forces. But reconfiguration of fighting groups, state or non-state, is nevertheless essential after civil wars, and the phased retraining of all local security forces would need management. The expectation of all fighters, from the security forces to the resistance militias, is that there will be, of course, some dividend or benefit from the peace. Exclusion from Development, Disarmament and Reconstruction (DDR) processes is known to encourage recidivism. Of more immediate concern, thanks to widespread devastation, is the need for medical support and the provision of essential services. The controlled return of the population by zone, equipped with the tools to commence their own reconstruction, needs further planning and preparation, as does the provision of water, food and fuel, at least in the early stages. Moreover, there often needs to be region-wide engagement to ensure that neighbouring states are reassured, can assist and do not interfere with reconstruction or attempt to exploit the situation for their own ends. That diplomatic effort requires planning and facilitation from the earliest stage. Critically, in the case of Syria, there would need to be a mechanism to change Russian policy from upholding state terror and greater responsibility in accordance with international humanitarian law. Such a transformation in Moscow would only seem likely after a prolonged period battling terrorism and insurgency.

Given the likelihood of 'upstream' efforts in certain regions of the world, including Syria, the UK government and armed forces would profit a great deal from consultation with local actors, aid agencies, those in the private sector and specialist academics. At the strategic level and in the long term preparatory phase, this input, especially consultation with a variety of local stakeholders, is vital. As one moves down to the operational and tactical level and in shorter time frames, so the government and professional military component becomes more important. The implication of this is that the questions change as one approaches the seat of the crisis, but there is no substitute for planning carefully, and considering the environment one is likely to encounter in the future.

Conclusions

The environment for 'upstream effects' is changing and will be significantly different in 2035 compared with the expectations of the 1990s or the experiences of Western military personnel in 2001–2014 in Iraq, Afghanistan and Libya. It is therefore a surprise to find that there is a widespread expectation that Western forces will continue to influence, shape, intervene and stabilise as they have done in the past, and that activities will be conducted 'upstream' as a measurable success. The idea that influence can occur to prevent armed conflict does not have a flawless track record. Indeed, it is difficult to find evidence that 'upstream' activities work very well, and certainly not as intended. There are many case examples that show upstream activities do not succeed. Intervention can destabilise, creating turbulence that can, in some cases, cause the very conflict it sought to avert. In Libya, attempts to bring Gadhafi into the international system did not last long, and the country has been in a civil war since 2011. In Syria, the efforts of the 1990s and early 2000s did not yield the results that were hoped for. In Yemen, there is little sign that 'upstream' engagement conducted since the 1990s has worked, and, at the time of writing, the country has been locked in a protracted civil war, fuelled by external regional powers.

It seems likely that in the next few years there will be considerable faith in the Western world in the ability of air power to deliver results. Paradoxically, air power cannot deliver humanitarian relief and yet it is the responsibility to protect which would act as the biggest driver for intervention. The air power instrument reduces liability, but that cannot be its sole metric for its utility.

The geopolitical context in which the West has intervened, supported or otherwise engaged with countries at risk of armed conflict is changing. While it is likely that various spheres of influence will appear, with contested boundaries, the Middle East is set to remain a zone of economic and strategic interest for all the world's leading countries. It is therefore likely to remain a subject of defence engagement efforts for the next few decades, but also a zone of contestation at the boundary of influence and competing national interests.

Both actors and technological developments will change and evolve too, and these developments may both assist and hinder any Western attempts to engage and influence local conditions. The conclusion is therefore that the parameters of Western calculations about 'upstream' engagement must change as the environment alters. As the cases of Iraq and Syria indicate, stabilisation in the near-term would be extremely problematic. By 2040, it might be a concept that has been entirely abandoned, not least because of fundamental changes in the future operating environment. In the short term, there needs to be a much more realistic and robust appraisal of ground truths, a jettisoning of favoured assumptions or ideological preferences, and a more pragmatic assessment of what is feasible, acceptable and affordable. Above all, any consideration of upstream engagement needs to accept risk, clarify strategic intent, and engage its local actors with cold realism.

References

Cain, Peter J., & Hopkins, Anthony G. (1993). *British Imperialism: Crisis and Deconstruction, 1914–1990*. London: Longmans.

Chilcott. (2017). *The Iraq Enquiry*. http://webarchive.nationalarchives.gov.uk/20171123123237/http://www.iraqinquiry.org.uk/. Accessed April 2018.

Darwin, John. (1987). *Britain and Decolonization: The Retreat from Empire in the Post-war World*. London: Macmillan.

Global Researcher. (2008). *Volume 2, 1*. http://depts.gpc.edu/~gpcglobe/Forms/ChinainAfrica.pdf. Accessed May 2016. There has been severe criticism of China for investing only in industries or sectors that benefit China and paid little regard to regimes with abysmal records in human rights abuses, including the allocation of the China Africa Development (CAD) Fund established in 2006, the sale of weapons or favourable trade deals with unaccountable and undemocratic governments. See 'China in Africa'.

Global Strategic Trends: Out to 2045. (2014). *UK Ministry of Defence*, 5th ed.

Guinn, Paul. (1965). *British Strategy and Politics, 1914–1918*. Oxford: Clarendon Press.

Hughes, G. (2009). 'A "Model Campaign": The Counter-Insurgency War in Dhofar, Oman, 1965–1975'. *Journal of Strategic Studies, 32*(2), xxxii.

Johnson, Robert. (2016). 'Out of Arabia: British Strategy and the Fate of Local Forces in Aden, South Yemen and Oman, 1967–76'. *International History Review, 39*(1): 143–164.

Melvern, Linda. (2004). *Conspiracy to Murder: The Rwandan Genocide*. London and New York: Verso.

Staff Blogs of the Department for International Development. (2016). https://dfid.blog.gov.uk/. Accessed May 2016.

UK Government. (13 August 2013). https://www.gov.uk/government/news/syria-chemical-weapons-attack. Accessed May 2016.

UN Commission on Refugees. (2016). http://data.unhcr.org/syrianrefugees/regional.php. Accessed 22 May 2016.

Worrall, James. (2014). *State-Building and Counterinsurgency in Oman*. London: I.B. Tauris.

CHAPTER 8

The Apocalyptic and the Sectarian: Identity, 'Bare Life' and the Rise of Da'ish

Simon Mabon

The emergence of Da'ish in the summer of 2014 is the story of the mobilisation of an apocalyptic vision and response to—and continuation of—the marginalisation of sectarian identities across the Middle East. These stories, when taken together, can explain how a group of people—emerging from the embers of Al Qaeda in Iraq—was able to gain control over territory in Syria and Iraq that was larger in extent than Great Britain and conduct terrorist attacks across the world. A growing number of people have begun to focus upon the first story, the tale of an apocalyptic vision (McCants 2015), but this chapter focuses predominantly upon the second story, of the politicisation and securitisation of a range of identities across the Middle East which are, of course, shaped by the first. While the capital of the self-proclaimed caliphate is the Syrian city of Raqqa and the Syrian Civil War has played a prominent role in helping the group to gain traction and support, in this chapter I focus on Iraq for four reasons: First, the group's roots can be traced back to Al Qaeda in Iraq, the group led by Abu Musa al-Zarqawi. Second, Abu Bakr al-Baghdadi, the leader of Da'ish is an Iraqi citizen. Third, a large number of the group's leading members were prisoners in Camp Bucca,

S. Mabon (✉)
University of Lancaster, Lancaster, UK

T. Clack and R. Johnson (eds.), *Before Military Intervention*,
https://doi.org/10.1007/978-3-319-98437-7_8

the American prison in Iraq. Fourth, as Abu Musa al Zarqawi noted, the "spark was lit in Iraq." He had claimed: "…and its heat will continue to intensify – by Allah's permission – until it burns the crusader armies in Dabiq" (al-Zarqawi 2014). As such, while the analysis can be extended to events in Syria, this chapter will focus solely upon events in Iraq.

To facilitate awareness of the emergence of Da'ish, the chapter begins by exploring ideas of sovereignty, albeit couched in a Western philosophical tradition. In doing so, it is possible explore a number of important issues that shed light on the nature of political interaction within a particular territorial area.[1] It then considers political organisation in Iraq across the twentieth century, focussing upon the rise and fall of the sovereign state. The argument then turns to the events of 2003 and the invasion of Iraq, considering the process of deba'athification, which resulted in a Shi'a government in Baghdad, mass unemployment and the onset of sectarian violence. The spread of religious identities across the region means that it is necessary to consider the penetration of the Iraqi state by external actors, namely Saudi Arabia and Iran, whose geopolitical agendas—framed within the context of support for sectarian kin—fed into the continued fragmentation of the state. From this, it is possible to see how Sunni communities became marginalised and securitised, resulting in what Giorgio Agamben (1995) has termed 'bare life', the exclusion from the political realm that shapes daily life.

This exclusion is not limited to high politics, rather, also refers to the deprivation of resources and opportunities, restricted by formal and informal structures. It is these conditions that gave rise to the emergence of Da'ish. From here, the argument turns to an exploration of the different types of support that the group is able to mobilise, from the active to the passive. In attempting to defeat the group, it is essential to engage with these questions. Essentially, the paper considers sovereign power and the regulation of political life across Iraq, questioning how inclusion, exclusion and spaces of indistinction have created bare life, pushing people to the margins of society.

[1]A different understanding of sovereignty is found when considering salafism, which holds that sovereignty couched in *tawahid*, the oneness of God. Fundamentally, this view means that democracy and power-sharing are incompatible with Islam. This position is at the core of Da'ish's ideology and much be acknowledged, but political understandings of sovereignty reveal a great deal more about dynamics on the ground in the Middle East.

As per other chapters within this volume, the argument contributes to discussion about the concept of upstreaming, by questioning what the rise of Da'ish can add to these debates. Upstreaming, a term initially found within the oil industry, deals with a range of processes with different objectives, but shaped by different temporal, geographical and scaler factors. Typically, these are comprised of small military teams operating at early stages of conflict curves. Within debates on the topic, it is clear that streams are rarely linear in one direction, either geographically or dimensionally, be that in terms of flows of people, finances, arms, ideas or contraband.

Sovereignty, 'Bare Life' and Political Organisation

To understand the rise of Da'ish it is important to locate it within the context of the political transition across Iraq that emerged following 2003 war which reversed decades of political marginalisation and discrimination and resulted in a Shi'a government in Baghdad. Yet such issues have their roots much earlier than events of 2003 and thus it is important to consider the long-standing grievances that were reversed in the aftermath of the toppling of Saddam Hussein. To this end, the following section provides a brief genealogy of the history of political organisation in Iraq after the formation of the state in 1921, although formal independence from British rule was only achieved in 1932. Yet before embarking on this survey, it is useful to consider ideas of sovereignty as a means of exploring political organisation and of locating the position of identity groups within the state along with understanding the nature of power relations with the sovereign.

Conventional understandings of sovereignty make a distinction between internal sovereignty and external sovereignty, with the former engaging in questions of political organisation within clearly defined territorial areas and the latter engaging with ideas of non-interference. Western approaches to sovereignty have shaped global understandings of questions about the nature of political organisation—couched in the establishment of the United Nations and norms of international politics—grounded in the work of scholars such as Thomas Hobbes (1651), Max Weber (2004), Carl Schmitt (1922), Stephen Krasner (1999), James Caporaso (2000), Michel Foucault (1976), and Giorgio Agamben (1995) among many others. These approaches, while different in the nuance involved, typically share a number of component parts, namely citizenship, territoriality, authority, and autonomy. The idea of sovereignty is largely accepted as a form of political and social control, with the continuation of sovereignty as an end in and of itself.

Problems arise when considering exceptions—and challenges—that are found within the state rather than as the external manifestation of another. Given the fractious nature of identity politics within a number of Middle Eastern states, ideas of sovereignty that are found in the more conventional approaches, grounded in ideas of citizenship and inclusivity become problematic. From this problem, it is important to consider alternative ways of engaging with political organisation. Underpinning this, of course, is the ability to control life, or, as Michel Foucault articulates, "the right to take life or let live" (1976: 136).

For Carl Schmitt, sovereignty refers to a power that is able to determine when the law should be suspended and a 'state of exception' can be declared (1922). The sovereign is then able to determine who remains inside and who is excluded, delineating the nature of political organisation in terms of people rather than territory. Such a position contains within it several assumptions about the ontology of such a form of political organisation, which become contested in the Middle East by competing sources of authority. Although Foucault's notion of sovereignty provides an integral underpinning to political organisation across the region, tension between citizenship, territoriality and authority are increasingly in tension with one another.

Moreover, when considering the supra-state nature of identities across the region, through tribal and religious affiliation, the idea of systems of governance within neatly defined territorial areas appears problematic and inappropriate. As John Agnew (1994) argues, such a conceptualisation of a state as a fixed unit of sovereign space is hugely problematic. For Agnew, "Social, economic, and political life cannot be ontologically contained within the territorial boundaries of states through the methodological assumption of 'timeless space'" (1994: 77). Such problems are compounded in the Middle East, when fused with the existence of tribalism and religious affiliation, which also have the capacity to challenge a regime's authority.

Foucault and Agamben seek to offer such an alternative, starting from the "decisive abandonment of the traditional approach to the problem of power" (1995: 5) and grounded in biopolitics, a Foucauldian approach to understanding the regulation of life by the state. Although for Foucault and Agamben, such conditions emerge from modernity and the capitalist system, with explicit reference to Western states, these ideas are also applicable in the non-Western world where different socio-economic conditions have given rise to a different form of political organisation, underpinned by religion. Biopolitics, as conceptualised by Foucault, suggests that human life is targeted and regulated by the organisational power of the state, yet for Agamben, there is a hidden tie between the sovereign power and biopolitics, born out of exceptionalism emerging from state sovereignty.

Agamben begins his exploration of sovereignty with a discussion of Schmidt and ideas of a state of exception, which play an integral role in the emergence of the condition of 'bare life', where political life and all that comes with it is stripped from them (discussed in detail below) as an effort to regulate life. It is through the enactment of the exception—and the suspension of the law—in which the conditions of bare life emerge. In a Western context, "the rule, suspending itself, gives rise to the exception and, maintaining itself in relation to the exception, first constitutes itself as a rule" (Agamben 1995: 18). Clearly, this is predicated upon the existence of a system within which the rule of law operates, for it is the suspension of the law that brings about the conditions of bare life. Yet such conditions may arise in non-Western contexts, where a state of emergency has been declared following the deterioration of the domestic security situation.

Of course, it is easy to suggest that such claims are only applicable to Western democratic states, given the nature of political organisation and broader, of the construction of the political. Yet as Wael Hallaq, a scholar of Islamic Law suggests, modern states possess five form properties to be considered as a state: constitution as historical experience; sovereignty and ensuing metaphysics; legislative monopoly; bureaucratic machinery; cultural hegemony within the social order (Hallaq 2013: 23). In the case of Iraq we can see that although a number of these form properties have been contested, they exist, allowing for exploration of Iraq through the lens of Agamben's work. In particular, the metaphysics of the state provides rich scope for empirical and ideological exploration, given Iraq's relationship with colonial powers and, perceived relationship between Shi'a groups and Iran. Amidst such conditions, exploration of the establishment of sovereign power is of paramount importance.

Central to Agamben's work is the premise that the law is used to regulate behaviour, determining which people are able to become involved in politics. Across his work, Agamben argues that politics is the process of rendering people vulnerable and maintaining a control over decisions of life and death, which can be applied in a range of political contexts, occurring beyond the formal structures of the state. If one accepts this, the status of bare life can be created in authoritarian states, although the journey to the destination differs from the Western context.

For Agamben:

> The realm of bare life – which is originally situated at the margins of the political order – gradually begins to coincide with the political realm, and exclusion and inclusion, outside and inside, bios and zoe, right and fact, enter into a zone of irreducible indistinction. At once excluding bare life from and capturing it within the political order, the state of exception actually constituted, in its very separateness, the hidden foundation on which the entire political system rested. (1995: 9)

From this, Agamben argues that it is the state that makes the distinction between bios and zoe, articulating a distinction between those recognised as fully human, who are participating in political life and those who are of a lesser classification, of bare life. Agamben's discussion takes place in Homo sacer, with the title a nod to such an individual, from ancient Rome, who is banned and may be killed by anybody, but not in a religious ritual, as his or her life is worthless (1995: 72). Yet their life is still controlled by the state, which retains the power of life and death over them. While those existing in bare life would most likely reject the idea that they are 'no longer human', this argument helps to locate and explore grievances and contexts that can marginalise people in a range of different ways including—but not limited to—power relations, questions about identity and inclusion, citizenship, control and ultimately, the conditions that give rise to violent groups.

What Agamben and Foucault show is how sovereign power is used to regulate life, to restrict political agency and maintain power. By preventing particular groups from entering the political realm, their agendas and arenas are pushed to the margins of political discourse, rendering their life worthless. This rendering of life as bare, without meaning, requires recourse to a range of different structures including political, legal, social, economic and normative, revealing the importance of contingency and local context. Let us now turn to a consideration of how context and contingent factors help to facilitate the emergence of bare life.

The Sykes-Picot Agreement and the Rise of the Sovereign State

In June 2014 a Norwegian-Chilean man, Bastian Vasquez, stood on the border of Syria and Iraq and uttered the following words:

> Bismillah ir-Rahman ir-Rahim. As you can see right now, I'm on the border of Iraq and al Sham. Right now I'm inside of As sham. As you can see this is the so-called border of Sykes-Picot. Alhamdulillah, we don't recognise it and we will never recognise it. Inshallah this is not the first border that we will break and inshallah, we shall break all the borders, but we shall start with this, inshallah. [...] Alhamdullilah there is nobody now except the soldiers of dar al Islam. So alhamdulillah inshallah we cross the border. Bismillah. [...] As you can see, this is under our feet right now. [...]As Abu Bakr Al Baghdadi used to say 'He is the breaker of barriers'. Inshallah we will break the barrier of Iraq, Jordan, Lebanon, all the county[sic] inshallah. Until we reach Quds. This is the first of many barriers we shall break inshallah. (Vasquez 2014)

Vasquez spoke of the agreement reached between Sir Mark Sykes and his French counter-part, Francois Georges-Picot, in 1916. Sykes and Picot sought to reach an agreement about how best to control land in the Middle East following the end of the Ottoman Empire. Yet as Sykes himself acknowledged, such an agreement never emerged. For Sykes, "imperialism, annexation, military triumph, prestige, White man's burdens, have been expunged from the popular political vocabulary; consequently Protectorates, spheres of interest or influence, annexations, bases, etc. have to be consigned to the Diplomatic lumber-room" (Dodge 2005: 13; Johnson 2018).

Yet as Toby Dodge (2005) and Robert Johnson (2018) argue, the narrative is all too often used to explain the roots of discontent across the region, despite its inaccuracies. Such a position leads to a number of serious problems when understanding the Middle East, reducing political affairs to religious organisation. Despite this, in dismissing the narrative entirely out of hand, one risks throwing the baby out with the bathwater; the Sykes-Picot narrative highlights the extent of the "perfidious interference" (Dodge 2014) of colonial powers in the region and it is here where the narrative gains much of its traction. Indeed, by stating the intent to destroy the Sykes-Picot agreement, Vasquez really demonstrated the intent to destroy the colonial legacy in the region.

After the redundancy of the Sykes-Picot Agreement, the victorious Allied powers convened a conference at San Remo in 1920, which determined the allocation of mandates following the fall of the Ottoman Empire. Under the Treaty of Sevres, signed four months after San Remo, Turkey was stripped of its Arabian possessions, ending colonialism with the establishment of mandates. As such, although the Sykes-Picot Agreement was not implemented, the legacy of external actors in Iraq is prominent. In tracing the history of modern Iraq one must begin with the fall of the Ottoman Empire and the involvement of the British in shaping the early years of political organisation. Indeed, this starting point serves to highlight the power of the narrative of colonial interference, resulting in claims such as that made by Bastian Vasquez.

British involvement in Iraq began as a consequence of strategic aims during the First World War, but the presence of oil across the Middle East would make the region increasingly important to London. Gaining control of territory following the fall of the Ottoman Empire and the establishment of a mandate, the British quickly concluded that a monarch was essential to create stability in Iraq (Tripp 2007: 43–50), yet they also sought to maintain their influence, choosing Faisal, the son of Sharif Hussein of Mecca, for the task. In doing so, a Sunni monarch was imposed to rule over a predominantly Shi'a population.

The challenge facing Faisal in the formative years of the Iraqi state quickly became apparent. T. E. Lawrence noted Faisal's concerns about the lack of a coherent Iraqi identity:

> There is still – and I say this with a heart full of sorrow – no Iraqi people but unimaginable masses of human beings, devoid of any patriotic idea, imbued with religious traditions and absurdities, connected by no common tie, giving ear to evil, prone to anarchy, and perpetually ready to rise against any government whatsoever. (Lawrence 1917)

To counter this, Faisal sought to build both a state and a national identity, two projects that were complementary yet difficult to achieve simultaneously while also retaining political power. This quest to fuse a state-building project with attempts to develop a coherent national identity, along with pushback from a range of sources that emerged from such a quest, would be a prominent feature of politics in Iraq. Domestic unrest would characterise the formative years of Faisal's rule and efforts to transform the lifestyle from the tribal nomadic, rural organisation to a sedentary, urban life would only add to these tensions.

Sectarian divisions would become increasingly fractious, as these identities became politicised as a means of ensuring control over key institutions and, ultimately, maintaining control over the state. This is perhaps best highlighted in the case of the Iraqi army at this time, in which an overwhelming percentage of officers were Sunni, with very little Shi'a representation in the officer class (Tripp 2007: 111). Such policies pushed Shi'a groups to the margins of political life, beginning to institutionalise religious difference as a mechanism of control. Central to such concerns was the fear that Shi'a influence would provide opportunities for increasing Persian influence, thus undermining the nascent Iraqi state's sovereignty (Bell 2015: 169).

Such schisms deepened as the political landscape of Iraq changed. The series of coups d'etat that shaped Iraqi politics in the 1950s and 1960s—ending monarchical rule in favour of military dictatorship—continued with recourse to the manipulation of sectarian dynamics, along with a number of draconian efforts to ensure the survival of particular regimes in the face of political flux (Quinlivan 1999). The rise of Saddam Hussein to power in 1979 ended the political turmoil that had plagued the upper echelons of Iraqi politics by purging Shi'a actors out of the political realm. Moreover, in order to get access to jobs—and influence—one had to be a member of the Ba'ath party, a fact largely missed in the aftermath of the 2003 invasion. Saddam faced a number of challenges that had become commonplace for rulers of Iraq to negotiate, namely questions of national identity and the integration of Shi'a and peripheral communities into the fabric of the state (Mabon and Royle 2017).

The brutality of Saddam's response to such challenges can be seen in exploration of the Halabja massacre (Hilterman 2007), where chemical weapons were used against the Kurdish population in 1988. Kurdish insurgencies had proved successful during the 1970s, resulting in distrust of Kurdish communities, and fearing defeat in the Iran-Iraq war, Saddam was limited in terms of resources to suppress the Kurdish offensive, resulting in the decision to use chemical weapons. The marginalisation and persecution of Shi'a communities continued, including the execution of Muhammad Baqir Al Sadr and a crackdown on radical groups such as Al Da'awa, which gained popularity among the persecuted Shi'a while pushing a number towards Iran (Alaaldin 2017).

Central to the survival of the Iraqi state under Saddam was the presence of a strong set of institutions falling within the security sector. Amidst political flux, Saddam established a range of institutions designed to protect his rule, watching and regulating each other (Quinlivan 1999). Central to this, however, was the role of the army, which served as both a source of national pride and a mechanism through which a particular vision of Iraq could be cultivated. The army was perhaps the most important institution across Iraq under Saddam and what would happen to the army in the years that followed the US-led invasion, would have catastrophic consequences.

The 2003 Iraq War and the Fall of the Sovereign State?

The idea of a sovereign state in the Middle East, free from external interference and led by a regime that was able to define the exception and determine which lives can live within a clearly delineated territory has become problematic. Tensions between regime and society became increasingly fractious, erupting in the Arab Uprisings of 2011, stemming from a frustration at socio-economic conditions across the region. This frustration was furthered by the denial and erosion of space for political discourse—and civil society—and with it, the channels for expressing political opposition and dissent.

In Iraq tensions were precipitated by the 2003 invasion and the removal of the Ba'ath regime, which increased scope for dissent. Ultimately, the US-led invasion of Iraq in 2003 would be fundamental in facilitating the rise of Da'ish through facilitating conditions that would allow an Al Qaeda franchise to engage in violence across the state. The invasion would also open up internal schisms within the state that would allow militias to gain power and influence, resulting in conditions that would prove integral to helping the group gain support from dissatisfied Sunnis.

In an attempt to prevent the resurgence of the Ba'ath Party, the Coalition Provisional Authority began a process of De-ba'athification, stripping out the institutional fabric of the state and in doing so, creating large-scale unemployment and a Shi'a government in Baghdad. Under the Prime Ministership of Nouri Al Maliki, the leader of the Shi'a Da'wa party that had long opposed the regime of Saddam Hussein, Iraqi politics took on an increasingly sectarian agenda, reversing decades of anti-Shi'a persecution. Following the Deba'athification of Iraq, many prominent opposition figures returned to Iraq, although, as Charles Tripp argues, it would be a mistake to "suppose that 'politics' returned to Iraq with the ingathering of the exiles" (Tripp 2007: 280). Rather, the return of figures such as Haider Al Abadi and Ahmed Chalabi would provoke a number of tensions among Shi'a communities, many of who had remained in Iraq to oppose Saddam's regime.

Under the Coalition Provisional Authority and both the Al Maliki and Al Abadi regimes, Sunni Iraqis were increasingly subjected to persecution while facing existential threats. They were marginalised politically, socially and economically and often found themselves caught between opposing coalition forces and the Shi'a government and militias. With the fragmentation of the state and the failure of key institutions to provide for the basic needs of the Iraqi people, an alternative set of structures emerged, run by sectarian militias, designed to ensure the survival of their sectarian kin. A number of militias gained prominence at this time, notably the Badr Corps and the Jaish al Mahdi (Ucko 2008) also known as the Mahdi army, which was led by the firebrand cleric, Muqtada Al Sadr. While both militias were Shi'a, the Badr Corps were formed in Iran during the 1980s and as such, received large-scale financial support from Tehran. Both engaged in conflict with coalition forces, yet it was within the context of Iraqi politics that their influence was most felt, with increasing sectarian violence emerging.

The influence of the militias was perhaps best noted by Jawad Al Hasnawi, who suggested that "the street is stronger than the Council of Representatives" (08BAGHDAD239_a 2008). The emergence of a number of powerful militias would have an undeniable impact upon the political landscape of post-invasion Iraq, especially as the state forces were much weaker than the militias (Semple 2006). In the North and West of Iraq, Sunni and Shi'a militias regularly clashed. However, in the Shi'a dominated south of the state, violence was intra-sect, driven by a desire to influence domestic politics (Bruno 2008).

At the same time as this burgeoning inter-militia rivalry, AQI was orchestrating a violent insurgency campaign against coalition forces. Simultaneously, it was targeting Shi'a groups in an attempt to drive apart Iraqi communities and, ultimately, to increase support for AQI. In an effort to counter the insurgency, Sunni tribal groups, self-generating, fought back against AQI, albeit unsuccessfully. Later, the US military sponsored a number of these groups to form a coalition to increase security in their local areas. Beginning in 2005, the so-called Sunni Awakening required groups to stop engaging in violence against coalition forces, instead, using their presence to maintain security against other insurgent groups. To continue with this, Awakening groups would be given financial incentives, paid for initially by the US military, and then, over time, by the Iraqi government under Al Maliki (Long 2008). Such a move led to serious problems.

Several serious errors fed into the fragmentation of the Iraqi state and the emergence of conditions that would help Da'ish emerge. The marginalisation of Sunni tribal leaders following the process of Deba'athification and the failure to bring the leaders of the Awakening movement into the fabric of the state was a serious miscalculation by Al Maliki and his key advisors, leaving influential Sunnis on the periphery of governance across strategically important provinces. After the US occupation, the security situation in Anbar deteriorated, yet Baghdad was either unable or unwilling to improve it, fuelling grievances among the Sunni tribes.

Geopolitics, Sectarianism and the "Iranian City of Basrah"

Rising violence along sectarian lines in recent years has propelled the academic exploration of sectarianism. While debates about the nature of the term continue (see Wallis 1975; Potter 2013; Ismael and Ismael 2010; Haddad 2013; Mabon and Royle 2017), a number of assumptions that come along with the term are generally accepted, including notions of othering and suspicion. Despite this, there is nothing inherently violent about sectarian difference; rather, it is when sectarian identities are securitised and politicised that differences can turn violent. It does, however, raise questions about the ontology of identity, whether such identities are primordial or whether they are constructed over time. As different sects have been able to co-exist peacefully at different times in history, the notion of sectarian difference being inherently violent should be rejected for it suggests that other factors must drive violence between different sects (Ismael and Ismael 2010). The fragmentation of political organisation within Iraq presented external actors with the opportunity to pursue their own agendas within the state. The penetration of Iraqi society adds to this process of marginalisation and securitisation, leaving groups caught between domestic political agendas and broader geopolitical calculations. In the case of Sunni communities, there was little opportunity for political leadership to emerge, leaving Sunni groups caught in a zone of indistinction, trapped between geopolitical competition and pushed to bare life within Iraq. To this end, it is important to examine the actors involved in the penetration and manipulation of sectarian groups along with the methods that actors have used to achieve this.

At the heart of this external penetration of the Iraqi state—and also a number of other Middle Eastern states—is a rivalry between Saudi Arabia and Iran, which, although couched in religious terms, is geopolitical in nature. Since the 1979 revolution in Iran, the two have become embroiled in a fractious rivalry that is increasingly taking place along sectarian lines. The two states have sought to support sectarian kin across the region and the fragmentation of political order across the region has provided opportunities for Riyadh and Tehran to do this, demonstrating the increased use of religion as a tool of geopolitics (Mabon 2013).

As US diplomatic cables released by Wikileaks document, Saudi Arabia was concerned as to the potential for increased Iranian influence in Iraq:

> The US "should not leave Iraq until its sovereignty has been resorted, otherwise it will be vulnerable to the Iranians. He said the Saudis will not support one Iraqi group over the others and that the Kingdom is working for a united Iraq. However, he warned that, if the U.S. leaves precipitously, the Saudis will stand with the Sunnis". (06RIYADH9175_a 2006)

This fear stems from events in the aftermath of the revolution, where it was suggested that Iran was involved in a series of coups d'etat orchestrated to undermine regional stability.[2] In the aftermath of the revolution, a spiral of vitriolic rhetoric emerged, escalating tensions across the Gulf. Ayatollah Khomeini stated that Iran would:

> export our experiences to the whole world and present the outcome of our struggles against tyrants to those who are struggling along the path of God, without expecting the slightest reward. The result of this exportation will certainly result in the blooming of the buds of victory and independence and in the implementation of Islamic teachings among the enslaved nations. (*The New York Times* 1987)

[2] See events in Bahrain, Lebanon and the perception of involvement in Saudi Arabia and Iraq.

The legacy of Shi'a thought would play a prominent role within the foreign policy of the newly established Islamic Republic. In particular, the narrative of events at Karbala, where Hussain was killed by corrupt members of the Yazid court, plays a prominent role in explaining Tehran's support for oppressed groups across the region (Worrall et al. 2015). This narrative was enshrined within Article 3.16 of the new Iranian constitution, which articulated an obligation to support the *mustazefin* of the Muslim world and can be seen in action through Iran's support for groups such as Hizballah.

Following the revolution, Iranian support for Shi'a groups would be a cause of much consternation across the Middle East, resulting in the perception that Shi'a minorities were 5th columns, possessing greater loyalty to Iran than to their host states. Coupled with this, demographic conditions across the region meant that Shi'a groups were often minorities or in positions of relative weakness compared to Sunnis and thus, Tehran's support was against the status-quo. In Lebanon, the Qods Force was instrumental in the establishment of Hizballah and continues to have a strong relationship with the Party of God (Worrall et al. 2015). In Bahrain, often considered the epicentre of sectarian tensions, an attempted coup d'etat undertaken by the International Front for the Liberation of Bahrain—a Shi'a organisation—was foiled in 1981. It later transpired that the coup was orchestrated by members of the Iranian Revolutionary Guards Qods Force.

Concern at the potential for Iranian manipulation of Bahrain's Shi'a majority led to the building of the King Fahd causeway, to facilitate easy access for Saudi forces to support the Al Khalifa, which was used in 2011 (Mabon 2012). Moreover, it was believed by many in Saudi Arabia that Iran was behind the unrest in the Eastern Province of the Kingdom which broke out during the 1980s, inspired—rather than directed—by events in Iran. Tensions between Saudi Arabia and Iran became more fractious during the Iran-Iraq war, which saw Riyadh side with Saddam Hussein's Iraq in an attempt to prevent Khomeini's revolutionary goals from spreading (Furtig 2002).

Since the events of 1979, the rivalry between Saudi Arabia and Iran has been increasingly fractious, with a number of events escalating the tensions between the two. In July 1987, 400 pilgrims on the Hajj were killed and debates as to where blame should lie led to the breaking of diplomatic ties between Riyadh and Tehran. On the 25th June 1996, a blast destroyed the Khobar Towers in Eastern Province of Saudi Arabia.

The attack was attributed to Hizballah Al Hijaz who were found guilty of the bombing in 2006, along with Iran (Leonnig 2006). Five years later, the US District Attorney, Eric Holder, revealed details of an Iranian orchestrated plot to assassinate the Saudi Arabian ambassador to the US. In January 2016, the execution of the Shi'a cleric, Nimr al Nimr, caused Iranians to storm the Saudi embassy in Tehran, resulting in the severing of diplomatic relations.

Over time, Riyadh became concerned about rising Iranian influence across the region and the onset of a number of proxy conflicts ensued. Iraq and Bahrain were of paramount importance to Saudi Arabia, given the proximity of both to the Kingdom and the establishment of a Shi'a government in Iraq evoked fears that Iran would galvanise a "Shi'a crescent" across the Middle East. These suspicions were raised by King Abdullah in a diplomatic cable released by Wikileaks:

> The King said he had "no confidence whatsoever in (Iraqi PM) Maliki, and the Ambassador (Fraker) is well aware of my views". The King said he had met Maliki early in Maliki's term in office, and the Iraqi had given him a written list of commitments for reconciliation in Iraq, but had failed to follow through on any of them. For this reason, the King said, Maliki had no credibility. "I don't trust this man," the King stated, He's an Iranian agent." The King said he had told both Bush and former Vice president Cheney "how can I meet with someone I don't trust?" Maliki has "opened the door for Iranian influence in Iraq" since taking power, the King said, and he was "not hopeful at all" for Maliki, "or I would have met with him". (09RIYADH447_a 2009)

The US diplomatic cables document many such fears about Tehran's penetration of the Iraqi state along with broader concerns about regional activity. This penetration and attempts to exercise influence in Iraq occurred in a number of different guises, ranging from support for the Al Maliki regime through formal channels to the more informal support for Shi'a militias. One cable documents how "Iranian sources, including the IRGC-QF, reportedly supported SCIRI and its affiliates with approximately \$100 million; \$45 million was specifically allocated to its militia arm, the Badr Corps" (05BAGHDAD3015_a 2005). The same cable suggested that Iranian supported actors are "implicated in the intimidation and assassination of Sunni Arabs in the southern provinces and in on-going attempts to penetrate and control the Basra police forces"

(05BAGHDAD3015_a 2005). Clearly, such penetration—if true—has serious implications for the strength of the Iraqi government along with perceptions of the government. Indeed, such penetration resulted in a much weaker government of Iraq and an increasingly strong set of militias, the existence of which challenged the sovereignty of the state (Mabon and Royle 2017).

The extent of the perception of Iranian penetration and influence across Iraq also caused Shi'a parties to distance themselves from Tehran:

> A growing anti-Iran sentiment among the Iraqi populace is compelling Shia parties to distance themselves publically from Iran [...] Even in Shi'a strongholds in Iraq, such as the southern province of Basrah, public sentiment about Iran is often characterised by suspicion and resentment. (10BAGHDAD22_a 2010)

For Sunnis, this served to fuel grievances about the manipulation and marginalisation of their identities by external actors, leaving them with little in the way of localised political leadership. Across Iraq, Sunni groups faced political, economic and social discrimination and, amidst the geopolitical struggle, indigenous concerns were lost (08BAGHDAD239_a 2008). These grievances would ultimately create fertile breeding ground for Da'ish to emerge and to gain control.

The Rise of Da'ish and Bare Life in Iraq

When tracing the roots and emergence of Da'ish, Al Qaeda in Iraq (AQI) under the leadership of the Jordanian Abu Musab Al Zarqawi, provides a useful starting point. Indeed, many members of Da'ish had also been members of AQI and had served time in the American prison, Camp Bucca (Chulov 2014). Abu Bakr Al Baghdadi, the self-proclaimed caliph, was born in Iraq and at the time of the 2003 invasion, is believed to have been a cleric in a mosque in Samarra, a city characterised by sectarian cleavages. It was at Camp Bucca where Abu Bakr Al Baghdadi was able to develop a network of contacts that would—along with former regime loyalists and disenfranchised Sunnis—become Da'ish.

Al Qaeda in Iraq was a splinter group from the main Al Qaeda organisation, often clashing with Osama bin Laden and Ayman Al Zawahiri over tactics and goals. Both AQI and Da'ish drew upon Salafist ideas but the latter would deviate from AQI and bin Laden, making brash claims about the takfirs and infidels that would result in an increase in sectarian violence that began under the leadership of Al Zarqawi. Rivalries with AQ and Al Nusra, the AQ affiliate in Syria, over ideology and methodology would spawn a more virulent Da'ish movement. While many suggest that the fundamentalist vision at the heart of Da'ish locates the group in the seventh century, such claims neglect the fact that the group embraces modern technology to spread its vision. In addition, both AQI and Da'ish group's leadership would propagate the narrative that the end of days was approaching, which resulted in tensions with Al Qaeda (Wood 2015). The seizure of the Syrian town of Dabiq would only serve to play into this narrative, as it is said that the 'Army of Rome' will be defeated there and, in this defeat, will bring about the countdown to the apocalypse. Of course, with the Da'ish's military defeats across the second part of 2016, such anachronistic and apocalyptic claims are discredited.

The onset of the Syrian Civil War in early 2011 would also provide an opportunity for Da'ish and other violent Islamist groups to gain strength and territory. The outbreak of war followed the violent repression of protesters in Syria who had called for the Assad regime to undertake political reforms. Of course, the ferocity of the government's response forced many to take up arms to protect themselves. The seizure of the cities of Ramadi and Mosul would gain the group much attention, by this point, controlling an area of land bigger than the United Kingdom. As violence intensified across Syria and Iraq, the conflict became increasingly internationalised, with media (and social media) outlets documenting the brutality of the conflict, increasingly fought along sectarian lines. From this a number of individuals crossing the Syrian-Turkish border to fight with groups opposing the Syrian regime.[3]

Over time, the rising power and influence of Da'ish led to declarations of allegiance from a range of actors across the Middle East and Africa. The emergence of Da'ish affiliates or wilayats would add an extra dimension to the internationalisation of the conflict. To date, groups in Egypt, Tunisia, Somalia, the Persian Gulf, Afghanistan, Pakistan, Yemen and Algeria have declared allegiance to Da'ish, extending the influence of the group. Whether such allegiance has been accepted and the extent to which the group's leaders maintain control over action is uncertain.

[3]It is worth noting that the foreign fighter phenomenon is not restricted to Da'ish or Isamist groups; rather, a range of individuals and groups have also travelled to fight against the group or in support of others involved in the conflict (Mabon 2015).

Within the context of this political fragmentation across Syria and Iraq, where individuals faced existential threats on a daily basis and acts of violence were conducted against them seemingly with impunity, individuals sought to escape such conditions. Da'ish was able to capitalise on these conditions and draw support from those communities marginalised by the state. In light of the fragmentation of Iraq and the attempts by external actors to manipulate identity groups within the state to achieve their own ends, political communities in the state bore the brunt of this violence. While the existence of direct violence is undeniable, structural violence against a range of communities across the state was also occurring. This structural violence, while initially perpetuated by the state, was also instigated by militias operating across Iraq, adding to the growing instability facing Sunni communities, leaving them in bare life, abandoned by the laws of the state yet also discarded from its protection.

The nature of sectarian politics pursued by the Al Maliki government would have a detrimental impact upon the nature of identity politics within Iraq, inverting decades of Shi'a marginalisation at the expense of the Sunni minority, many of whom were also experiencing serious socio-economic challenges following the Deba'athification process. Although the economy was decimated by the legacy of sanctions following the Gulf War in 1991, the restructuring of the state following the 2003 war would pose serious problems to a number of communities across Iraq.

An International Crisis Group report documents the destruction of Sunni communities and the inclusivity of political organisation within Iraq. The extent of this destruction demonstrates the intent behind it:

> Prime Minister Nouri al-Maliki has implemented a divide-and-conquer strategy that has neutered any credible Sunni Arab leadership. The authorities also have taken steps that reinforce perceptions of a sectarian agenda. Prominent officials – predominantly Sunni – have been cast aside pursuant to the Justice and Accountability Law on the basis of alleged senior-level affiliation to the former Baath party. Federal security forces have disproportionately deployed in Baghdad's Sunni neighbourhoods as well as Sunni-populated governorates (Anbar, Salah al-Din, Ninew, Kirkuk and Diyala). Al-Iraqiya, the political movement to which Sunni Arabs most readily related, slowly came apart due to internal rivalries even as Maliki resorted to both legal and extra-judicial means to consolidate power. (International Crisis Group 2013)

Here we see the extent of Sunni discrimination, with the regulation of life within Sunni tribal communities working towards the dismantling of political and social infrastructure. Ultimately, this recourse to legal and extra-judicial means reveals the severity of efforts to regulate life and maintain control. This penetration and control over Iraq included the security sector, with Shi'a officials dominating the prominent positions. Moreover, state institutions increasingly fell under the control of Shi'a militias, further adding to notions of marginalisation and persecution that were taking hold among Sunni communities. This 'sectarianisation' of state security institutions was documented by a US diplomatic cable that noted how "Police brigades are controlled not by the MOI but by ISCI/Badr, particularly in Karbala, Diwaniyah, and Nasiriyah" (08BAGHDAD239_a 2008).

Such conditions had a serious impact upon younger members of Sunni communities, which, when coupled with suspicions about connections to Al Qaeda, will feed into longer-term grievances. These concerns were exacerbated by the violence conducted by militias across the state. The rising violence orchestrated by groups such as the Badr Brigades and JAM involved the targeting of Sunnis across the state, often undertaken under the guise of being state officials, resulting in the onset of bare life. Violence against Sunnis was not restricted to direct violence, with instances of structural violence also feeding into—and facilitating—marginalisation and persecution. Structural violence also serves to aid the process of dehumanisation, which is a prominent part of the transition into bare life.

When coupled with socio-economic conditions and the growing existential concerns facing the Sunni minority, it is hardly surprising that hatred and violence along sectarian lines became increasingly prominent in Iraq. As Abu Muhammad Al Adani, a spokesperson for Da'ish stated, we "need to settle our differences with you [...] These differences go back a long way. We will settle our differences not in Samarra or Baghdad, but in Karbala, the filth-ridden city, and in Najaf, the city of polytheism" (Bazzi 2014). While there are clear theological aspects inherent in Al Adani's comment, the policitisation of sectarian identities and the changing security environment meant that such a message found resonance among Sunnis, many who had been subjected to increased violence over the past decade. As noted previously, sectarian difference need not necessarily be violent, but when such identities—even names—become securitised, the descent into violent behaviour appears all but inevitable.

From this, it is easy to see how conditions of 'bare life' emerge across Sunni communities in Iraq. Of course, one may easily suggest that this can be understood as a lack of representation, or fear, yet this should go much further. The organisation of religious communities within the state meant that certain provinces were predominantly occupied by members of one sect. Anbar Province, for instance, is dominated by Sunnis, meaning that conditions of bare life could easily emerge in particular areas. The marginalisation of Sunni communities from political life diminishes the role of Sunnis within the state and the increasing levels of structural and direct violence highlights the challenges facing many across the state. The interaction of normative and economic factors, plus an apparent existential threat to life along with the perceived reluctance of the ruling elite to protect them, it is possible to get a much greater awareness of the transition from zoe to bios. Perhaps most importantly, however, is that the identification of factors that lead to bare life can help to create appropriate responses.

Typologies of Support

While Da'ish has been able to cultivate support from those existing in bare life, it would be inappropriate to suggest that all of this support is the same. To this end, it is important to flag up how the creation of bare life has stimulated the actions of others domestically and internationally. In embarking on this task, Brandon Boylan suggests that it is important to make the distinction between "behavioural (active and passive) and induced (enticed and coerced) continuums of support" (2015). To facilitate this it is important to break up the supporters of the group into a number of different categories.

At the heart of the group are the core ideologues, led by the caliph Al Baghdadi, while underneath are four councils: the Sharia, Shura, Military and Security (Lewis 2015). This structure is replicated across the wilayats and attempts to create an Islamic and secure system of governance. Supporting this group are the devout followers of the ideology espoused by Al Baghdadi and those operating at the heart of the group's governance structure. Many of these individuals spent time in Camp Bucca or other US-run prisons, having previously been members of AQI. These members fill prominent positions within governance structures, having demonstrated loyalty to the cause.

Supporting this group is a growing number of foreign fighters who travelled to the caliphate to join the group and fulfilled a range of different roles. Within 18 months, by the end of 2015, it was estimated that there were 27,000 foreign fighters in Iraq and Syria, from 86 states (*The Guardian* 2015). There are a number of reasons as to why people wanted to travel to Syria and Iraq to participate, ranging from sectarian concerns to a crisis of modernity. The brutality of the conflict and extreme violence facing sectarian kin would be a key motivation for a large number of those who travelled. Others struggled to find meaning in the West, where struggles for certainty within the context of a crisis of modernity made the strengthened the appeal of Da'ish's message (Mabon 2015). It is worth stressing that while people wishing to participate in the conflict in Syria and Iraq had a range of different groups that they could join, the fundamentalist implementation of the Salafist interpretation of the Shari'a meant that a majority of those who travelled from Europe and beyond sought to join Da'ish.

In addition to this, a distinction must be made between the behavioural supporters and the induced supporters, with each category then subject to further clarification. The behavioural supporters can be broken into the active and the passive on the grounds of their involvement within the group's range of activities and distinctions should be drawn between individuals who fight for the group and individuals who work in hospitals or schools. Within the context of Iraq, many of the residents of Sunni cities would fall within the definition of passive supporters, located within the territorial borders of the caliphate, pushed to the group as a consequence of militia and government oppression yet not necessarily sharing the group's ideological vision.

For those supporters who were induced, another distinction must be made between those who were enticed and those who were coerced. Those who were enticed to support the group do so for reward or gain while those who were coerced to do so act under duress. Such an acknowledgement—and categorisation of support—helps to gain insight into the inner workings of the group, although empirical data to help differentiate between this support is currently lacking. It is pertinent to note that not all of the people located within the territorial dimension of the caliphate are supporters of the group, in whatever form. Indeed, a number of individuals have engaged in acts of resistance against Da'ish, perhaps best documented by the blog Mosul Eye. For them, Da'ish governance structures have now also created bare life.

Conclusions and Upstream Operations

Upstream operations, by their very nature, involve the interaction of a complex set of variables, within particular boundaries of time and space and when considering the case of Da'ish, a number of factors must be considered. Boundaries of time and space are integral to understanding the challenge facing an upstream operation, yet these boundaries are rarely clearly defined and as such, interactions can draw in a range of different actors (and agendas) from a number of different times. Causal relationships within these bounded areas need not necessarily be direct; rather, indirect causal links can play a powerful role in determining the nature of the environment within which the operation is occurring. Thus, those engaging in an upstream operation would do well to be reminded of the need to consider neighbouring environments to the arenas in which they are operating. Moreover, there is a need to identify direct and indirect links between actors in arenas that lie in close proximity.

The impact of upstream operations across Iraq is easily seen in the post 2003 context, both in the presence of the US-led coalition but also military efforts to regulate life amidst an increasingly unstable political environment. Within spatial confines of the Iraqi state, the deployment of military personnel was done with specific aim of toppling the regime of Saddam Hussein but not necessarily prepared for the increasingly volatile political aftermath.

Two themes emerged from upstream operations at this point, which both serve to re-inforce the creation of bare life across the state. The first stemmed from the evisceration of Ba'ath party infrastructure which erased the prominent Sunni position across the state, creating a vacuum for Shi'a parties and groups to exert power and influence. The nature of this post invasion context involved the reification of religious identities in the form of political parties and militias, which, in turn, fed into the historic cultivation of bare life. The second concerns the impact upon Sunni communities who had political meaning stripped from them in the post invasion context and, as a consequence of the political and security environment at the time, meant that Sunni communities found themselves trapped between coalition forces, Shi'a groups and militias, and Al Qa'ida. Essentially, Sunni groups were forced into bare life with little opportunity to exert agency.

To understand the emergence of Da'ish, it is clear that one must look at a number of different interpretations and consider how they interact. The fragmentation of political organisation across Iraq resulted in a number of basic needs not being met. When coupled with serious threat to life—actions seemingly conducted with impunity—the emergence of bare life forced people to turn away from the state to a range of alternative actors in search of security and basic needs. Such an acknowledgement can help to discover how groups such as Da'ish are able to cultivate support from local communities and from this, it is possible to develop strategies that can reduce their influence. While the desire to defeat the group is undeniable, such efforts fail to explore the conditions within which it was able to emerge and thrive.

The establishment of a caliphate and implementation of a system of governance derived from a fundamentalist interpretation of the Shari'a would ultimately feed into the cyclical process of bare life. This demonstrates the cyclical nature of bare life within Iraq, evolving from conditions impacting on the Shi'a, to Sunnis, to opponents of Da'ish within the caliphate. Although grounded within a Western philosophical tradition, the concept allows for an exploration of the conditions within which violent groups can emerge. Moreover, through such an acknowledgement, responses to violent groups can be developed, aimed at reducing the support received from more passive facets of the support base.

The creation of bare life is a seemingly unavoidable consequence of political systems which by their very nature require the ability to suspend the law to respond to emergency situations. While the need to respond to emergencies in a timely and responsible manner is important, the potential repercussions may pose existential challenges to the very nature of the political project. While all political projects are by their very nature exclusionary, the creation of permanent exclusion through bare life risks creating a permanent schism at the heart of political organisation, creating its own downfall. States thus contain the seeds of their own demise which can easily emerge in times of perceived crisis and amidst efforts to maintain security. Although political projects are inherently exclusionary, they must retain their sense of inclusion since if they fail to do so—as we have seen with the case of Iraq—the risks are far greater.

References

05BAGHDAD3015_a. 2005. Building a House on Shifting Sands–Iran's Influence in Iraq's Center-South. [online] Available from https://www.wikileaks.org/plusd/cables/05BAGHDAD3015_a.html. Accessed 4 November 2016.

06RIYADH9175_a. 2006. Saudi Moi Head Says If U.S. Leaves Iraq, Saudi Arabia Will Stand with Sunnis. [online] Available from https://wikileaks.org/plusd/cables/06RIYADH9175_a.html. Accessed April 2016.

08BAGHDAD239_a. 2008. "The Street Is Stronger Than Parliament:" Sadrist Vows Opposition to Ltsr. [online] Available from https://wikileaks.org/plusd/cables/08BAGHDAD239_a.html. Accessed 4 April 2016.

09RIYADH447_a. 2009. Counterterrorism Adviser Brennan's Meeting with Saudi King Abdullah. [online] Available from https://wikileaks.org/plusd/cables/09RIYADH447_a.html. Accessed April 2016.

10BAGHDAD22_a. 2010. Iraqi Views on Events in Iran and Impact on Iraq. [online] Available from https://wikileaks.org/plusd/cables/10BAGHDAD22_a.html. Accessed April 2016.

abu mus'ab az-zarqawi. 2014. The Return of Khalifah. *Dabiq*, 1.

Agamben, G. 1995. *Homo Sacer: Sovereign Power and Bare Life*. Stanford: Stanford University Press.

Agnew, J. 1994. The Territorial Trap: The Geographical Assumptions of International Relations Theory. *Review of International Political Economy, 1*(1), 53–80.

Alaaldin, R. 2017. The Islamic Da'wa Party and the Mobilization of Iraq's Shi'i Community, 1958–1965. *Middle East Journal, 71*(1), 45–65.

Bazzi, M. 2014. The Sistani Factor. *Boston Review*, 12 August. [online] Available from http://bostonreview.net/world/mohamad-bazzi-sistani-factor-isis-shiism-iraq. Accessed 12 August 2014.

Bell, G. 2015. *A Woman in Arabia: The Writings of the Queen of the Desert*. New York: Random House.

Boylan, B.M. 2015. Sponsoring Violence: A Typology of Constituent Support for Terrorist Organisations. *Studies in Conflict & Terrorism, 38*(8), 652–670.

Bruno, G. 2008. Badr vs. Sadr in Iraq. *Council on Foreign Relations*. [online] Available from http://www.cfr.org/iraq/badr-vs-sadr-iraq/p15839. Accessed 4 April 2008.

Caporaso, J. 2000. Changes in the Westphalian Order: Territory, Public Authority, and Sovereignty. *International Studies Review, 2*(2), 1–28.

Chulov, M. 2014. Isis: The Inside Story. *The Guardian*, 11 December. [online] Available from http://www.theguardian.com/world/2014/dec/11/-sp-isis-the-inside-story. Accessed 11 December 2014.

Dodge, T. 2005. *Inventing Iraq*. New York: Columbia University Press.

Dodge, T. 2014. Can Iraq Be Saved? *Survival: Global Politics and Strategy, 56*(5), 7–20.

Foucault, M. 1976. *The Will to Knowledge: The History of Sexuality—Volume 1*. London: Penguin.

Furtig, H. 2002. *Iran's Rivalry with Saudi Arabia Between the Gulf Wars*. Reading: Ithaca Press.

Haddad, F. 2013. Sectarian Relations in Arab Iraq: Contextualising the Civil War of 2006–2007. *British Journal of Middle Eastern Studies, 40*(2), 115–138.

Hallaq, W. 2013. *The Impossible State*. New York: Columbia University Press.

Hilterman, J.R. 2007. *A Poisonous Affair: America, Iraq, and the Gassing of Halabja*. Cambridge: Cambridge University Press.

Hobbes, T. 1651/2008. *Leviathan*. Oxford: Oxford University Press.

International Crisis Group. 2013. *Make or Break: Iraq's Sunnis and the State*. Middle East Report No. 144. [online] Available from http://www.crisisgroup.org/~/media/Files/Middle%20East%20North%20Africa/Iraq%20Syria%20Lebanon/Iraq/144-make-or-break-iraq-s-sunnis and-the-state.pdf. Accessed 12 October 2015.

Ismael, J., and Ismael, T. 2010. The Sectarian State in Iraq and the New Political Class. *International Journal of Contemporary Iraqi Studies, 4*(3), 339–356.

Johnson, Robert. 2018. The de Bunsen Committee and a Revision of the 'Conspiracy' of Sykes-Picot. *Middle Eastern Studies, 54*(4), 1–27.

Krasner, S. 1999. *Sovereignty: Organized Hypocrisy*. Princeton: Princeton University Press.

Lawrence, T.E. 1917. Faisal's Table Talk Report to Colonel Wilson. FO 686/6.

Leonnig, C.D. 2006. Iran Held Liable in Khobar Attack. *The Washington Post*, 23 December. [online] Available from http://www.washingtonpost.com/wp-dyn/content/article/2006/12/22/AR2006122200455.html. Accessed 23 December 2010.

Lewis, A. 2015. Islamic State: How It Is Run. *BBC*, 22 May. [online] Available from http://www.bbc.co.uk/news/world-middle-east-32829096. Accessed 22 May 2015.

Long, A. 2008. The Anbar Awakening. *Survival, 50*(2), 67–94.

Mabon, S. 2012. The Battle for Bahrain. *Middle East Policy, 19*(2), 84–97.

Mabon, S. 2013. *Saudi Arabia and Iran: Soft Power Rivalry in the Middle East*. London: I.B. Taurus.

Mabon, S. 2015. ISIS: Sectarianism, Geopolitics and Strong/Weak Horses. *E-International Relations*. [online] Available from http://www.e-ir.info/2015/04/10/isis-sectarianism-geopolitics-and-strongweak-horses/. Accessed June 2018.

Mabon, S., and Royle, S. 2017. *The Origins of ISIS*. London: I.B. Tauris.

McCants, W. 2015. *The ISIS Apocalypse: The History, Strategy, and Doomsday Vision of the Islamic State*. New York: St. Martin's Press.

Potter, L. 2013. *Sectarian Politics in the Persian Gulf.* London: C. Hurst & Co.

Quinlivan, J. 1999. Coup Proofing: Its Practice and Consequences in the Middle East. *International Security, 24*(2), 131–165.

Schmitt, C. 1922. *Political Theology. Four Chapters on the Concept of Sovereignty.* Translated by G. Schwab, 2005. Chicago: University of Chicago Press.

Semple, K. 2006. Militias Battle for Iraqi City as Shiite Rivalry Escalates. *The New York Times*, 21 October. [online] Available from http://www.nytimes.com/2006/10/21/world/middleeast/21iraq.html?pagewanted=print. Accessed 20 June 2015.

The Guardian. 2015. Number of Foreign Fighters in Iraq and Syria Doubles in a Year, Report Finds. *The Guardian*, 8 December. [online] Available from http://www.theguardian.com/world/2015/dec/08/isis-foreign-fighters-iraq-syria-doubles-report. Accessed 8 December 2015.

The New York Times. 1987. Excerpts from Khomeini Speeches. *The New York Times*, 4 August. [online] Available from http://www.nytimes.com/1987/08/04/world/excerpts-from-khomeini-speeches.html. Accessed 1 December 2010.

Tripp, C. 2007. *A History of Iraq*. Cambridge: Cambridge University Press.

Ucko, D. 2008. Militias, Tribes and Insurgents: The Challenge of Political Reintegration in Iraq. *Conflict, Security & Development, 8*(3), 341–373.

Vasquez, B. 2014. The End of Sykes Picot, 28 June. [online] Available from https://www.youtube.com/watch?v=i357G1HuFcI. Accessed 7 May 2015.

Wallis, R. 1975. *Sectarianism: Analyses of Religious and Non-religious Sects.* London: Peter Owen.

Weber, M. 2004. *The Vocation Lectures.* Translated by R. Livingstone. Chicago, IL: Hackett Books.

Wood, G. 2015. What ISIS Really Wants. *The Atlantic*, March 2015. [online] Available from http://www.theatlantic.com/magazine/archive/2015/03/what-isis-really-wants/384980/. Accessed 1 April 2015.

Worrall, J., Mabon, S., and Clubb, G., 2015. *Hezbollah: From Islamic Resistance to Government.* Santa Barbara: Praeger.

CHAPTER 9

The Unintended Consequences of Upstreaming: Western Engagement in Iraq

Gareth Stansfield

Western involvement in Iraq, since 2003, has assisted in transforming the country arguably beyond all recognition. Compared to how Iraq was governed before 2003, with the Ba'th regime holding all power, and with the Shi'i and Kurds excluded from having any meaningful access to the key offices of state, the situation could not be more different. From being a country with a strong state controlled by an authoritarian one-party regime, Iraq is now, officially at least, a federal state that sees the transference of power between governments taking place through a multi-party four-yearly election process. The government of Iraq is now dominated by political parties representing the Shi'i community, with parties representing Kurdish and Sunni interests being minority blocks within the Iraqi parliament (the Council of Representatives), and being included in the formation of governments through a power-sharing system (known as the muhasasa system) that gives a semblance of unity across ethnic and sectarian groupings, but in actuality maintains an

G. Stansfield (✉)
University of Exeter, Exeter, UK

T. Clack and R. Johnson (eds.), *Before Military Intervention*,
https://doi.org/10.1007/978-3-319-98437-7_9

overwhelming weight of power in the hands of the leading Shi'i parties (Boduszyński 2016).

In terms of unity, too, Iraq has, officially at least, changed beyond recognition. While the country was officially unitary in its design before 2003, the Kurdistan Region existed as a de facto entity, protected by Western powers and accommodated, to varying degrees, as a useful enclave in Iraq by Turkey and Iran in particular. Today, the Kurdistan Region exists as a codified federal region of Iraq—the only one, in fact—and has constitutionally-defined rights, responsibilities and competences that never existed before 2003 and the Region's leaders now plan to hold a referendum on their possible secession from Iraq in September 2017. Iraq is also far more openly communalised than it was previously. Whether ethnic and sectarian sub-state identities were strongly prevalent under Saddam's regime, or were instead generated by Western, US-led, policies that somehow simplified Iraq's politics down to the level of a three-way interaction between Sunnis, Shi'is and Kurds is an interesting and emotive debate that has strong adherents on both sides. But the reality is that, today, Iraq's political life is dominated by these identities, by how they mobilise politically and, increasingly, militarily and para-militarily, and by how Western powers chose to engage with them.

This chapter focuses particularly on the manner in which Western powers engaged with military organisations in Iraq since 2003 and some of the unintended consequences of these engagements. Western powers were heavily involved, and remained so after 2004, in the military affairs of Iraq from initially being occupying forces with a heavy and overwhelming military footprint, to being partners with fledgling Iraqi military institutions from 2005, operating under a Status of Forces Agreement (SOFA). Western forces were then drawn into the ferocious sectarian conflict that engulfed Iraq from 2006 to 2008, with US forces being increased to meet the challenges posed by the increasing threat of Sunni jihadist groups operating under the banner of Al-Qaeda Iraq (AQI). Even though the Ba'th regime had been removed in 2003, a Transitional Administrative Law (TAL) passed in 2004 that formed the basis of the permanent Constitution of Iraq in 2005, which was passed by a popular referendum, followed by the election of Iraq's first fully-empowered post-2003 government, a sectarian conflict had erupted between Sunnis and Shi'is, with Iraq's mixed cities, and especially Baghdad, degenerating into armed sectarian enclaves by the end of 2006 (Sky 2011). Western engagement was critical in bringing not only the sectarian conflict under control, but then in ending the far more dangerous intra-communal conflicts that had broken within the ranks of the Sunnis, and between Shi'i groups, from 2007 onwards. Ultimately, Western, US-led, counter-insurgency (COIN) efforts proved to be successful in quashing what was the antecedent of ISIS—the AQI organisation led a range of figures, with the most notable being Abu Musab al-Zarqawi—and in ending the threat posed by the firebrand Shi'i cleric Muqtada al-Sadr and his Jaish al-Mahdi militia. With regard to the former, Sunni partners that could be persuaded to oppose AQI were embraced, trained and equipped to do so, while those who remained loyal to AQI would feel the full wrath of the US-led COIN initiative as prosecuted by the Joint Special Operations Command (JSOC). The Sadrist militia were given a similar choice—to either end their insurgency, or to be eliminated with the clinical efficiency that still seems to remain the preserve of Western special forces units, with many of these units melting away, only to reappear several years later in the form of new, highly sectarianised, militia units, such as Asa'ib Ahl al-Haq and Kata'ib Hezbollah, that would receive direct Iranian tutelage as they confronted ISIS forces.

While these initiatives were not strictly 'upstreaming', in the terms preferred by Western defence establishments that have sought to revision their own roles in times of heightened austerity and public aversion to engagement in debilitating foreign ventures, they did engage with local forces and promulgated a range of lessons for future practitioners of COIN operations for when Western forces and their allies would deploy again. But there was also, arguably, an unintended consequence to the sharpening and codifying of COIN doctrine, as those actors that had been exposed to the highly efficient Western-led COIN response—whether as partners or as adversaries—would also reflect upon their experiences and learn lessons accordingly, with their education being made manifestly easier by the open availability of COIN materials on Western military establishment websites (JDP-05 2016; JDP 3-40 2009; FM 3-24 2006). Not only had these forms of upstreaming served to strengthen the then partners of the day, but it had also it seems, informed those planning insurgencies, in Iraq, Syria and elsewhere, for opportunities as they arose in the future.

The first part of this chapter addresses the first decade of Iraq's post-2003 development, but focuses not upon how US-led military forces ended the sectarian conflict, denuded the AQI threat, and removed the challenge to the Iraqi state posed by the Jaish al-Mahdi. There are many excellent academic and journalists' accounts of these subjects. Instead, it identifies a counter-intuitive dynamic—that at least some of the seeds of the future ISIS insurgency were sown during the period of the defeat inflicted by Western forces, not only in terms of facilitating connections between key individuals in detention centres (as is well documented), but in terms of inadvertently providing lessons to future adversaries—jihadists as well as 'nationalist' insurgents—keen to take the fight back to what was seen as an illegitimate, Shi'i-dominated and Kurdish supported, government of Iraq. The environment that then allowed these seeds to germinate and grow was then provided for by the policies and actions of the government of Iraq, which was itself supported by Western powers whom remained silent as Sunnis were persecuted to such an extent that they would support those organisations best placed to protect them. The subsequent backlash—from Shi'is in particular—witnessed the rapid expansion of militia units previously limited by the US-led forces, but which now were reinvigorated by the threat of the ISIS opposition arrayed against them and emboldened by the COIN lessons they had paid such a high price in learning from the US-led coalition several years before, and supported and guided by the region's experts in insurgency and counter-insurgency operations, the Al-Quds Force (sepah-e Quds) of Iran's Islamic Revolutionary Guards' Corp (IRGC).

The second part of the chapter then moves forward to the present period, as Western-led forces are once again engaged in Iraq, this time rebuilding the Iraqi Security Forces (ISF) after their mauling by ISIS fighters in 2014, and the Kurdistan Region's peshmerga forces as they too recovered from a near-death experience in August of the same year (Stansfield 2014). Again, whether these initiatives fit neatly the definitions of 'upstream engagement' would be debatable, as the conflict had already broken out, and Western powers—alongside Iran—moved quickly to ensure that Iraqi and Kurdish forces did not collapse even further, and were then regrouped, reorganised, retrained and re-equipped to take the fight back to ISIS in 2016. As such, the initiative was more accurately one of emergency reinforcement followed by an extensive train and equip plan, alongside close military planning, logistics support and deployment of Special Forces units at key areas of the frontline. The plan also looks to be succeeding, although the retaking of the city of Mosul and the wider Nineveh governorate has taken longer than initially envisaged. But the key question, again, emerges as to what the longer-term implications, or unintended consequences, of this defence engagement with Iraqi organisations will be. The situation in Iraq is now very different to that of 2003, when Western forces began training the new ISF, as it was.

Today, Iraq's political structure has been fragmented into three distinct areas. There is a Shi'i dominated space stretching from the eastern border with Iran, at Jalawla, to the town of Samarra to the north of Baghdad, and then taking in the capital and the heavily populated areas of the mid-Euphrates, the Shi'i holy cities of Najaf and Karbala, and the oil-producing province of Basra, with its eponymous city at the head of the Gulf. There is then a Kurdistan Region of Iraq, as approbated in the Constitution of 2005, which included the three northern governorates of Dohuk, Erbil and Suleimania, and eastern parts of Kirkuk governorate, that was then augmented in the summer of 2014 with the inclusion of the oil-rich city of Kirkuk and a significant tranche of northern Nineveh governorate, to the west, north and east of Mosul city.

There is then, finally, the Sunni-dominated space that includes the governorates of Anbar and Nineveh, and parts of Salahadin and Diyala to the east. This area was largely taken and held by ISIS from 2014 and was in opposition to the government of Iraq beforehand. However, the liberation of Islamic State-held lands will progress, it is distinctly possible that the conditions that led to the rise of ISIS in the period from 2011 onwards may well remain in place, or even become magnified, in the period following the Islamic State's defeat in Mosul, Tal Afar and Hawijah, whenever that will happen (Stansfield 2016). With this in mind, understanding the ability of capable Arab Sunni leaders to learn the lessons from the demise of IS and to remobilise in the future should be viewed as a continuing serious threat, particularly if "the day after" strategies implemented by the government of Iraq, and supported by their Western and Iranian advisers, prove to be inimical to the interests of the Sunnis of the area (Abdulrazaq and Stansfield 2016).

Western Upstreaming in Iraq and the Rise of the Islamic State of Iraq and al-Sham

The precursor to the Islamic State (IS—in Arabic *al-Dawla al-Islamiyya*) was the Islamic State of Iraq and al-Sham (ISIS—in Arabic *al-Dawla al-Islamiyya al-Iraq wa al-Sham*), which itself was a development of the Al-Qaeda affiliated Islamic State of Iraq (ISI—in Arabic *Dawlat al-Iraq al-Islamiyya*). ISI itself had emerged as the successor to Abu Musab al-Zarqawi's AQI that itself had formed from his earlier Tawhid organisation (Buchanan 2015).[1] The Islamic State, IS, was declared as being established on 29 June 2014, following the spectacular sweep of ISIS forces across Iraq's northern territories, south of the Kurdistan Region, in the summer of 2014. Its leader, Abu Bakr al-Baghdadi, became known as Caliph Ibrahim upon the declaration of the Islamic State's formation.

For the purposes of this section, it is the rise of the insurgent group ISIS that is of particular interest, rather than the formation and operation of the subsequent insurgent state, IS. And, with regard to understanding the ramifications of 'upstreaming', the case of ISIS may provide some compelling and also concerning lessons. Most analyses of ISIS's formation and subsequent development focus upon it being the latest in a line of Sunni jihadist organisations to operate in Iraq, but one that was also a complex amalgam of a range of different Sunni insurgent groups brought together over a period of years (Cockburn 2014; Lister 2014, 2015; Hashim 2014; Weiss and Hassan 2015; Stern and Berger 2015; McCants 2015). These entities were varied in terms of their ideologies and aims, with some of them not being particularly religious in their orientation, like ISI, but rather hailing from nationalist insurgent groups associated with the deposed regime of Saddam Hussein, such as the Army of the Men of the Naqshibandiyya Order (*Jaish Rijal al-Tariqa al-Naqshibandiyya*—JRTN) and the General Military Council (*al-Majlis al-Askari al-Amn li-Thuwwar al-Iraq*—GMC). Abu Bakr and his lieutenants also managed to reach out to those disaffected Sunni tribes that had, previously, been part of Western COIN strategies to train and equip them to fight AQI and ISI—only for the promises made to them by US, and UK, forces to be ignored by the Iraq government of Nouri al-Maliki.

[1] ISIS is also referred to as ISIL (Islamic State of Iraq and the Levant) and *daesh*, which is an acronym derived from the name of the organisation in Arabic. It has also been suggested that the acronym *daesh* sounds similar to the Arabic word *daas*, which means 'to trample'. Both the US and the UK government decided that daesh would be the title of official usage by them, perhaps indicating that they viewed the word as somehow demeaning, and it would therefore serve to insult and even delegitimise the organisation. This belief, however, is perhaps somewhat misguided and unfounded. While reports suggested that the ISIS leadership banned the use of the name daesh, it was probably because they needed to further legitimise the notion of 'The Islamic State'—*al-dawla al-islamiyya*—and any name other than this would serve to dilute this position.

What they therefore had in common was their opposition to the government of Iraq, and in particular the domination of the government by Shi'a political parties. They also felt marginalised and disenfranchised by the political process in Iraq, considering that the established political parties that claimed to represent Sunni interests in Baghdad were in reality vehicles for corrupt politicians to advance their own fortunes. This situation came particularly stark from 2010 onwards, as the government of Iraq pursued policy of further marginalising Sunni Arab communities targeting the demonstrations and suppressing their leaders, thus creating a fertile environment in which violent jihadist groups opposed to the state could recruit, operate and ultimately challenge the power of the state in these areas.

ISIS as a Manifestation of Western-Led Upstreaming

But ISIS was not merely the latest and most successful of the line of Sunni Arab dominated insurgent movements, however. As noted, it was also a reaction, in part, to the earlier Western-led COIN mission against the ISI/AQI, and it would seem that there were two parts of this reaction.

The first was ISIS being the logical output of a lesson learning process, with the successes and perhaps more importantly the failures of previous insurgent groups feeding into the design doctrine and operations of the new organisation. With this in mind, ISIS was an unintended consequence of Western upstreaming conducted in Iraq since 2003. Perhaps it was even a product of it, as it seems likely that Sunni fighters would have reflected upon their engagement with the MNF-I, and the Iraqi forces they were building, and considered how Western COIN approaches were being applied, and how they could be countered. It now seems to be clear that the ISIS leadership—at least in the military and intelligence organisations—were largely, perhaps even wholly, previously officers and officials of the military, special forces and intelligence services of Saddam's state. As such, they would have been highly trained, with some of them having had experience at first, or second, hand of Western training in staff colleges in the 1980s, and with intelligence officers having had long experience of dealing with Western, and Eastern counterparts, over many decades. Saddam's experienced people would also have known the benefits of analysing their opponents' successes, and learning from them (Sly 2015).

There remain a plethora of 'unknowns' concerning ISIS, but the question of how it managed to change from being merely the latest in a line of increasingly violent but marginalised jihadist outfits into being an extremely capable, organised and agile organisation needs to be answered carefully. Its willingness to learn from opponents as well as predecessors, and perhaps comparatively as well, is likely one of those core differences.

While conjecture to be sure, it would seem that Abu Bakr recognised early on that the success of the Western-led upstream intervention in 2007—which saw a 'surge' of US troop numbers from 150,000 to 178,000—was as much to do with the sociology of nationalism as it was to do with physical kinetic force. Under Zarqawi's leadership, and that of his successors, ISI had become associated with foreign fighters, with Iraqi tribes in particular viewing them, and their puritanical approach to Islam, as a threat to their own way of life and, ultimately, power. This cleavage saw the commencement of the tribal 'awakening' break out in Anbar first, and then other provinces, as Iraqi tribes began to challenge ISI/AQI. It was this local development that the US and her allies, including the UK embraced. Local Iraqi tribes and community organisations in cities were placed upon the US payroll then trained and equipped to defeat what was now seen as a foreign force in the form of ISI. The plan was ultimately successful, and it would seem it was a lesson that the leadership of ISIS learned well. While they recruited foreign fighters extensively, the leadership of ISIS was totally Iraqi. Recruitment was also very local, and power seems to have been devolved to a range of geographically-defined emirates, all with emirs that hailed from the locality.

It seems that the counterpoint to this Iraqi-first strategy was also copied from the US COIN manual from the period of the 'surge'—that those who could not be 'reconciled' would be eliminated. Thus, ISIS embarked on a series of campaigns that were designed to swell its ranks with loyalists, such as Breaking the Walls campaign of 2012–2013, that saw Iraqi prisons targeted in eight assaults, releasing several hundreds if not thousands of prisoners (Suadad al-Salhy 2013; Lister 2015). Following this, the next ISIS programme of activity ran from the summer of 2013 and into the following year, and arguably never stopped. Known as Operations Soldiers' Harvest—which also seems to be somewhat reminiscent of Western military language—ISIS Special Forces units undertook a systematic campaign of targeting known opponents and potential threats among the Iraqi population. These figures, who were usually former senior members of Saddam's elite military and intelligence units, but also leaders of other jihadist groups that were unaligned with the increasingly homogenising ISIS, were targeted and killed in operations that seemed more reminiscent of US Special Forces raids of the Joint Special Operations Command (JSOC) of Genera Stanley McChrystal than they did of the earlier efforts of AQI guerillas in Iraq's civil war of a decade before. Soldier's Harvest was also bolder than this, however. Recognising that their main enemy was the ISF, ISIS units also targeted ISF units across northern Iraq so that, when the assault on Mosul happened in the summer of 2014, the ISF was already demoralised with its capabilities denuded by the invidious effects of ISIS's own counter-COIN campaign.

Western "De-Upstreaming"

Just as there are dangers to an 'upstreaming' initiative with military forces, or initiative of active political engagement, there are also potentially debilitating effects of not 'upstreaming' in the first place, and maybe even greater negative consequences if the 'upstreaming' initiative is not comprehensively undertaken and completed. Arguably, this 'de-upstreaming' is what happened in Iraq between the end of the period of the 'surge' in 2008 and the fall of Mosul to ISIS fighters in the summer of 2014. The consequences of 'de-upstreaming' were arguably significant and, while they cannot fully explain the rise of ISIS, the collapse of the ISF, and the fracturing of Iraqi political life, the impact of each of them needs to be carefully considered by Western policy makers as the problem of how to normalise 'post-IS' Iraq following the recapture of Mosul begins to take on pressing importance.

Three facets of 'de-upstreaming' occurred in the period between 2010 and 2014, whereby Western powers, and principally the US, failed to fully implement their early plans to completion, or to ensure that the political conditions necessary for these plans to succeed were maintained. Each facet is important in its own right, and each are linked with the others, thus presenting a complex set of processes, feedback loops and interaction conditions that would underpin the rise and consolidation not only of ISIS is an organisation, but of the Islamic State as a concept, an idea, in opposition to a Shi'a dictatorship in Baghdad, Kurdish traitors and apostates in the north, Western occupiers, and Shi'a Persian aggressors.

The first of these 'de-upstreaming' facets concerns the fate of those Sunni tribal groups brought into the US-led train and equip programme, as part of the 'Awakening' initiative. By December 2007, the US had recruited some 75,000 fighters onto their books, with each receiving on average $350 per month. As part of the deal, they also had to register with the US military, which included the taking of biometric data. But, for the salary, training and the promise that they would then be integrated into the state's security structures in the near future, while their political leaders would also assume positions of authority in key state institutions, it seemed to be a reasonable deal to make. However, the US had little leverage over the Iraqi Prime Minister, Nouri al-Maliki, who had remained unsupportive of a project that he viewed as being a direct challenge to his own security services, and instead furthering the agendas of Sunni Arabs—who he viewed with increasing amounts of suspicion and animosity—in their bid to return Iraq to Sunni domination and Shi'a subjugation. Impervious the US pleas, Maliki brought the Awakening forces under his direct control, which also gave his security and intelligence organisations direct access to the biometric data collected by the US military. The Sunni tribes were not brought into the state security organisations, but instead were targeted by the government's security forces, with intimidation and arrests of prominent sahwat leaders becoming commonplace. For those among the Sunnis who had trusted the Americans in the 'upstreaming' initiative, only to be left to the mercy of Maliki as promises made to them proved to be hollow, the lessons were blatantly clear—that the US could not protect them, and the Iraqi government was an enemy, not a partner or ally.

The second 'de-upstreaming' facet then followed the first, in terms of timing. Maliki, upon gaining control over the US's successful military upstreaming initiative, then began to unravel the delicate threads of democracy that had been woven in Iraq since 2003 by consolidating power around him and by removing not only threats from within the Sunni community, but from within his own Shi'i community as well. Maliki moved against the Jaish al-Mahdi militia of Muqtada al-Sadr in Basra in 2008 and introduced a system of directly appointing members of the officer cadre to the ISF. Staffed with loyalists, the ISF would increasingly become Maliki's praetorian guard. But it would also damage ISF command capabilities when faced with a threat of the size posed by ISIS in 2014, when US forces would not be on hand to support them as they were in 2008. But perhaps the most damaging aspect of this second 'de-upstreaming' episode came in 2010. The parliamentary elections of that year saw Maliki present himself as the head of the State of Law coalition (Dawlat al-Qanun) and the defender of a unified, centralised, Iraqi state that opposed the continued presence of US forces beyond 2011. However, due to internal splits with other Shi'a parties, the list supported mainly by Sunni Arabs, the Iraqiyya block of Iyad Allawi, achieved a surprise, albeit narrow, victory over Maliki. With 91 seats to Maliki's 89, Allawi had every reason to be confident in succeeding Maliki and Sunnis viewed Iraqiyya's success as heralding a new start in Iraqi politics. But Maliki refused to recognise the legitimacy of the result, accusing his opponents of fraud and with a political stalemate then leaving Iraq with parliament reconvened in the summer, but with no government.

The subsequent Erbil Agreement of November, brokered by Kurdish leader Massoud Barzani, promised far reaching changes that would see Iraqiyya control the security, military and intelligence apparatus, if Maliki were to remain prime minister, which he agreed to. But, once in office, he simply ignored the claims made by Allawi and his team and instead turned his attention to removing the threat posed to him by what were now clearly capable, popular and influential Sunni political leaders. Meanwhile, the US, under the new Obama administration, had little interest in becoming embroiled with the fractious and possibly dangerous world of Iraqi electoral politics, and other Western powers did not have the capability or leverage to effect any sort of change in favour of what had been a democratic outcome. And, so, the lesson for the Sunni Arabs was again clear—that even when elections are won, they will still be denied a rightful place in the state. Thus, a political, social and security environment was beginning to form that would prove to be receptive, even supportive, of a group such as ISIS that would stand against the Maliki government, against what was seen as the Shi'a ISF, and seek to return them to power by force of action and not the ballot box.

The first two facets therefore relate to developments within Sunni Arab society and how they facilitated the rise of ISIS. The third facet focuses upon the 'de-upstreaming' in the Iraqi security sector, and the cessation of meaningful 'upstreaming' with the ISF, before the ISF would be able to operate effectively against a determined opponent. The US presence in Iraq had been ordered and mandated by a SOFA signed by Iraq and the US in December 2008, and which allowed for the basing of US combat troops until the end of 2011. Under Obama, and even under Bush before him, the US seemed to have become less enamoured with the need to stay in Iraq beyond the end of the SOFA term and, while negotiations did take place between the US and Iraq to extend the SOFA beyond 2011, neither Maliki nor Obama seemed fully engaged with the process. For Maliki, Shi'a popular opinion had become very anti-American, and to support an extension to the SOFA was, for him, politically unworkable. Obama, too, had to contend with popular opinion turning against the US's involvement in the costly and bloody Iraq campaign, and so the SOFA expired and the final US combat troops left Iraq with little fanfare along the desert highway to Kuwait at the end of the year. While driven by political expediency in both Baghdad and Washington, the withdrawal of US forces at this time left the ISF woefully exposed. Not yet fully trained and capable of combating a serious insurgency by themselves, the ISF was no longer able to undertake the missions necessary to further limit the threat posed by still-active insurgents, and it would quickly lose its cohesion as a Western-designed military force without having Western advisers and instructors in place to consolidate the improvements that had been made to date. Indeed, Maliki himself was already undermining the professionalism of the officer corps of the ISF by making direct appointments, and the breakdown of the cohesion of the ISF would be exposed to terrible effect by the rampaging of ISIS forces throughout the north in 2014.

The Future of a "Post-Mosul" Iraq: The Legacies of Upstreaming in a Fractured Political Setting

ISIS forces had begun to operate with relative impunity across Sunni-dominated Iraq since mid-2013, with Fallujah and Ramadi following under ISIS control in early 2013 and with ISIS becoming increasingly dominate in the rural areas of Nineveh province. ISIS had also secured control of Raqqa in Syria, and the border area, thus giving them strategic depth, strong supply lines and access to significant supplies of Syrian Army weapons. And an assault was expected. For several months, the Governor of Nineveh, Athil al-Nujaifi, had complained about sectors of his city, in the west, becoming uncontrollable, and Kurdish intelligence agencies had become aware of the threat emerging on their southern border, but neither Baghdad nor Western capitals were willing to act upon these warnings (Smith 2014).

The assault commenced on 4 June, with some 1500 ISIS fighters overrunning an ISF presence of some 30,000 personnel organised into 5 divisions of army and federal police units. By 9 June, ISF officers had largely fled the city, leaving their units without commanders, allowing the main ISIS assault to simply move quickly through the city of 3 million people before then spreading out into the Arab-dominated areas of Kirkuk province to the south east. The Kurdish leadership in the north was shocked by the advance, but more because the ISF had collapsed rather than due to any threat posed to them by ISIS forces. Before the fall of Mosul, Prime Minister Maliki and President Barzani had been engaged in their own sabre-rattling brinkmanship over a range of issues, but mainly with regard to the status of the disputed territories of Kirkuk. Now, with the ISF eliminated as a threat, the Kurdish leadership ordered the occupation of the Kurdish-dominated parts of the disputed territories, including Kirkuk, areas of north and north east Nineveh, and parts of Diyala, with most of these territories being under Kurdish, peshmerga, control by 10 June.

The Peculiar Interregnum

The fall of Mosul, traumatic though it was, ushered in a peculiar interregnum—a transitional period that saw the Iraq as a country, society and state undertake a transformation from what it was before the fall of Mosul, to what it was to become following its liberation. The nature, scale and ramifications of these transformations have still to be understood, but they include the emergence and consolidation of Shi'a majoritarianism as the principal means of ordering the state, rather than the pre-2014 model of informal power-sharing; the further distancing of the Kurdistan Region, politically, from the rest of Iraq, with the possibility of their holding a referendum as the first stage in a process of secession being very likely; and, most pertinently from a military viewpoint, the transformation of security sector actors in Iraq, with the ISF's role, capabilities and monopoly as the legitimate military forces of the state, being challenged and even subordinated by the various Shi'a militias that had expanded, and formed, in response to the threat posed by IS.

During the interregnum, Western policy was not focused on security sector reform in its traditional sense, or even on "upstreaming", in terms of taking pre-emptive measures to manage foreseeable issues on the horizon. Rather, Western policy was focused almost wholly on containing and then removing the presence of IS in Iraq, and then in Syria. To achieve this, the United States allocated a $1.6 fund in 2015 as part of the Iraqi Train and Equip Fund (ITEF) to provide arms for Iraqi soldiers, with the fund largely being used to procure weapons, armour, and other equipment for ISF units to use against the still-advancing IS forces (Stewart and Spetalnick 2015). The scale of the ITEF was breathtaking, with over 1200 military transport vehicles, 20,000 small arms and heavy weapons and 2000 AT-4 anti-tank missiles being supplied, alongside many other pieces of equipment (US Department of State 2017). One of the main beneficiaries of this programme was the elite Counter-Terrorism Service (CTS), known in Iraq as the 'Golden Division'. Set up as a dedicated counter-terrorism unit, the CTS remained a small organisation of 12,500 that received intense training and support from their western instructors. Seen as Iraq's Special Forces, the CTS was increasingly deployed in the fight against IS and was largely responsible for the retaking of eastern Mosul in 2016–2017 (Knights and Mello 2017). The UK was also an active participant in standing up Iraqi forces against IS. In September 2015, the Ministry of Defence announced that 2000 Iraqi personnel had been trained by British troops, with the number rising into 2016, with some 3000 peshmerga and 5000 ISF troops being trained as part of Operation SHADER (Defence Committee 2016: 23).

The Rise of the Hashed al-Sha'bi

These numbers and statistics, impressive though they may be, need to be placed within the context of what was happening in Iraq during this interregnum. Most significant perhaps, were the actions taken by Iraqi Prime Minister Maliki, in June 2014 following the Iraqi army's collapse in Mosul, to form the Commission for the Popular Mobilization Forces (hay'at al-Hashed al-Sha'bi). The Commission was tasked with coordinating the several Shi'a militias that had already formed in a move that directly contravened the Iraqi constitution, but which nonetheless, due to the threat posed by the IS advance, was enacted. Maliki's legitimisation of the Shi'a militia was then inadvertently then further strengthened by the issuing of a fatwa by Grand Ayatollah Ali al-Sistani—the most senior religious figure of the Shi'a community in Iraq—which called upon all Iraqis to join the security forces. While not explicitly communal in its nature, the fact that the fatwa was issued by the Shi'a Grand Ayatollah, in response to a terrifying threat that was strongly associated with Sunni jihadists, meant that Maliki and commanders of the Shi'a militias were able to further expand recruitment while also undermining the Iraqi army by smearing their actions to date against IS (Mansour and Jabar 2017).

The Shi'a militias would increase massively in size, with estimates ranging from 60,000 to 140,000 across some 30 individual groups (Mansour and Jabar 2017: 13). These groups fall into three clusters that have distinct aims, agendas and lines of command and control. The pro-Khamanei cluster consists of those militias that are linked to the IRGC of Iran. Sometime these links are obvious, with Iranian military advisers being openly visible, and sometimes they are more circumspect. But it is these groups—such as the Badr Army, Saraya Khurasani and the Asa'ib Ahl al-Haq that are seen not only as the most militarily capable of the Shi'i militia forces, but also the most transformative in terms of their impact upon the nature of the Iraqi state. Far from simply responding to an earlier call to arms, these militias expect to see the further institutionalisation of the Hashed forces so that they, maybe, become the Iraqi equivalent of Iran's IRGC. In such a model, the 'regular' armed forces are deemed to be of secondary importance to the formations of the Revolutionary Guard and, just as the IRGC has become not only the pre-eminent military organisation in Iran but also one with great political influence and economic power, so too would the future manifestation of the Hashed in Iraq hold such positions of prominence in the country.

Challenging this cluster are the two other groupings, often referred to as "pro-Sistani" or "pro-Najaf", and "pro-Sadr". These organisations in the pro-Sistani cluster swear allegiance to Grand Ayatollah Ali al-Sistani—the most senior Shi'a cleric in Najaf, and one who eschews a different view of the relationship between clerics and the state than his counterparts in Iran. From a position known as 'quietism', Sistani and his associates in Najaf have tended to distance the religious establishment from the affairs of state, and only issued the fatwa of military mobilisation as an emergency response to the threat posed by the Islamic State. And, so, once that threat has subsided, so too will the need to have so many thousands of men under arms and the militias of the pro-Sistani cluster will then disband. The final cluster is composed of one great—the Peace Brigades (Saraya al-Salam) which are loyal to the Shi'a leader Muqtada al-Sadr. Himself the scion of the powerful Sadr family, Muqtada has transformed himself over the last decade, from fiery Shi'a rebellion leader against foreign occupiers, to being an Iraqi nationalist

Shi'i leader who seems to be opposed to Iran as much as he is to the US. As an off-shoot of the earlier Jaish al-Mahdi, the Peace Brigades are numerous and potentially powerful, but their role in the Hashed is unclear, as is the overall political aims of Muqtada himself.

The rise of IS therefore presented Western powers with an inverted situation, compared to what they had experienced before 2014. Previously, they had engaged wholly with the established and legal military forces of the Iraqi state, in the form of the ISF. Western upstreaming engagement was invested into the ISF, in the form of training, advisory work, equipping and general support, and the ISF Special Forces units in particular received a great amount of attention from their Western counterparts. Western forces not only did not engage with the Shi'a militias, they purposefully avoided them. This was not only a political statement being made by Western forces keen to show their support for the legal institutions of the state. It was also a sensible security precaution to take, as many of these entities had fought with MNF-I in the past and remained of the view that Western forces had to be removed from Iraq at any cost.

It was then the Iranian military and intelligence organisations that continued to work with what was, until 2014, very much a secondary set of militias, in terms of capabilities and influence, compared to their legitimate ISF counterparts, moved in. Under the umbrella of legitimacy granted by the government of Iraq's empowerment of the militias combined with Grand Ayatollah Sistani's fatwa, Iran's IRGC Al Quds Brigade began to emulate the train and equip programmes being implemented by Western powers with the ISF, but according to their very own specific model of building not only reliable military organisations, but ones that would be loyal, ideologically acceptable to the government of Iran, and extremely capable. For some analysts, Tehran's initiative would resemble that of building the Hezbollah organisation in Lebanon. But, in reality, the analogy would be found in Iran itself. Far from building a militia proxy, Tehran's IRGC seems to be attempting to build an IRGC for Iraq. Rather than building a pliant set of militias, the model would instead be to construct an entirely new military and intelligence structure, but one that would not be in parallel with the extant organisations such as the ISF, but superior to them.

The Western focus on removing the threat of ISIS in Mosul has undoubtedly strengthened this initiative. With the most capable ISF units, including the CTS, being deployed in the first stages of the missions to retake Mosul, in the east of the city, ISF units suffered appallingly heavy losses, with the CTS alone reportedly having 40% battle losses, and with regular ISF Divisions perhaps faring even worse (Knights and Mello 2017). This then left the way clear for Hashed forces to be more involved in the liberation of western Mosul—with the Ministry of Interior's Emergency Response Division (ERD), which itself is closely aligned with the Shi'a militia, taking the lead. With Mosul liberated, the only organisation that could remotely have presented itself as 'Iraqi' rather than "Shi'a" to the inhabitants of these Arab northern governorates have now been largely marginalised, while those forces aligned with the most hardline and pro-Khamane'i of the Hashed al-Shabi reap the spoils. This, then, leads to a most perplexing question for Western policy makers to grapple with: should they continue with their attempts to "upstream" with the ISF, when the ISF itself is in such a weakened position within the Iraqi security structure that it seems unlikely that a return to the status quo ante can be achieved?

Conclusion

Western engagement with the security situation in Iraq, since 2007, has shown that 'upstreaming' can succeed, and it can have very impressive results. But it has also shown that incomplete "upstreaming", or even "de-upstreaming", can have deleterious ramifications that could act as a catalyst in the emergence of extremely negative political and security scenarios. By 2008, Western upstreaming initiatives had been responsible for strengthening a local Iraqi Sunni initiative to combat AQI/ISI and had also seen the progressive and rapid consolidation of the capabilities of the ISF. Yet the failure to complete these upstreaming initiatives, and to facilitate the creation of a political environment that would de-escalate rather than escalate sectarian and inter-communal tensions, would contribute to backlash from within the Sunni community that would find its expression in the actions and atrocities committed by ISIS and then the Islamic State.

As Iraq enters a new, post-Mosul Operation if not post-IS, period, Western policymakers again need to reflect upon the wisdom, aim, and agenda of a policy of upstreaming with Iraqi security organisations. With the pro-Iranian Shi'a militia of the Hashed al-Sha'bi being in the ascendency—in political as well as security terms—Western engagement with the ISF may not only be superfluous, as the ISF is increasingly subordinated to the Hashed, but it may also ultimately be dangerous, as Iraq of 2017 may be much more similar to the anti-Western Iraq of 2004–2007 than it is to the Iraq of 2007–2008. A further challenge also exists in the north, in the Kurdistan Region, and one that needs further reflection upon beyond the scope of this paper. With Western forces 'upstreaming' so effectively with the peshmerga, they may find themselves as de facto allies with the Kurds as they seek to seceded from Iraq, which would then, perversely, make them associated with the Kurds' adversaries not only in the Hashed, but also in the ISF. The strategy of upstreaming in Iraq should therefore be considered very carefully as the situation will become far more complex, in the post-Mosul Operation environment, than it was during the relatively stable interregnum provided by the existence of the Islamic State.

References

Abdulrazaq, Tallha, and Stansfield, Gareth. 2016. 'The Day After: What to Expect in Post-Islamic State Mosul.' *The RUSI Journal*, Vol. 161, No. 3: 14–20.

Boduszyński, Mieczysław. 2016. 'Iraq's Year of Rage.' *Journal of Democracy*, Vol. 27, No. 4.

Buchanan, Rose Troup. 2015. 'Daesh: What Does the Word Mean? Is David Cameron's Use of It significant?' *The Independent*, 2 December.

Cockburn, Patrick. 2014. *The Rise of Islamic State: ISIS and the New Sunni Revolution*. London: Verso.

Defence Committee. 2016. House of Commons UK Military Operations in Syria and Iraq: Second Report of Session 2016–17. September.

FM 3-24. 2006. US Counterinsurgency Manual at http://usacac.army.mil/cac2/Repository/Materials/COIN-FM3-24.pdf. Accessed June 2018.

Hashim, Ahmed S. 2014. 'The Islamic State: From Al-Qaeda Affiliate to Caliphate.' *Middle East Policy*, Vol. XXI, No. 4 (Winter): 69–83.

JDP 3-40. 2009. Security and Stabilisation: The Military Contribution, November 2009. https://www.gov.uk/government/publications/shaping-a-stable-world-the-military-contribution-jdp-05. Accessed June 2018.

JDP-05. 2016. UK's Shaping a Stable World, 8 March.

Knights, Michael, and Mello, Alex. 2017. 'The Best Thing American Built in Iraq: Iraq's Counter-Terrorism Service and the Long War Against Militancy.' *War on the Rocks*, 19 July.

Lister, Charles. 2014. 'Profiling the Islamic State.' Analysis Paper, No. 13, Brookings Doha Center, Doha, November.

Lister, Charles. 2015. *The Syrian Jihad: Al-Qaeda, the Islamic State and the Evolution of an Insurgency*. London: Hurst & Co.

Mansour, Renad, and Jabar, Faleh. 2017. The Popular Mobilization Forces and Iraq's Future, Carnegie Middle East Center, April.

McCants, William. 2015. *The ISIS Apocalypse: The History, Strategy, and Doomsday Vision of the Islamic State*. New York: St. Martin's Press.

Suadad al-Salhy. 2013. 'Al Qaeda Says It Freed 500 Inmates in Iraq Jail Break.' *Reuters*, 23 July.

Smith, Hannah. 2014. 'Warnings on Iraq ISIS Attack Ignored—KRG Official.' *Asharq al-Awsat*, 20 June.

Sky, Emma. 2011. 'Iraq: From Surge to Sovereignty.' *Foreign Affairs*, March/April.

Sly, Liz. 2015. 'How Saddam Hussein's Former Military Officers and Spies Are Controlling ISIS.' *The Independent*, 5 April.

Stansfield, Gareth. 2014. 'The Islamic State, the Kurdistan Region, and the Future of Iraq: Assessing UK Policy Options.' *International Affairs*, Vol. 90, No. 6.

Stansfield, Gareth. 2016. 'The Looming Problem of Tal Afar.' *The Wilson Center*, 1 November.

Stern, Jessica, and Berger, J. M. 2015. *ISIS: The State of Terror*. London. William Collins.

Stewart, Phil, and Spetalnick, Matt. 2015. 'U.S. Quietly Starts Channeling Arms from $1.6 Billion Fund to Iraq.' *Reuters*, 5 June. http://uk.reuters.com/article/us-mideast-crisis-iraq-usa-idUKKBN0OL1N520150605. Accessed June 2015.

US Department of State. 2017. U.S. Security Cooperation with Iraq Fact Sheet, 20 January. https://www.state.gov/t/pm/rls/fs/2017/265953.htm. Accessed June 2018.

Weiss, Michael, and Hassan, Hassan. 2015. *ISIS: Inside the Army of Terror*. New York: Regan Arts.

Index

T. Clack and R. Johnson (eds.), *Before Military Intervention*, https://doi.org/10.1007/978-3-319-98437-7

The manufacturer's authorised representative in the EU is Springer Nature Customer Service Centre GmbH, Europaplatz 3, 69115 Heidelberg, Germany. If you have any concerns regarding our products, please contact ProductSafety@springernature.com

Printed and bound by CPI Group (UK) Ltd, Croydon, CR0 4YY
22/09/2026
02220990-0002